33025350

INGLORIOUS DISARRAY

RORY MILLER

Inglorious Disarray

*Europe, Israel and the Palestinians
since 1967*

HURST & COMPANY, LONDON

First published in the United Kingdom in 2011 by
C. Hurst & Co. (Publishers) Ltd.,
41 Great Russell Street, London, WC1B 3PL
© Rory Miller, 2011
All rights reserved.
Printed in India

The right of Rory Miller to be identified as the author of
this publication is asserted by him in accordance with the
Copyright, Designs and Patents Act, 1988.

A Cataloguing-in-Publication data record for this book
is available from the British Library.

ISBN: 978-1-84904-116-4 *hardback*

This book is printed using paper from registered sustainable
and managed sources.

www.hurstpub.co.uk

CONTENTS

ACKNOWLEDGEMENTS

I would like to thank Michael Dwyer at Hurst and the editors at Columbia University Press for their support of this project. Over the last decade I have taught the subject of Europe and the Middle East to numerous MA students from all over Europe, North America and the Middle East. The idea for this book came from many the hours spent discussing the issues raised here in and out of class, and for that I am very grateful to all who participated in these discussions. In particular, I would like to thank two of my former students—Giuditta Fontana and Reyhaneh Fallah-Noshiravani—for their research assistance with this book.

My main debt is to Michelle whose copy-editing skills were only matched by her support, patience and encouragement. This book is for her.

ABBREVIATIONS AND ACRONYMS

ACM	Arab Common Market
API	Arab Peace Initiative
AUT	Association of University Teachers
BAM	Border Assistance Mission
CSCE	Conference for Security and Cooperation in Europe
CSFP	Common Security and Foreign Policy
DFLP	Democratic Front for the Liberation of Palestine
EAD	Euro-Arab Dialogue
EEC	European Economic Community
EFTA	European Free Trade Association
EJP	European Jewish Press
EMP	Euro-Mediterranean Partnership
EMU	Economic and Monetary Union
EPC	European Political Cooperation
ESDP	European Security and Defence Policy
ETA	Basque Fatherland and Liberty Organisation
EU	European Union
FLN	Front de Libération Nationale
GDP	Gross Domestic Product
GMP	Global Mediterranean Policy
IDF	Israel Defence Forces
IRA	Irish Republican Army
MBFR	Mutual Balance Force Reductions
MEI	Middle East International
MFO	Multinational Force and Observers
NAFTHE	National Association of Teachers in Further and Higher Education

ABBREVIATIONS AND ACRONYMS

NATO	North Atlantic Treaty Organisation
OAPEC	Organisation of Arab Petroleum Exporting Countries
OPEC	Organisation of Petroleum Exporting Countries
PA	Palestinian Authority
PASOK	Pan-hellenic Socialist Movement
PBC	Palestinian Broadcasting Corporation
PEDWG	Palestine Economic Development Working Group
PFLP	Popular Front for the Liberation of Palestine
PLO	Palestine Liberation Organisation
PNC	Palestine National Council
PSC	Palestine Solidarity Campaign
R&D	Research and Development
REDWG	Regional Economic Development Working Group
SALT	Strategic Arms Limitation Talks
TEU	Treaty on European Union
UAR	United Arab Republic
UN	United Nations
UNEF	United Nations Expeditionary Force
UNGA	United Nations General Assembly
UNIFIL	United Nations Interim Force in Lebanon
UNRWA	United Nations Relief and Works Agency
UNSC	United Nations Security Council

INTRODUCTION

A CAUSE LOOKING FOR AN OPPORTUNITY

'The conflict in the Middle East is dangerous for us. We are not just here, as the good guy who says please do not fight between you. We need this conflict to be finished because of its impact on life in Europe.'

Josep Borrell Fontelles

Since that fateful week of war in June 1967, when Israel's speedy military victory over the Arab states redrew the map of the Middle East, generations of European policy-makers have believed that a permanent settlement of the Israel-Palestine conflict on the basis of a two-state solution is not only vital for the Middle East but is, in the words of the former European Union foreign policy chief Javier Solana, 'fundamental to our own security'.[1]

Bound to the Middle East region, so the argument goes, by geography, history, culture, trade and strategic ties, Europe—or at least those parts of it involved in the ever-expanding move towards economic and political union—has both a right and a duty to play a key role in mediating an end to this 'festering crisis in a region so near',[2] as then Italian Prime Minister Bettino Craxi described it in the mid-1980s. During his time as British Prime Minister, Tony Blair went further and described the search for a solution to the Israel-Palestine conflict as the 'single most pressing political challenge in our world'.[3] In 2006, Spain's Prime Minister José Rodríguez Zapatero argued that 'peace between Israel and the Palestinians means to a large extent peace on the international scene'.[4]

The global perspective expressed by Blair and Rodríguez Zapatero reminds us that the ultimate aim of the founding fathers of the European

1

project was political rather than economic. Men like Jean Monnet, Walter Hallstein and Robert Schuman intended to create, though gradually and through economic cooperation in the first instance, a new centre of power in the world capable of developing and implementing its own policies independent of the United States (US) or the Soviet Union. As Hallstein said, 'We are not only in the business of business, we are in the business of politics'. The establishment of this European Union was a slow and difficult process and, as Schuman explained, Europe would 'not be built all at once, or as a single whole: it will be built by concrete achievements which first create de facto solidarity'.[5]

From the late 1960s onwards, the story of how the Community, just six members strong and a decade old at the time of the June 1967 Arab-Israeli War, attempted to involve itself in the Israel-Palestine conflict is also the story of its attempt to achieve the 'de facto solidarity' needed to establish itself as a major global political power.

It would be incorrect to argue that the Palestine issue provided the lowest common denominator for the Community's attempt to get into the business of politics, but it was certainly true that in the post-1967 era, European political cooperation evolved first and foremost as part of the European Community's attempt to deal with the challenges and opportunities arising from the Israel-Palestine conflict.

This book documents Europe's evolving, albeit stilted and often frustrating, attempt to insert itself into the politics of the Palestine issue and how this impacted on its relationship with Israelis, Palestinians and the Arab world. It also explores how its own internal political and economic development affected its role in the conflict and how the conflict, in turn, had an impact on the expanding Community's strategic positioning on the global stage.

For the most part, over the past four and a half decades Europe has not succeeded in becoming what Marc Otte, the EU's Special Representative for Middle East peace, recently termed 'a full player'[6] in the politics of the Palestine conflict. In fact, one can make the case that nowhere has the gap between European rhetoric and action been more obvious, and nowhere has the accusation that Europe is an 'economic giant but a political pygmy'[7] been more true.

This has to do with the often insurmountable differences born out of distinct national interests in a diverse Community. Time and again historic feuds, local jealousies, domestic politics, and intra-European competition have prevented the 'consensus [and] the basis for a common policy'[8] that the Belgian statesman Henri Simonet rightly argued was necessary for joint action in the Middle East and everywhere else.

Another factor examined throughout this book is Europe's inability to compete with the US in the Middle East. By the mid-1970s, the US had established itself as the dominant external political and military power in the region. Since then no other nation or grouping of nations has been able to convince Israel, the Arab states or the Palestinians that they have more to offer them in the role as mediator, guarantor and sponsor than Washington.

The most important explanation for this has always been, and still remains, the United States' special relationship with Israel. As the late Yitzhak Rabin acknowledged in a speech to the Knesset (the Israeli parliament) in 1992: 'Sharing with us in the making of peace will be the US, whose friendship and special closeness we prize. We shall spare no effort to strengthen and improve the special relationship'.[9] Since 1967, successive Israeli governments have viewed the US, regardless of whether the Democrats or the Republicans occupy the White House or hold a majority in Congress, as the only viable intermediary with the Arabs, as well as the only external party committed to Israel's strategic security. The US has gone to great lengths, both rhetorically and in terms of providing practical support to Israel, to promote and consolidate this view. As President Clinton stated in 1993, the US goal in fostering peace was to 'provide Israel with such generous military, economic and political support, that it feels confident about taking risks for peace'.[10]

A US commitment aimed at reassuring Israel of its strategic security has been central to all Israeli moves towards peace since 1967. Prior to the Oslo era such a commitment was evident in the 1975 Sinai II Accord and the 1979 Camp David Accords, as well as the 1981 US-Israeli Memorandum of Understanding on Strategic Co-operation. Following the signing of the Oslo Accords in 1993 the US gave similar assurances at times of deadlock to move the peace process forward, most notably in the Wye River Accords of 1998. Since the collapse of the Oslo process in 2000, American envoys like George Mitchell have also been careful to place Israeli security concerns at the forefront of their own efforts at peace promotion.

As we shall see in the course of this book, Israel, though it has never ignored Europe, has rarely trusted its motives for involvement in the peace process and has regularly questioned the goodwill and intent of the emissaries, peace missions and special representatives dispatched to the region on behalf of Brussels or national governments.

No less important among the obstacles Europe faces in its attempt to play a central role in the politics of peacemaking has been the Arab awareness of the US-Israeli special relationship. This has engendered an unshakeable Arab belief that Israel's economic, strategic and diplomatic reliance on the US has left it vulnerable to US pressure and persuasion and that only the US can guarantee any concessions for peace made by Israel. During the late 1970s, President Anwar Sadat of Egypt encapsulated this attitude. As Sadat explained, both Egypt and Israel looked to the US to the exclusion of any other external party during its peace negotiations because 'America is the only partner that has got cards in this game…we need someone that can be trusted by both of us to come and help us create confidence'.[11]

As this book will show, even in the 1970s and 1980s when the US refused to deal with it or recognise its claim to represent the Palestinian people, the Palestine Liberation Organisation (PLO) held a similar view of the importance of the US-Israeli special relationship for the achievement of its primary objective, the establishment of a Palestinian state. Following Israel's legitimisation of the PLO with the signing of the Oslo Accords in 1993, Europe could rightly claim that its long-time support for the PLO had been vital to sustaining the group during its wilderness years when the US refused to consider it a legitimate partner. But despite this, and the fact that during the Oslo era Europe established itself as the major contributor to the socio-economic development of the Palestinian Territories, the Palestinians continued to look to the US to play the primary external role in the political process.

Since the collapse of the Oslo peace process in 2000, Europe has continued to consolidate its position as the international community's lead donor to the Palestinians and Israel's number one trading partner. Yet, contrary to the claims of the former US President Jimmy Carter that the Europeans 'occupy an equal position with the US',[12] both Israel and the Palestinians still see US diplomacy, not European money, as the key to achieving a final political settlement.

Having said this, one should not be overly critical of the European failure to bring about a final negotiated settlement. Even the US has only succeeded in overseeing the moves towards peace by Israel and the Arabs when both parties have been ready to move forward. The key turning points—President Sadat's courageous visit to Jerusalem in 1977 and the secret Oslo meetings between Israeli and PLO representatives in 1993—were not initiated by the US. At times when Israel and the local Arab parties have not wanted to make concessions or bring lasting change, the US has been powerless to make them act against their fundamental interests.

Moreover, the argument made by some members of the Israeli political elite, that as long as Israel has the support of Washington the European position is irrelevant, is untrue. The EU's relentless attempts to transform its economic power into political influence may not have succeeded in helping it assert itself as a key player in mediating an end to the conflict. However, they have meant that when a Palestinian state is finally established the EU will play a crucial role in the socio-economic development of the new nation. This makes Europe important to both Israel and the Palestinians. But none of this changes the fact that when it comes to finding a political role in the Israel-Palestine conflict commensurate with its economic weight, Europe, to borrow Henry Kissinger's classic description of Russian foreign policy, has been, and remains, a cause looking for an opportunity.

1

THE FRENCH (DIS)CONNECTION

'If de Gaulle had wanted to barter the affection of the Arabs against the admiration of the Israelis, he certainly succeeded. But we know that that was not—and never was—his purpose. A friend neither of the Arabs, nor of Israel, but only of France.'

Jean Lacouture

A 'series of cataclysmic convulsions'[1] was how the well-known Swiss commentator F.R. Allermann described President Charles de Gaulle's approach to major foreign policy issues in 1963. At that time Allermann was primarily thinking of the French leader's recent decisions to abandon Algeria, veto British entry into the European Economic Community (EEC) and distance his country from the US and the heart of the Atlantic alliance.

But four years later de Gaulle would engage in another 'cataclysmic convulsion' when he ended France's long-time strategic relationship with Israel and sided with the Arab world at the time of the Arab-Israeli War of June 1967. This move by the French president would have profound implications for Europe's subsequent involvement in Arab-Israeli diplomacy and for the development of a more united foreign policy approach among members of the EEC.

The immediate events that led to the outbreak of war and de Gaulle's realignment of France in the Middle East can be traced back to 18 May 1967 when the United Arab Republic[2] (UAR) terminated its consent to the presence of the United Nations Expeditionary Force (UNEF) on Egyptian territory and requested its immediate withdrawal. Without

7

consulting the UN Security Council, UN Secretary-General U Thant quickly acceded to the demands of Egypt's President Gamal Abd al Nasser, the charismatic local champion of Pan-Arabism. He recalled the UN force that had been created in November 1956 to patrol the Egyptian-Israeli armistice and demarcation lines delineated in the 1949 armistice accords between the two countries.[3]

Four days later, on 22 May, President Nasser declared his intention to reconstitute the blockade of Israel in the Straits of Tiran. This, far more than the earlier expulsion of UNEF forces, constituted a direct threat to regional peace. In the face of economic and diplomatic isolation in the Arab world, Israel was very sensitive to Arab attempts to cut its vessels off from the international shipping lanes of the Middle East. Ten years earlier, on 1 March 1957, Israel's then foreign minister Golda Meir had stated at the UN General Assembly that 'interference, by armed force, with ships of Israel exercising free and innocent passage in the Gulf of Aqaba and through the Straits of Tiran, will be regarded by Israel as an attack entitling it to exercise its inherent right of self defence under article 51 of [the] UN Charter'.[4] To emphasise that Israel's position had not altered in the ensuing decade, Gideon Rafael, Israel's UN ambassador, re-read this section of Meir's speech into the UN record on 24 May.

At a lavish reception in Paris in December 1966, de Gaulle had advised the Israeli ambassador, Walter Eytan, that 'since you are strong, you should also be peaceful'.[5] Six months later, the French president was unmoved by the symbolism of Rafael's act at the UN in New York. In a meeting with Abba Eban in late May, de Gaulle told Israel's gifted foreign minister that the closing of the Straits of Tiran should not be regarded as a *casus belli*. A view that was reiterated by French officials, some of whom even argued privately that Nasser might have a strong legal case in closing the Straits.[6] At the same time the French government called on the three other Great Powers (the US, the Soviet Union and Great Britain) to join France in making a joint declaration opposing the use of arms by Israel or its Arab opponents. On 2 June, de Gaulle's government went even further with a statement that made it clear that the party to initiate hostilities would 'not have either her [France's] approval and even less, her support'.[7]

Three days later, at 3.10 am on 5 June 1967, the president of the UN Security Council, Hans Tabor of Denmark, was informed by Ambassador Rafael that Nasser's land and air forces had moved against Israel and that

Israel had responded. Twenty minutes later the Egyptian UN representative informed Tabor of a premeditated Israeli attack against his country. Israel had indeed initiated military action and, following the cessation of hostilities, de Gaulle stuck to his original position that France would withdraw support from the party that started the fighting. This new French stance towards the Arab-Israeli conflict was seen clearly during a five-week period of intense diplomacy at the UN that included 16 meetings of the Security Council (between 5 and 14 June) and 33 meetings of the UN General Assembly Special Session (between 17 June and 21 July), 17 of which were devoted to a general debate on the crisis.

France played a central role in all the UN deliberations on the crisis. Most notably, during the General Assembly Special Session, France voted in favour of the Yugoslav-sponsored Non-Aligned draft resolution on 4 July. This had originally been introduced to the debate on 28 June on behalf of 18 Non-Aligned states. The original text called on Israel 'immediately to withdraw all its forces behind the armistice lines' and concluded with a demand that only 'after Israel withdraws its forces behind armistice lines' should the Security Council give consideration to wider questions relating to the area. On 30 June, an amended version was introduced that replaced the call for Israel to withdraw its forces 'behind armistice lines' with a call for it to withdraw to 'positions they held prior to 5 June 1967', after which the Security Council should 'urgently [examine] all aspects of the situation in the Middle East'.[8]

France's support for this Non-Aligned draft, with its emphasis on an Israeli withdrawal independent of, and prior to, a settlement (or even an agreement to recognise Israel's right to exist), placed it squarely in the Soviet and Arab camp on the issue of the Middle East conflict in the summer of 1967. So did the subsequent decision to abstain on a General Assembly draft resolution more sympathetic to the Israeli position, put forward by the group of Latin American states.[9] Even the French vote in favour of the landmark 'land for peace' Security Council Resolution 242 in early November 1967, which was welcomed by Israel but rejected by the Palestinian Arab delegation at the UN as a 'treasonable act',[10] did little to improve Franco-Israeli relations. In part this was due to the fact that the official French text, which though a translation of the Resolution was equally authoritative, included the definite article 'the' in the demand for an Israeli withdrawal 'from the territories occupied in the recent conflict'; Israel had chosen to infer from the absence of the definite article in the English text that the Security Council agreed that in any future peace there would not be a return to borders as they existed before the war.[11]

The Franco-Israeli rift widened when de Gaulle used a late November press conference to castigate Israel as 'an elite people, sure of itself and overbearing'.[12] He followed this up by describing Franco-Arab cooperation as the 'fundamental base of our foreign policy'.[13]

The Israeli response to the evolving French stance was a mixture of disillusionment and anger. 'We thought we had a friend and we had only a supplier', was how one Israeli official was summed up at the time.[14] Others went further. 'One day, two or three generations from now', wrote the otherwise Francophile Elie Wiesel, 'they will mention Charles de Gaulle and say...he did a lot for his people but he was an anti-Semite'.[15]

Emotions aside, the faith that Jewish and Israeli leaders, from Wiesel to Moshe Dayan and Shimon Peres, the architect of the ties with the French, had placed in de Gaulle was, in the words of one very well-informed contemporary commentator, 'a little naïve and quite misplaced'.[16] It is true that during the 1950s France developed into Israel's closest Great Power ally, as evidenced by the Franco-Israeli-British invasion of Egypt in late 1956 following Nasser's decision to nationalise the Suez Canal.[17] France also became Israel's primary supplier of military equipment, and between 1955 and 1965 almost half of its total arms exports went to the Jewish state. This culminated in France's agreement in the wake of Suez crisis to build Israel a nuclear reactor in the Negev, at Dimona, complete with a separation plant for extracting plutonium, a substance integral to the construction of a nuclear bomb.[18]

This patron-client relationship, at its height between 1955 and 1958, was driven by a specific set of circumstances that existed during these years, including a shared antagonism towards Nasser. The French viewed the Egyptian leader as the major sponsor of the anti-French rebels in Algeria. For its part Israel faced continuous guerrilla attacks from Egyptian-controlled Gaza, and in April 1956 Egyptian artillery initiated a sustained assault, also from Gaza, on Israeli settlements in the Negev. At the same time, French ties with the Arab world were severely damaged by events in North Africa during the era of decolonisation. Most notably, all Arab nations except Lebanon broke diplomatic ties with Paris during the Algeria crisis, leaving it almost as isolated in the region as Israel.

With the fall of Guy Mollet's Socialist-led government in May 1957, the 'almost complete identification'[19] with Israel that had defined the latter half of the 1950s came to an end. In 1960, only two years after he came to power, de Gaulle temporarily suspended French aid to the Israeli nuclear project. The following year the annual staff level meetings between the French and Israeli militaries were ended. The minor Israeli role in the 1965 abduction of the Moroccan political dissident Mehdi Ben Barka in Paris led de Gaulle to order an inquiry into the nature of Franco-Israeli military cooperation. On top of all this, from 1962 onwards, having extricated France from its brutal attempt to suppress Algerian independence, de Gaulle had begun re-evaluating his country's close political ties to Israel.

In the diplomatic sphere French representatives at the UN in New York began distancing themselves from the Israeli position in debates. France also set out to rebuild its practical role across the region. By 1967 there were over 26,000 French teachers and technicians working in the Arab world, compared with just 33 in Israel.[20]

This process of normalisation was almost complete by the summer of 1967. In May, officials from the Quai d'Orsay and embassies across the region met in Beirut to review France's Middle East policy. This occasion was heralded by Hervé Alphand, secretary-general at the foreign ministry, as evidence that France had rediscovered its 'traditional role in the Middle East'.[21] Following the Beirut meeting Alphand met Nasser in Cairo. A few weeks later, at the height of the war, he confided in a European diplomat stationed in Paris that even after meeting the Egyptian President he had 'not expected that a crisis, so near to boiling point, existed in the Middle East'.[22]

Some senior officials at the time would subsequently present the June crisis as a 'problem' for de Gaulle.[23] Certainly, in the wake of the Suez crisis and the debacle in Algeria, nothing threatened to set back French attempts to regain past influence in the Arab world like a new round of fighting in which it backed Israel. But the French President, the 'chief European champion of non-ideological power politics',[24] saw an opportunity to regain *la gloire* in a crucial region by using the June conflict to realign French policy in a dramatic, rather than a gradual, fashion. Decades later de Gaulle's foreign minister, Maurice Couve de Murville, would explain that the 1967 crisis was only 'one incident' and that the decision to adopt a position of 'complex objectivity' went back to the late 1950s.[25]

True as this was, President de Gaulle's highly visible and unprecedented involvement was widely criticised across a society whose radio stations and newspapers, led by *Le Monde*, provided blanket coverage of the affair. Shocked by the government's abandonment of Israel, many French citizens agreed with Raymond Aron that the President was 'gratuitously aggressive' towards Israel.[26] Aron, the philosopher and political commentator, was de Gaulle's most vocal domestic critic during the crisis. But foreign observers in Paris reported that French public opinion also viewed Nasser's actions leading up to war as 'insupportable and irresponsible acts of aggression' and 'reacted…in a manner uniformly sympathetic to Israel'.[27]

Within the French elite, many Gaullists and even some Communists and Left-wing intellectuals noted for their outspoken opposition to such imperialist actions as the war in Vietnam came out in favour of Israel's right to self-defence. Many within the military and scientific establishment, who had developed deep and resilient connections with their Israeli counterparts in the previous decade, found it harder to abandon their working relationship with Israel than their head of state—despite the official line one French general could not resist telephoning the Israeli Defence Attaché in Paris to congratulate him on his country's military victory in June.[28]

There is no doubt that what Aron characterised as this 'diplomatic slide out of neutrality and into solidarity with the Arab countries'[29] went down well with its intended audience in the Middle East. There were pro-French demonstrations outside French embassies in various Arab capitals during the summer of 1967. Mohamed Hassanein Heikal, editor in chief of the influential Egyptian newspaper *Al Ahram* and a confidant of President Nasser, summed up the general attitude at all levels of Arab society when he paid tribute to de Gaulle for standing by the Arabs.[30]

In particular, de Gaulle's harsh criticism of Israel during his notorious November 1967 press conference was held up as a vindication of the Arab position. This was especially so as it came in the wake of the Khartoum summit, at which the Arab states had passed the infamous 'Three No's' resolutions of 'no peace, no recognition and no negotiation' with Israel.[31] In the wake of de Gaulle's November speech Nasser praised him as 'a man of principle' and the 'only Western Head of State on whose friendship the Arabs can depend'.[32] The Lebanese Prime Minister, Rashid Karami, described him as a man of honour and awarded the French President the title of 'Napoleon of the Century'.[33] Not content with words alone, a grateful President Abdul Rahman Arif of Iraq travelled to Paris to 'stretch out our hand to him who wants to befriend us'.[34]

By the end of 1967 even *The Times* of London, an organ loath to credit de Gaulle's foreign policy, had to admit that 'French diplomacy…has been having a prodigious year in the Middle East'.[35] But rising prestige in the Arab world aside, de Gaulle's dramatic realignment in the Middle East failed to breathe life into his attempt to achieve French dominance of the EEC in the realm of international affairs.

Israel still enjoyed widespread sympathy across Europe in the days and weeks following the war. In West Germany, Italy, the Netherlands, Britain Denmark and Norway, public opinion was overwhelmingly pro-Israel. So was popular sentiment in Europe's neutral states of Switzerland, Ireland, Sweden and Austria. Years of vocal Arab threats, Nasser's more recent expulsion of UNEF forces, and his attempts to deny Israel access to the Straits of Tiran, as well as the UN Secretary-General's seemingly ignominious abandonment of the UN mandate, were all viewed as evidence of Arab belligerence, UN impotence and the legitimacy of Israel's war of self-defence.

Inside the Community there was also added anger over de Gaulle's decision to break with Israel without consulting his European partners, all the more so as the French move had caused a number of minor political crises across the continent. Thus, during the summer of 1967, Belgium, Italy, Luxembourg and the Netherlands took a totally different position from France on the issue. Research published subsequently by the Beirut-based Institute of Palestine Studies characterised the stance of the four countries at the UN General Assembly during those dramatic days as either 'strongly' or 'very strongly' pro-Israeli, while France was the only EEC member to be classed as 'strongly pro-Arab'.[36]

The Federal Republic of Germany (West Germany) was not a member of the UN at this time. But it also found ways to make its distaste for the French position very apparent. Relations with Israel remained an extremely sensitive issue in Germany given the country's responsibility for the extermination of six million European Jews in World War Two. Over the previous two decades, bilateral ties between Bonn and Jerusalem had developed gradually. In September 1952 West Germany agreed to pay significant financial reparations as compensation for Nazi crimes against Europe's Jewish population. Relations culminated in March 1965 with the commencement of diplomatic relations. Though this decision led to the withdrawal of all but three (those of Tunisia, Morocco and Libya) of the twelve Arab ambassadors in Bonn, it was viewed as a major contribution to the rehabilitation of Germany on the world stage and also forced many Israelis and Jews to rethink their understandably negative, if not deeply hostile, view of the German state.[37]

Bonn sent 20,000 gas masks to Israel at the outbreak of the 1967 war, and though officially neutral the West German government was openly sympathetic to the Israeli position. In April, a month before the start of the conflict, a senior official dismissed an Arab League call for Bonn to refrain from extending military, economic and financial aid to Israel and to contribute 100 million marks to the Palestinian cause, on the grounds that 'no self respecting government would accede to such demands'.[38] In the immediate term the war actually appeared to help Israel in its major objective of replacing its 1964 economic agreement with the Community (which was due to expire in June 1967) with an association agreement.[39] As the Dutch foreign ministry noted during the war, the conflict had created a 'wave of sympathy for Israel [and] is likely to help considerably the conclusion of some form of agreement of association'.[40]

On 7 June 1967, one day after the outbreak of the war, the European Commission adopted its report to the Council of Ministers containing suggestions for the new phase of trade negotiations between Israel and the Community. This report included a recommendation calling for the negotiation of a preferential trade agreement with Israel on the basis of Article 111 of the Treaty of Rome. As the press noted this was both 'politically provocative [and]…a major innovation in the Community's foreign policy'.[41]

It also demonstrated that despite de Gaulle's 'shock tactics' France did not have the power to sway events in Europe, let alone the Middle East or the wider world. The French decision to endorse the Yugoslav draft resolution at the UN Special Session, in the company of the Soviet Union and the Arabs, and the refusal of its European allies to follow suit further underlined that France was a second-rank power whose decisions carried little practical weight.

If in early June 1967 de Gaulle, the 'master-builder'[42] of France's Arab policy, was confident enough to avoid consulting any of France's EEC allies prior to breaking with the previous pro-Israel policy, within months greater political consensus, at least rhetorically, became the order of the day. Arriving in Bonn in mid-July 1967, de Gaulle summed up this new thinking: '…there are two possibilities: one can accept things as they are…it is the easy way. Or there is the second possibility.…that is to safeguard our own personality. The first condition of this is that French and Germans should not drift asunder...the second is that what we have built for six years in the economic field be maintained'.[43] Of course, such cooperation would be on French terms or not at all. Hence the French abstention on a December 1967 resolution calling for 'real political cooperation within the alliance based on mutual consultation' adopted by the six other members of the Western European Union (WEU), a body made up of the EEC member states and Britain.[44]

At a meeting in Rome, on the eve of the 1967 War, Community leaders chose to ignore the worsening crisis in the Middle East and instead focused their discussions on the candidacies of applicant states.[45] During the ensuing crisis and the subsequent summer of international diplomacy there was little attempt to deal with the issue at the Community level. This reluctance to get involved was mocked by Raymond Aron who noted sarcastically that the Community 'was concerning itself with beetroot during these historic days'.[46] The European Parliament was no less critical and passed a resolution deploring 'the failure of the Community to date to frame a common policy [on the crisis]'.[47] Even when the UN Security Council adopted Resolution 242—which, though subject to widely differing interpretations, has since been accepted by all parties as the basis for any final settlement—in November 1967, the only official statement made by the Community was that 'we affirm our approval of the resolution which constitutes the basis for a settlement'.[48]

Despite this detachment it was becoming increasingly hard for the Community to ignore the evolving conflict in the Middle East. The June 1967 war did not mark the beginning of a Palestinian refugee crisis but it did result in the displacement of a further 200,000 Palestinians, which exacerbated the existing problem. By the winter of 1967 only a tiny fraction of those Palestinian Arabs who had fled the West Bank in June had returned to their homes and the future looked bleak for the rest.

As the Arab and Israeli negotiating positions crystallised it became increasingly difficult to separate the humanitarian issue relating to the refugees from the political issue concerning the Israeli occupation of the West Bank and Gaza Strip. At the same time the debate over the relationship between a solution to the Palestinian refugee problem and a settlement of the Arab-Israeli dispute intensified. This deeply affected European attitudes in coming years. So did the fact that Israel's victory in June 1967 and, in particular, its occupation of territories captured during the fighting transformed the European view of the Jewish state: from being a victim of Arab aggression it was now seen as a 'self-confident, coldly efficient', and even colonial, occupying power at a time of growing European sympathy for Third World causes and anti-colonial ideology.[49] Or as a long article on Israel published in the *Irish Times* in February 1970, entitled 'Adolescent David feels the loss of love', put it: 'the fact of the matter is that Israel is growing up and nobody loves the assertive spotty, adolescent David quite as much as they did the schoolboy'.[50]

Until June 1967 the international community, including the EEC, viewed the Palestinian issue overwhelmingly in humanitarian terms and there was little support for the political aspirations of the Palestinian people, who for the most part lived as refugees in Arab states or under Egyptian and Jordanian control in Gaza and the West Bank respectively. Following the 1967 war the Arab-Israeli military conflict entered a new phase characterised by an upsurge in Palestinian guerrilla warfare and terrorist operations. This enhanced the belief that Zionism was an anachronistic, even illegitimate, ideology while the Palestinian struggle was one of liberation.

In 1964, the Palestine Liberation Organisation (PLO) was founded under Egyptian auspices, in part because of President Nasser's belief that Israel had successfully marginalised the Palestine issue in the West.[51] In the same year Fatah, Yasser Arafat's power base in the Palestinian movement, began organised guerrilla operations against Israel from its base in Ba'athist Syria. Since its founding in the late 1950s, Fatah had been comparing itself to the Front de Libération Nationale (FLN) in Algeria and the National Front for the Liberation of Southern Vietnam (NLF), better known as the Viet Cong.[52]

Over the next decade, Arab regimes and their media organs began playing up to the anti-colonial atmosphere in the Western world by hailing the Vietnamese offensive against US backed forces as a precedent for the Palestinians and promoting an Algerian or a North-Vietnamese model of liberation against Israel. As Israel's Foreign Minister Abba Eban confided in Nicholas Katzenbach, the acting US Secretary of State, this new approach of mimicking what had been 'practiced in Algeria, Vietnam' had 'created a major problem' for Israel both on and off the battlefield.[53]

Edward Said, the celebrated Palestinian-American academic later described by the *New York Times* as the 'Bright Star of English Lit and the PLO',[54] described 1969 as the 'year of legitimacy' for the Palestinians.[55] During that year Fatah gained control of the Palestine National Council (PNC), the governing body of the PLO, and under Arafat Fatah's 'nouveau riche dynamism',[56] as it was called at the time, energised the PLO and quickly succeeded in creating a new identity for the Palestinians.[57] Fawaz Turki captured this. 'Suddenly', he recalled, 'Palestine became the Palestinians, the Palestinians became the PLO, and the PLO became in an age that looked romantically at such things, a national liberation movement'.[58]

The new reality became even harder to ignore as the upsurge in Palestinian violence was not confined to targets inside Israel's borders, but was increasingly being carried out in Europe or against European property. For example, between July 1968 and the end of 1972, Palestinian terrorists were responsible for attacks on Israeli, European or American airlines or aviation facilities in Rome (three times), Athens (three times), Zurich (twice), Munich (twice), Jordan (twice), Amsterdam (once), Beirut (once) and Brussels (once). The first of the three attacks on Rome, in July 1968, was unprecedented. The Popular Front for the Liberation of Palestine (PFLP) had hijacked an El Al aeroplane bound for Tel Aviv, primarily in order to create an international media event. As Zehdi Labib Terzi, the PLO's chief observer at the UN in the mid-1970s, acknowledged, this 'aroused the consciousness of the world and awakened the media and world opinion much more—and more effectively—than 20 years of pleading at the UN'.[59]

So did the expulsion of the PLO from Jordan in September 1970 (known subsequently as 'Black September') and the 1972 Munich massacre, the murder of 11 members of the Israeli Olympic team in full view of the world's press. The Munich operation has been described as marking the beginning of global information warfare.[60] No less important, Munich also underlined the fact that, as one sympathetic Western observer put it, '"Palestinian" is [now] identified with the commando warrior rather than with the downtrodden displaced person'.[61] Such actions increasingly fuelled the belief within Europe that a solution to the wider Arab-Israeli conflict first necessitated a resolution of the Palestine problem. As an *Economist* headline argued in mid-1969, 'Palestine is the key'.[62]

This growing focus on the political aspect of the Palestinian issue offered a disunited Community an opportunity to come together on an issue on which there was increasing consensus. An editorial in *The Times* in mid-1969, at a time when disagreement was rife inside the Community on numerous issues, drew attention to this when it noted that 'an apparent paradox may be true—that the best means of ensuring détente in Europe is to concentrate on extra-European matters such as...the Middle East'.[63]

That was certainly the thinking behind the specially-convened WEU meeting early in the same year. As the British Foreign Secretary Michael Stewart explained, the Palestine issue had been chosen as the focus for this discussion as a 'concrete example' of European political consultations, and a 'decided step forward in European unity'.[64] France refused to participate in this meeting; its foreign minister Michel Debré dismissed the talks as pointless. Other French officials threatened that France would withdraw from the WEU if Britain continued to use it as a 'pretext' for creating an alternative to the EEC in the political sphere.[65] Even taking into account the French boycott, the meeting was a success and led to a series of political consultations on the Middle East between Britain and France's five EEC partners within the WEU framework. This in turn resulted in a further agreement between those participating to consult one another on important matters of foreign policy before taking up firm national positions.[66]

Despite the French distaste for Britain's central role in this process, there was no ignoring its message to Paris that France's EEC partners were deeply frustrated by the ongoing failure to present a united front on foreign policy and would look elsewhere (in this case to the WEU) if necessary to achieve this. It also underlined what had become increasingly apparent—substantive European political consultations, and even agreement, were possible if the evolving Arab-Israeli conflict, in particular the Palestinian issue, topped the agenda of any foreign policy discussions.

Following the establishment of the EEC in 1958, Israel's first Prime Minister David Ben-Gurion was of the view that the 'closely knit community...would become a central force in world affairs' and Israel needed to forge close ties with it.[67] Accordingly, Israel was the third country after the United Kingdom and the Republic of Ireland to establish a diplomatic mission with full ambassadorial status in Brussels.[68] In 1964, despite considerable diplomatic pressure from the Arab world, the Community signed its first non-preferential trade agreement in the Middle East with Israel.[69] By January 1967, the Israeli delegation in Brussels was expressing its interests in a Customs Union in the industrial sector.[70]

In December 1967, as the longer term ramifications of the previous summer's war began to coalesce, the European Council debated EEC-Israeli trade relations. The Commission restated its support for a preferential agreement with Israel, possibly extending, in the future, to association. This was supported by West Germany, the Netherlands, Belgium and Luxembourg. Even Italy (a direct competitor of Israel in several agricultural product areas) was prepared to consider a preferential agreement, or even association, if the Israeli negotiations took place in the context of general enlargement that did not focus exclusively on the Mediterranean. However, France refused to discuss the nature or extent of any future economic links with Israel. Over the following years it opposed improved economic ties with Israel on the grounds that a preferential agreement that abolished customs duties was out of proportion with Israel's economic importance to the Community. It even adopted the Italian call for expansion northwards as a way of avoiding progress with Israel.[71]

It was only in late 1969, and in return for the Netherlands agreeing to abandon its own opposition to improving economic ties with North Africa and exploratory talks with Lebanon and the UAR, that France agreed to remove its veto on an agreement with Israel.[72] The upshot of this trade-off was the Israel-EEC agreement of June 1970. This extended preferential treatment to industrial commodities and granted the most significant staged-tariff reductions on Israeli industrial exports up to that point.

With this out of the way, France was now determined to make 'tenacious efforts'[73] to bring its EEC partners into line with its political approach to the Palestine question, in order to regain its influence at the heart of the Community. In preparation for the European Summit in The Hague in December 1969, the French government, led by President Georges Pompidou, stepped up diplomatic efforts to initiate political cooperation in the foreign policy sphere so as to enable the Community to play a major role in world affairs.[74]

At this summit, EEC leaders reaffirmed their 'belief in the political objectives which give the Community its meaning and purport, their determination to carry their undertaking through to the end', and confidence in the final success of their efforts. More practically, they also agreed to launch a framework for European Political Cooperation (EPC). Until the establishment of the EPC framework there existed no formal mechanism for joint European policy, and foreign policy was excluded from the Community process. The Luxemburg Report of 1970, though cautious, built on the new initiative by calling for 'regular exchanges of information and consultations, a better mutual understanding on great international problems…[to] strengthen solidarity by promoting the harmonisation of their views, the coordination of the positions, and where it appears possible and desirable, common actions'.[75]

The Palestine issue held centre stage in discussions at the Hague meeting, and it was also a key focus of subsequent meetings of the EPC framework during 1970. Yet the fact remained that European Political Cooperation at this time was both tenuous and unpredictable, even on the Palestine question. Disunity on the issue was apparent at the first political cooperation meeting in Munich in November 1970, where there was significant disagreement on the Middle East. It was also seen in Community members' voting at the UN. For example, on 4 November 1970, France voted in favour of a General Assembly draft resolution on the Palestine issue. The Netherlands voted against and Denmark, Belgium, Luxembourg and Italy abstained. On a second vote on the same day, France voted against while Denmark, Italy, Luxembourg, the Netherlands and Belgium voted in favour.[76]

Nevertheless, by the time of the May 1971 meeting of EEC foreign ministers in Brussels convened to discuss political co-operation in the international arena, the Palestine issue once more topped the agenda. Israeli leaders had taken little comfort in the statement by Michel Debré the previous year that his country's attitude towards Israel had been 'grievously misunderstood'.[77] Instead, prior to this meeting there was deep concern over the possibility that (in the words of Prime Minister Golda Meir) France's 'one-sidedly anti-Israel'[78] policy could radicalise its Community partners. Hence, on the eve of the Brussels talks, Abba Eban met his West German counterpart Walter Scheel to urge him not to follow the 'French adoption of the Soviet-Arab line'. The Israeli foreign ministry also took the unusual step of sending notes to the governments of Belgium, Italy, the Netherlands and Luxembourg asking them not to succumb to the French position.[79]

According to the French foreign minister, Maurice Schumann, the Brussels meeting was a 'good start' as the Community had 'considerably narrowed the gap between our points of view'.[80] The meeting led to the drafting of a document named after Schumann that was unanimously approved by the six EEC foreign ministers on 13 May. The paper restated the Community's support for UN Security Council Resolution 242; an Israeli withdrawal (with minor adjustments) to lines occupied on 4 June 1967; and the internationalisation of Jerusalem. But it also broke new ground in supporting the right of Palestinian Arab refugees either to return to their former homes or to be compensated.[81]

The Schumann memorandum was never officially published, and although it directly addressed the Palestine issue, most notably in regard to the hugely controversial matters of the final status of Jerusalem and the repatriation of refugees, it also dealt with a number of issues relating to the wider Middle East conflict. In addition, the rest of the Community was still not willing to accept French hegemony in the political sphere by bowing to its will on the Palestine issue. This prevented any agreement over the document's value, with German and Dutch officials dismissing it as 'a working paper' of no real importance.[82]

Despite the reluctance of the Community to embrace this French-sponsored approach to the Middle East conflict, the Schumann document did have the dual effect of alienating Israel further and focusing the Community's Middle East policy increasingly on the politics of the Palestine issue.[83] Its circulation was followed by an expression of sympathy by the Italian Foreign Minister, Aldo Moro, for the Palestinian struggle for a homeland, as well as the Belgian government's announcement of its 'preoccupation' with the future of the Palestinian people.[84] 1971 also saw the beginning of official EEC aid to the Palestinians under the auspices of the United Nations Relief and Works Agency (UNRWA). In November 1972, it was announced that over the next three years the EEC would provide food worth 22 million francs to Palestinian refugees through UNRWA.

Though ostensibly a humanitarian gesture, this decision was part of the attempt to develop a common European approach in the foreign policy sphere. As Le Monde noted at the time, this idea of bringing united EEC financial assistance to the Palestinian refugees had come about not at a meeting on aid, but at a meeting convened to discuss unanimity in EEC diplomacy.[85] These 'politico-humanitarian' contributions to UNRWA, as the British Foreign Office termed it, were embraced across the Community.[86] In late 1970 Patrick Hillery, Ireland's foreign minister, justified an increase in aid to UNRWA 'on political grounds [as a way of] demonstrating in a practical manner the government's wish to assist in alleviating the cause of tension in the Middle East'.[87] A similar argument was made subsequently by France and Italy for their decision to use UNRWA to fund two Palestinian schools and a hospital.[88]

This growing capacity for agreement on international affairs, even if it was only in regard to the Palestine issue, was undoubtedly helped by the resignation of de Gaulle in late April 1969. His departure marked the end of what the distinguished Dutch historian Peter Geyl termed 'attempts to subject [the Community] to his leadership inspired by dreams of French grandeur'.[89] From the late 1940s onwards the concept of European unity was driven to a large extent by France and it was a Frenchman, Jean Monnet, who had championed the idea of a united Europe. This idea of creating a new centre of power in the world capable of developing and implementing its own policies gained the support of a US foreign policy establishment that viewed increased European unity as desirable in the face of the Soviet threat. But upon his return to power in 1958 de Gaulle was hostile to European political integration and France became the most implacable opponent of the European idea. Instead, he promoted the idea of '*l'Europe des Patries*', which rejected both European supra-nationalism and Atlanticism.[90] Under his watchful eye, over the next decade, French policy makers were unwilling to concede even that minimum of Community decision-making necessary for a real European role. This led Monnet to tell de Gaulle that if he continually put France to the forefront he was going to kill the European idea for ever.[91]

De Gaulle's preoccupation with the grandeur of France and his determination that the Community should exist to serve French interests was not a purely personal phenomenon. His successor Georges Pompidou, described by a well-known commentator as de Gaulle's 'own invention',[92] also represented a powerful nationalist tradition in French politics. Pompidou would continue to challenge American hegemony during his presidency, complaining that Washington was not keeping Europe informed on key developments—including the decision of President Richard Nixon to go to Moscow in October 1971, the Strategic Arms Limitation Talks (SALT I), and the ongoing US-Soviet discussions on Mutual Balance Force Reductions (MBFR).

The same was true in the matter of the Middle East. Like his predecessor, Pompidou explicitly continued to promote French national interests in the region, telling the National Press Club in Washington in February 1970 that 'it is sufficient to look at a map to see that France has a direct

interest in all that happens in the Mediterranean'.[93] A view more eloquently expressed by Michel Jobert, Pompidou's foreign minister, who
noted that 'the memory of France, for a large part, is Mediterranean'.[94]
Pompidou was particularly critical of the failure of the US administration
to consult him on the Middle East peace efforts undertaken by the Secretary of State, William Rogers, in 1969.[95] In his first Elysée press conference Pompidou spoke of the 'human and political problems posed by the
existence and rights of the Palestinian people'. Soon afterwards, he
acknowledged the 'political character' of the Palestinian problem.[96] In
1970 France voted in favour of UN General Assembly Resolution 2628
which linked the Palestine refugee problem to the 'inalienable rights of
the people of Palestine', and which was dismissed by Israel as 'one-sided
and harmful'.[97]

These efforts gained much praise in the Arab world. In 1971 Ghassan
Tueni, the Lebanese politician and newspaper editor, spoke for many in
the region when he expressed the hope that the EEC would now take
its place as a 'new force…that is prepared to consider the Middle East as
its natural extension, its natural partner'.[98] But Pompidou's stance infuriated pro-Israel constituencies almost as much as de Gaulle's. In February
1970, for example, the New York Mayor John Lindsay boycotted a meeting with Pompidou in New York in protest at his pro-Arab stance, while
on the same visit Pompidou's wife was harangued by pro-Israel activists
in Chicago.[99]

However, the end of the de Gaulle era did see the end of the French
obsession with keeping Britain out of the EEC, a preoccupation that
more than anything else had isolated France and retarded increased
political cooperation in Europe during the previous decade. France apart,
there had been great relief inside the Community following the July 1961
British application to enter the EEC. Just four months earlier, the Dutch
government had vetoed a French proposal for co-operation on international policy, because of concerns that France was looking to dominate
the Community. As the Belgian Prime Minister Théo Lefèvre put it, the
smaller EEC states wanted Britain to join to ensure equilibrium in
Europe.

Just as de Gaulle chose not to consult his partners prior to his decision
to end France's pro-Israel policy in 1967, he did not consult them prior
to his decision to veto British entry in January 1963. Across Europe this
veto was met with 'dazed resentment', in the words of Lord Gladwyn,

the former British ambassador to both Paris and the UN.[100] For the remainder of his time in power de Gaulle made no secret of his distrust of the pro-Anglo-Saxon and pro-Atlanticist tendencies of his European partners. As he told the British ambassador in Paris in February 1969, in a conversation subsequently leaked to the media by the British Foreign Office, while France had achieved an independent position it was impossible for its EEC partners to follow suit.[101]

Britain's re-application for entry into the EEC in mid-1967 was also vetoed by de Gaulle. But de Gaulle's subsequent withdrawal from public life and a new British application in 1969 provided cause for optimism. All the more so because senior British officials like Foreign Secretary Stewart 'made clear' that they supported the development of a Community that would 'remove the danger of French dominance … and the consequent danger of estrangement from the US'.[102] Although there were no illusions that either de Gaulle's departure or British entry would bring about the full integration of European foreign policy in the short term, the British attitude encapsulated by Stewart was music to the ears of officials in Italy, West Germany and the Benelux countries. By 1971 there was a real sense of optimism that the time was near for what Anthony Hartley termed a 'regional Europe' able to 'exercise economic and political influence on geographically adjacent areas—in the first place in the Mediterranean'.[103]

There were, of course, some naysayers who were sceptical of the impact of British entry on Europe's political development in the face of the global realignment following the thaw in US-Chinese relations and the West German Chancellor Willy Brandt's embrace of *Ostpolitik*. Others saw the challenges in less strategic and more cynical terms. The well-known Italian commentator Luigi Barzani dismissed both the motives for British entry and its capacity to make a difference, arguing instead that the British joined the EEC reluctantly like 'decayed aristocrats obliged by adverse circumstances to eat in a soup kitchen'.[104] Nevertheless, by the beginning of the 1970s the Community had entered into a new stage in its development. In late 1970 the Davignon Report was approved. It called for bi-annual meetings of foreign ministers, as well as the convening of summit conferences and the establishment of a committee of EEC political directors drawn from national foreign ministries. For the first time EEC ambassadors began receiving common policy papers and even some joint instructions on how to respond to various foreign policy issues. The following year, in an unprecedented ruling, the European Court of Justice widened its interpretation of the Community's treaty-making powers and hence its ability to engage in international affairs.

All this was not lost on the international community, and by 1972 almost 100 countries maintained accredited representatives to the EEC in Brussels. At the Paris Summit of October 1972, there was a further endorsement of the EPC framework. In particular, there was an attempt to improve cooperation in international affairs by having foreign ministers meet four times a year instead of twice. As the meeting's final communiqué noted, it was hoped that this would help 'deal with problems of current interest and, where possible, to formulate common medium-and long-term positions'. The same communiqué also expressed the Community's desire to 'establish its position in world affairs as a distinct entity'.[105] The meeting also announced the political goal of a European Union by 1980. As one commentator summed up, if the Treaty of Rome was the Community's Old Testament, then the Paris communiqué was its 'New Testament'.[106]

The 'ambitious catalogue of the Paris summit of October 1972',[107] as *The Times* put it, added to a sense that there now existed a real opportunity to build on systematic cooperation between governments in order to develop collective policies. It also opened the way for a meeting of Community foreign ministers in The Hague in December 1972 to agree that following the entry of Britain, Ireland and Denmark, the newly enlarged EEC should try to coordinate its position on foreign policy, especially at the UN in New York. Sir Christopher Soames, a former British Ambassador in Paris and an early EEC Commissioner, summed up this optimism only months after British entry:

A few months ago, a new entity was born—the enlarged Community, with over 250 million people. We have no precedents on how such a Community should order its international relations. Our economic agglomeration gives us tremendous political potential. Such political potential inevitably imposes on us, here and now, a heavy political responsibility to live up to the role that we can play for the good in the world—not simply within Europe, but well beyond its shores. To take part in shaping such policies is an exciting no less than an exacting task.[108]

There were still major obstacles to overcome, but the acrimonious disunity that existed in the final years of de Gaulle's presidency was no more. The second Copenhagen Report consolidated the EPC framework and explained that 'as a general rule' member states would no longer look to take up 'final positions [on common European foreign policy issues] without prior consultation with its partners'.[109] The Community, with its new British member (as well as the smaller nations of Denmark and Ireland), had come along way from the summer of 1967 when Raymond Aron castigated France for having 'broken away both from her partners in the Common Market...she has broken with those to whom she is the most closely tied by her economy, her culture, her ideals'.[110]

Even the arch-realist, the US National Security Adviser Henry Kissinger, got into the spirit. In a speech before the Associated Press' annual dinner in New York in April 1973, he expressed the belief that over the coming year Europe would 'match and dwarf the great accomplishments of the past decades'. Kissinger did not stop there. Nineteen seventy-three, he announced, would be 'the Year of Europe'.[111]

2

'INGLORIOUS DISARRAY'

'It immediately became clear that oil was an issue upon which a frightened community would be unable to maintain solidarity. There was a distinct air of "every man for himself" and we were soon in inglorious disarray.'

Garret Fitzgerald

'A pious and pointless irrelevance'[1] was how Michael Howard, a leading British commentator, described Henry Kissinger's declaration of the 'Year of Europe'. The British Prime Minister Edward Heath went further. Kissinger's 'mistaken creation of the Year of Europe was rather like my standing between the lions in Trafalgar Square and announcing that we were embarking on a year to save America!'[2] For its part the French government, whose then foreign minister Michel Jobert saw the affair as evidence of the 'clumsiness of the Nixon-Kissinger team',[3] was confused as to whether the US was offering the Community a compliment or an insult. Unsure which was worse, President Pompidou joked about it in public, and Jobert submitted a list of questions to Washington on just what exactly Kissinger meant.[4]

By the end of the 1973 it hardly seemed to matter. By then the newly-operational EPC framework had shown itself to be wholly unsuited to the foreign policy challenges Europe faced and the Community was in the midst of its most serious challenge since the French vetoed British entry a decade earlier. But this time the crisis arose from political and economic challenges extraneous to Europe. As Jobert eloquently put it, the 'true origins of the crisis [were] as distant as its consequences were immediate'.[5]

A view echoed by a powerful editorial in the Italian newspaper *Corriere della Sera* entitled 'Faraway causes and immediate effects'.[6]

On 6 October 1973, the forces of Syria and Egypt invaded Israel on Yom Kippur, the holiest day of the Jewish calendar. Taken by surprise, the Israel Defence Forces (IDF) failed to block the Arab offensive, and this enabled the Egyptians to occupy the Bar Lev defensive line and Syrian tanks to destroy Israeli defences in the southern sector of the Golan front. This opened the way for a push deep into Israel's pre-1967 territory. Facing what seemed to be an existential threat, the Israeli government looked for political and military support from the Western alliance.

After some high-level debate, the US administration agreed to provide a massive airlift to an embattled Israel. Inside the European Community, though some member states such as Italy called for 'immediate consultations',[7] no special meeting was convened to deal with the outbreak of war. Instead the matter was addressed in the course of the pre-scheduled EPC meeting of 11–12 October.[8] The only official Community statement on the matter had no more substance. It restated support for Security Council Resolution 242, which clarified little given the differing interpretations of that resolution among EEC member states. Even the previously outspoken French decided on a 'wait and see' policy, which prompted a letter from Colonel Muammar Qadafi of Libya condemning France's 'reserved attitude'.[9]

As the conflict progressed it became apparent that no European country was willing to follow the US precedent and provide any practical support to the Jewish state. France had initiated an arms embargo on Israel in the wake of the 1967 war. During the 1973 crisis Britain followed suit and refused Israel spare parts for its British-made Centurion tanks. In response to media reports that Israeli ships with American arms were leaving German ports en route to Haifa, the West German government banned arms supplies to Israel from US stocks in the country and publicly rebuked Martin Hillenbrand, the US Ambassador in Bonn.[10]

Nor did any Community member agree to allow the US air convoy sent to re-supply Israel during the war to use its air space or territory for landing or refuelling. Despite this, on 17 October 1973, 11 days into a war that saw 18 days of fighting, representatives from Kuwait, Saudi Arabia, Iraq, Abu Dhabi, Qatar, Libya and Algeria met at the Kuwait Sheraton Hotel. Following this meeting these seven Arab members of the Organisation of Petroleum Exporting Countries (OPEC), the oil producing cartel, announced that they would cut back oil production by five per cent every month until Israel withdrew from occupied Arab territories and restored Palestinian rights.[11] Kuwait and Saudi Arabia went further and threatened an immediate reduction of 10 per cent.[12]

Two days later, all seven Arab states declared that they were in the course of drawing up a list of their 'friends' and 'enemies' in Europe. Oil exports to the 'friendly' nations of France, Spain and the United Kingdom would remain at September 1973 levels. All other European countries would face a 5 per cent monthly cut in deliveries until Israel agreed to Arab demands. That meant all European countries except Portugal and the Netherlands, who along with the US faced an immediate and total Arab oil embargo: Portugal for providing the US with permission to re-equip Israel via the Azores, and the Netherlands for being the most pro-Israeli nation in Europe.

From the late 1950s, vast oil reserves and its involvement in the process of decolonisation had established the Arab world as an increasingly significant economic and strategic player. In Europe there was some awareness of the potential power of oil in swaying attitudes to the Middle East conflict. As an editorial in an Irish national paper presciently noted in 1963, exactly a decade before the oil crisis: 'if it comes to a matter of competition for the friendship of Israel or of the Arab League, nobody can doubt what the outcome will be: the oil-rich Arab states possess an attraction denied to Israel'.[13]

For the most part, the founding of OPEC in 1960, and the growing power of the organisation over the ensuing decade, aroused little attention or concern. Even less notice was paid to the founding of the Organisation of Arab Petroleum Exporting Countries (OAPEC) in January 1968. This body comprised all the Arab members of OPEC, as well as those Arab states whose oil exports were not high enough to qualify them for membership of OPEC (Egypt, Syria and Bahrain). Despite its centrality to global energy supplies OAPEC was studiously ignored. It only received two mentions in the pages of the *New York Times* in the two-year period following its establishment.

In part this indifference was due to the fact that there had been regular predictions of crises in the oil markets since the late 1920s and all had failed to materialise. This led to a widely held view into the 1960s that regardless of political developments there would be affordable oil supplies long into the future. This complacency was further reinforced when warnings, on the eve of the 1967 war, of the 'possibility of an interruption in the flow of oil'[14] failed to materialise. Instead, all that took place was a half-hearted and disjointed attempt by a minority of Arab states, notably Libya and the new Ba'athist regime in Syria, to halt oil supplies to a number of European nations for their perceived support of Israel during the war.

On top of this, Saudi Arabia, which controlled the largest oil reserves in the region, had repeatedly come out against the use of the oil weapon in relation to the Palestine issue. As far back as 1947, the kingdom's founder, Abdul Aziz Ibn Saud, had been opposed to imposing economic or oil sanctions on the West over the Palestine issue. The Saudi representative speaking at a special session of the Arab League's political committee in Lebanon in September 1947 argued that oil sanctions would be divisive and that the oil producing countries would be the main losers in such a move.[15]

Two decades later, Ahmed Zaki Yamani, the flamboyant Saudi Minister for Petroleum Affairs, argued in a similar vein that any oil boycott in response to the 1967 war would hurt producers more than consumers.[16] Soon after, his ruler King Faisal was even more adamant: the Arabs should not allow oil to be used as a political weapon and 'oil and politics should not be mixed'.[17]

There were others, admittedly less powerful, who saw the role that oil could play in the Arab world's political relationship with Europe. One was Cecil Hourani, the veteran Arab intellectual and former adviser to President Habib Bourguiba of Tunisia, who argued in 1969 that 'Arab oil, and the very considerable cash holdings which it generates…could play an important role in giving us influence in the economic and financial life of Europe, with a consequent political influence'.[18]

By 1971, parts of the European media were warning of the 'stranglehold' that Arab oil suppliers now had on Europe.[19] At the same time, credible commentators on the oil industry were warning that the balance between the oil producing and consuming countries had 'shifted decisively in favour of the producing countries', and that 'the political effectiveness of OPEC unity, of unilateral action and of the threat of embargo—these are realities which consuming governments must now begin to address'.[20] However, conventional thinking in Europe on the issue very much echoed the view of Parker Hart, president of the prestigious Middle East Institute in Washington and a former US ambassador in the region. In mid-1971 he was categorical that the 'oil supply today cannot be manipulated successfully for political goals by producing states against major consuming countries'.[21]

Perversely, the fact that the Western world, with Europe in the lead, was virtually the only customer able to buy the quantity of oil produced by the Arabs gave credence to the argument that the producers could not tolerate an interruption of oil supplies as it would reduce their income, thus restricting their ability to service their massive debt and fund infrastructural development.[22] Given this, national efforts to address the issue—such as the 1972 British decision to invest heavily in the coal industry, which had long been in decline—were primarily motivated by a preoccupation with national prestige rather than national security.

Not even the fifteen separate threats in 1972 by senior Arab officials from across the oil-producing states that the oil weapon would be used in the future against their 'enemies'[23] had any noticeable impact on attitudes. The issue of energy was near the bottom of the agenda at the October 1972 heads of government summit and, when in May 1973 the Community held its first ministerial level meeting on energy for almost three years, it failed to agree on a common policy—though by this time Henri Simonet, the highly regarded Belgian politician who held the Commission's Energy portfolio, was openly acknowledging that 'oil is 90 per cent politics'.[24]

In late 1973, when the Arab countries of OPEC did initiate what the French foreign minister Jobert termed a 'selective embargo',[25] the newly-enlarged and totally unprepared Community fell to pieces. On a political level, the next few months would severely test the Community's capacity to act in a united manner in critical situations and the Atlantic alliance would face one of its gravest tests since the Suez crisis of 1956. Matters were made worse as the crisis came at a time when a number of EEC member states were facing domestic political turmoil. Between November 1973 and May 1974 governments fell in Britain, Italy, West Germany and Belgium.

There were also significant economic implications. Between late October and early November, the crisis led to an implied contraction of 13 per cent in the supply of crude oil on the international market and a barrel of crude oil more than doubled in price from US$2.40 to over US$5. The targeting of the Netherlands also had notable implications because of the strategic importance of Rotterdam, through which some two million barrels of petroleum passed daily to the rest of Europe.

Undoubtedly the oil crisis was a dramatic event. Yet the Arab embargo did not cause either an immediate or long-term crisis in supplies, and at no time was there a real shortage of petroleum on the European market. In mid-December 1973 the *Economist* ran an article entitled: 'How Scarce is Oil?'[26] 'Not very' was the answer. Between October 1973 and April 1974, the reserve of oil products in the EEC countries never fell below the 80-day equivalent of consumption.

In fact, during this period those oil producing countries that had refused to join the boycott, including Iran, increased their production and supply. This meant that between December 1973 and March 1974, the availability of petroleum was reduced by 16 per cent in the Netherlands, 12 per cent in West Germany, seven per cent in France and less than one per cent in Britain. It increased by four per cent in Italy, which even managed to register a six per cent increase in consumption of energy at the height of the crisis.[27]

From the moment that the embargo started a majority of EEC member states quickly looked to distance themselves from the US and the Netherlands. West German and Danish efforts to persuade the rest of the Community to stand by the Dutch were rejected by Britain, France and the smaller EEC states on the grounds that the Dutch had brought the boycott on themselves by their openly pro-Israeli position. Or, as one confidential British Foreign Office memorandum of the time summed up, 'the Dutch put their foot in it'.[28] More publicly, a Belgian diplomat, displaying an obtuse understanding of both diplomacy and the principles of democratic politics, told a group of journalists in Brussels: 'Eight European countries have observed strict neutrality. The ninth has followed public opinion. It is only normal that it should suffer the consequences'.[29]

In 1967 the Netherlands had openly blamed Arab aggression towards Israel for the conflict and had championed the Israeli position inside the six-member Community.[30] The Dutch government even agreed to represent Israeli interests in Moscow when the Soviet Union broke off diplomatic ties with Israel in the wake of the war. When the 1973 crisis began the Netherlands was the most outspoken Community critic of the Arab invasion.[31] A group of well-known Dutch figures, including three former prime ministers, even ran a full-page advertisement expressing solidarity with Israel in the *Jewish Chronicle*, a newspaper published in London.[32] But in practical terms, the Netherlands maintained a strictly neutral position during the war. Israeli ships calling at Dutch ports were prevented from loading arms and KLM, the Dutch national airline, can-celled all flights to Israel at the start of the conflict and refused to trans-port volunteers planning to go to Israel's aid.

As at the time of the 1967 war, European public opinion during the 1973 crisis was sympathetic to Israel. According to polls 45–50 per cent of British respondents and 57 per cent of those in France sided with Israel. Only 6 per cent in Britain and 16 per cent in France supported an Arab victory.[33] Despite this, Community governments refused the Netherlands' requests for help in meeting its oil shortage. Britain's foreign secretary Sir Alec Douglas-Home justified his government's refusal to supply Holland from its reserves on the grounds that it would only have got the rest of Europe onto the Arab boycott list.[34] The French government, also on the Arabs' list of 'friendly' nations, fully subscribed to this view. Pompidou's oil minister explained that his government would not break the oil boycott of Holland because it wanted to develop a 'confident, balanced and lasting' relationship with the Arab oil producers.[35] During a visit to London in November 1973, Pompidou was more forthright, telling Prime Minister Heath that standing by those allies who were singled out by the Arab oil producers 'was more likely to result in [us] being attacked by the Arabs and treated by them in the same way'.[36] No doubt Pompidou's stance can be explained, though perhaps not defended, by a French determination not to 'fall prey to the same panic as its European partners', as Jobert put it.[37] Yet, this 'sauve qui peut approach',[38] as it was regularly described at the time, showed little regard for communal cohesion.

Abandoning the Dutch was not in itself enough to guarantee the favour of the oil suppliers. On 6 November 1973, the Community went further. It issued a declaration on the Arab-Israeli conflict, which it described as its 'first contribution' to the 'search for a comprehensive solution'.[39] This statement called for both sides to return to their 22 Octo-ber 1973 positions and for negotiations along the lines set out in UN Security Council Resolutions 242 and 338 (the latter was passed by 14 votes to zero on 22 October 1973[40]). It expressed support for the right of each state to live in peace within secure and recognised borders, an implicit acceptance of Israel's right to exist. However, this was linked to a much more explicit statement that there would only be a just and last-ing peace if the 'legitimate rights of the Palestinians' were taken into account. It also stressed the need for Israel to 'end territorial occupation' of land gained in 1967.[41]

In the immediate wake of the publication of the November 1973 declaration Foreign Office officials argued that the British position 'had not moved a centimetre'. The European statement, they argued, was simply a reiteration of British support for UN Security Council Resolution 242.[42] In truth, it was anything but the standard inoffensive and bland joint communiqué traditionally issued at the end of EEC get-togethers. Rather, it was the first time since 1967 that the Community collectively placed the Palestinian issue at the centre of the political debate. This was followed by a joint Franco-Tunisian communiqué of 17 November, issued during Jobert's two-day visit to the North African nation. It restated the need for Israel to withdraw from lands occupied in June 1967 and demanded a role for the Arabs in any peace conference.

Most important, and directly challenging British official claims at the time, was the fact that by stating 'the need for Israel to end the territorial occupation which it has maintained since the conflict of 1967', the November declaration was lining up the newly-enlarged Community behind the French position since 1967—that Resolution 242 could only be interpreted as a withdrawal from all the territories occupied by Israel in the June war. This would have major repercussions for future British involvement in the politics of the Palestine question. In mid-1975, for example, the French government found it 'difficult to understand' the British reluctance to support any European guarantee of a peace that called for a full Israeli withdrawal to June 1967 borders, on the grounds that the Heath government, in endorsing the November 1973 declaration, had accepted the French reading of Security Council Resolution 242.[43]

The same was true for West Germany. In the summer of 1971 its foreign minister, Walter Scheel, was adamant that in regard to UN Security Council Resolution 242, there were 'differences between the French and West German positions...the attitude of Bonn supports the interpretation given by Washington and London'.[44] But in endorsing the November declaration, West Germany was now 'walking a tightrope'[45] between its commitment to Israel and its obligations to its EEC partners. Even the Dutch government, despite subsequent denials to the contrary by the foreign minister van der Stoel, appeared to accept the French position on Resolution 242 by supporting the November statement.[46]

Just weeks into his new job as US Secretary of State Henry Kissinger took a dim view of the Community's November declaration, which he had only heard about while on a visit to Cairo. Israel reacted even more negatively. Writing in *Ha'aretz*, the well-known commentator Joel Marcus described the declaration as 'the debacle of the anti-Israeli resolution of the EEC'.[47] Israel's Prime Minister Yitzhak Rabin argued that 'in effect the [European declaration] accepts the Arabs position on the political issue in everything regarding the Arab-Israeli conflict'.[48] The foreign minister, Abba Eban, urged the Community to 'reconsider the content and spirit of their declaration', adding that the EEC's new-found interest in Palestinian rights had more to do with 'oil for Europe …than peace for the Middle East'.[49] A view restated by Yigal Allon, Eban's successor as foreign minister, who told the Western media in 1975 that 'during the Yom Kippur [1973] war most European countries behaved in an un-European way. They bowed to pressure. They bowed to blackmail'.[50]

Douglas-Home rejected accusations of blackmail as 'nonsense',[51] but Allon had a point. It was later confirmed by senior OPEC officials that the French and British governments, among others, provided guarantees, including support for the boycott of the Netherlands, in return for keeping their places on the 'friendly' nations list. Subsequently, Heath would have no reservations in acknowledging the link, at least in his mind, between the 6 November 1973 Middle East declaration and the oil crisis, noting that 'in recognition…we were treated, along with France, as a "friendly" nation'.[52]

Heath's recollection does not match the actual timeline, as Britain was placed on the list of 'friendly' nations prior to the publication of the November declaration. However, this was published at the height of European anxiety that the embargo might be extended. On 1 November, just five days before the EEC declaration, Libya, which along with Saudi Arabia provided two thirds of West Germany's oil needs, threatened Bonn with a total boycott if it failed to show what it termed 'positive neutrality'.[53] Just two days before the November declaration, eight of the ten OAPEC member states met in Kuwait to discuss tightening the oil embargo. Given this, even *Le Monde*, which was generally supportive of the European approach throughout the crisis, published a piece in which André Fontaine criticised the EEC declaration as a 'revelation' of the political impotence of Europe in the face of the oil crisis.[54] This view was given credibility by the fact that public Arab threats regarding possible future reductions of up to 25 per cent in oil supplies to Europe ceased immediately following the publication of the 6 November declaration.

At their summit meeting in Algiers in late November 1973, the Arab Heads of State called the EEC's declaration 'significant'.[55] They also expressed a desire to develop closer relations with the Community, adding that 'we look forward with greater concern to the signs of understanding of our position which have begun to appear in the States of Western Europe'.[56] Secret clauses excluded from the original Algiers Declaration, but published subsequently in the Arabic press, called for the 'Arab nation' to build on what President Sadat of Egypt termed 'signs of understanding' in Europe in order to 'develop the political stance'.[57]

The Algiers meeting was important for other reasons also. It agreed to set up PLO information offices in Community capitals under the auspices of the Arab League. Also, by designating the PLO as the 'only legitimate representative of the Palestinian people', a resolution officially confirmed by the Arab summit in Rabat in October 1974, this gathering of Arab leaders placed the Palestinian question and the role of the PLO at the top of the Arab agenda. This would have a significant impact on both Euro-Arab and Euro-American relations over subsequent years.

In the short term, while the crisis dragged on, these moves by Arab states were significant because they provided a pretext for European leaders to defend their decision to make concessions to the Arabs in response to the oil crisis. Jobert, for example, countered accusations of appeasement by critics in the French National Assembly by noting the Arab 'determination at the Algiers Summit' to play a major role.[58] Prior to the 1973 war, the Arab governments had been frustrated over what they saw as their inability to gain political influence in Europe. In late 1972, Egypt's recently-appointed foreign minister, Muhammad Hassan al-Zayyat, made his first official visit overseas to London, Rome and Brussels. On his return he acknowledged that the Arab effort to improve diplomatic ties with Europe had failed in the face of counter-efforts by pro-Israel forces inside the Community.[59] But this changed in late 1973 when, as Mohamed Hassanein Heikal would later note, the political as well as economic power of the oil producing Arab world 'increased enormously'.[60] From this point on, in the words of a British Foreign Office assessment of early 1974, 'our future dealings with the Arabs world will be on the basis of equality and interdependence'.[61]

The events of late 1973 altered for ever the relationship between the oil-exporting Arab nations and the industrial West. Senior Arab officials suddenly found that they had unfettered access to Europe's most senior politicians and policy-makers. On 5 November 1973, al-Zayyat met Pompidou and Jobert in Paris. This was followed by a tour of European capitals by the Saudi oil minister Ahmed Zaki Yamani and Dr Beleid Abdul Sallam, the Algerian Minister of Industry and Energy. In these meetings European leaders pleaded for the Arab world to refrain from jeopardising European unity.[62] In turn the two Arab representatives pressured their hosts to take a firmer stand against Washington's policy in the Middle East in order to protect Europe's oil and other strategic interests in the future.

Such demands did not fall on deaf ears. One major consequence of the oil crisis was that it highlighted the very different realities that Europe and the US faced in dealing with the Middle East.

The rotating presidency of the European Council gives smaller member states the opportunity to interact at the highest levels of the international system. When Ireland's foreign minister Garret Fitzgerald took over this role in the mid-1970s he was surprised on discovering the great 'divergence of attitudes of the Community and the US administration on the Middle East'.[63] The first and most immediately apparent difference related to dependence on Arab oil. Pompidou told Kissinger at the height of the crisis: 'You only rely on the Arabs for about a tenth of your consumption. We are entirely dependant upon them'.[64] The French President was actually overestimating US reliance at this time. In 1973, the US imported just four per cent of its oil from the Arab world, whereas Britain imported 30 per cent, West Germany, 38 per cent, France, 53 per cent and Italy 60 per cent of their oil from the same suppliers.[65]

The Arabs had originally planned to use the embargo to punish the US. Notably, Saudi Arabia's decision to halt oil supplies to the US was accompanied by a demand that Washington 'modify its Middle East policy'.[66] But the focus of the boycott quickly switched to Europe when it became apparent that it was far more vulnerable than the US because it relied far more on oil imports and used a higher proportion of imported oil for essential consumer and industrial needs.[67]

The Arab hope was that if Europe began to feel the impact of an oil shortage it would pressure the US into rethinking its policies towards the Middle East. Or if that did not work, then the aim was to isolate the US and place it in an untenable position among the Western states. In this connection it should be noted that Gideon Rafael, Israel's ambassador in London in 1973, recalled that 'repeatedly' in discussions with Israeli leaders at the time of the first EEC enlargement, 'Washington had pointed to the lack of European support for Israel as a handicap to the US in granting its own'.[68]

This Arab strategy benefited from the fact that even before the 1973 conflict it was already widely accepted inside the Community that the US was largely indifferent to the damage its Middle East policies were doing to European interests. In May 1973, for example, a diverse group of parliamentarians, academics, churchmen and writers from across Europe published an open letter to President Richard Nixon claiming that Europe, not to mention the US, had 'suffered because of the subordination of American policy in the Middle East to Israeli interests'.[69]

Once the crisis got under way this argument gained increased currency. It was noted, for example, that the Arab decision to divide Europe into 'friendly' and 'enemy' nations and to embargo the Netherlands was announced on the same day as President Nixon requested US$2.2 billion from Congress to pay for the military airlift to Israel. An editorial in *Middle East International*, a leading Arabist magazine published in London, summed up this attitude in an editorial of late 1973:

Washington can expect no support from Europe for a policy which ignores UN resolutions as well as the rights of the Arabs ...Nor is Europe's impatience likely to be decreased by the fact that this time its political judgement of the rights and wrongs in the Middle East is reinforced by the painful awareness that its collective economic wellbeing is in jeopardy.[70]

Tensions were compounded by the wave of statements emanating from US administration officials; Congressmen, Middle East experts and newspaper columnists charged Europe with having disgracefully capitulated to oil blackmail and having 'hurried to subscribe to political formulations demanded by the Arabs',[71] as one prominent US academic put it at the time.

It is true that in late October 1973 President Nixon acknowledged that Europe was under severe pressure due to the ongoing turmoil in the region and that this made it necessary to 'avoid another Mideast crisis so the flow of oil continues'.[72] But such statements of understanding were far fewer and garnered far less coverage in Europe than the very critical comments on the European position by more junior officials such as the State Department spokesman Robert McCloskey.[73]

But this growing divide between the Community and the US was due to more than anger over Washington's perceived neglect of European interests in the Middle East or resentment over critical briefings against Europe by mid-level Nixon administration officials. Many news organisations and commentators in Europe were no less scathing of European policy at the time. Italy's *Corriere della Sera* noted how 'blackmail has envenomed the oil crisis', and the *Economist* argued that in shutting its eyes and running around in circles the Community 'managed to combine the behaviour of the ostrich and the hen'.[74] West Germany's *Die Welt*, a newspaper with a track record of support for Israel, argued that the Community's decision to sell out Israel for Arab oil 'must make every German pale with disgust'.[75]

Transatlantic differences had deeper, more profound roots. For much of his time in the White House, President Nixon had been preoccupied with ending the Vietnam War, developing bilateral ties with China and pursuing détente with Moscow. European allies and Middle East conflict were well down his list of priorities. However, by 1973 the Nixon administration had shifted its foreign policy priorities away from South East Asia and towards a diplomatic initiative in the Middle East, as evidenced by Secretary of State Kissinger's lunch in New York for all Arab foreign ministers attending the UN General Assembly in September. America's disentanglement from the Vietnam quagmire and its new focus on the Middle East were greeted positively by some in Europe. Others expressed concerns over the impact they would have on European attempts to develop a common foreign policy independent of Washington on a wide range of issues, not least the Middle East.

From the late 1940s and into the 1950s successive US administrations had openly urged Europe to play a greater role in international affairs as it moved towards economic and political integration. But those days now seemed long over. European leaders had not forgotten Kissinger's 'Year of Europe' speech the previous April, with its assertion that the US 'has global interests and responsibilities. Our European allies have regional interests'.[76] The more informed even recalled that in 1965, prior to entering government service, Kissinger had written that 'a unified Europe is likely to insist on a specifically European view of world affairs, which is another way of saying that it will challenge American hegemony'.[77] Many now agreed with Jobert that the US 'did not have the slightest desire to bring to life a super-national Europe like the USA'[78] and that Kissinger was taking 'evident pleasure'[79] in using events in the Middle East to reassert US dominance over Europe in the region. These suspicions were fuelled by press reports that Kissinger had berated a group of European parliamentarians visiting Washington during the crisis for interfering in an American area of interest.

This major deterioration in US-European relations was all the more notable and noticeable because it occurred at a time when Downing Street was home to the least pro-American British prime minister since World War Two. Noting his 'passionate Euro-centrism', Kissinger recalled that Edward Heath was the 'only British leader I encountered who not only failed to cultivate the "special relationship" with the US but actively sought to downgrade it and to give Europe pride of place in British strategy'.[80]

The Middle East crisis highlighted this very clearly. Prior to British entry into the Community in January 1973, Israeli leaders were not as optimistic as the critic and novelist Rayner Heppenstall who, condemning France's 'repulsive foreign policy', had hoped that British membership would be a prelude to a renaissance in Israeli-European relations.[81] But just as there had been hope across the EEC that British entry would counterbalance French influence on any number of issues, there had been hope in Jerusalem that British entry would go some way towards counterbalancing the French effort to steer the Community's evolving Middle East policy towards the Arab position. As a British Foreign Office memorandum acknowledged during the first year of British EEC membership, 'there is an inclination…to regard us, the new boys in the Community, as having special capabilities in influencing Europe'.[82]

At the same time there was a very real awareness in Jerusalem that since coming to power in June 1970, Heath's Conservative government had moved closer to the French position on the Palestine issue. This belief gained further credence following the Foreign Secretary Douglas-Home's widely publicised speech on the Middle East in Harrogate in October 1970, which among other things called for an Israeli withdrawal behind 1967 boundaries. He would later recall that the Arab world was 'very welcoming and the Israelis angry'[83] following his landmark speech.

Certainly, Israeli statements in Middle East debates at the UN General Assembly at the time of British entry into the Community expressed a real concern that the British government was falling into line behind the French position on the Palestine issue. Such claims were dismissed by British officials who argued that if the government had shifted its position to any extent it was because Israel's hard-line stance since 1967 required a more pro-Arab emphasis to balance out the British position.[84] Heath explained his government's response to the 1973 crisis in similar terms when he described it as an effort to balance the Nixon administration's abandonment of an 'even-handed approach' to Arab-Israeli affairs.[85]

Whether he truly believed this or not, the war did provide Heath with an opportunity to consolidate his pro-European credentials and to underpin the British efforts to promote a united policy on the Middle East inside the Community. Heath's attempt to use the crisis to move away from the US was poorly received by the Nixon administration, which publicly described the British as 'uncooperative'.[86] Washington took particular offence at what it saw as a British breach of a promise to co-sponsor a UN Security Council resolution calling for an armistice.

Heath's position was warmly welcomed by the West German Chancellor Willy Brandt who, in November 1973, warned that the world's 'destiny cannot and should not be determined by two superpowers alone', and asserted that 'Europe has become self-confident enough and independent enough to regard itself as an equal partner'.[87] Thinking along the same lines, in late September 1973, only weeks before the outbreak of the 1973 war, Pompidou had proposed the convening of a Community summit intended to be a broad review of future foreign policy needs. 'It seems to me to be absolutely necessary', he told reporters, 'to provide manifold proof of the solidarity behind the construction of Europe and her capacity to help in settling the world's problems'. He also said events in the Middle East demanded that the Community take some 'positive common stand' and the upcoming summit should lay the basis for European political co-operation.[88]

Pompidou's call for a major Community summit before the end of 1973 was dismissed by many, with the well-known commentator M.F. Revel cuttingly remarking that this meeting would most likely be attended by historians.[89] But in the wake of the war, in late November, Pompidou and Heath endorsed such a meeting and agreed on the need for closer European political cooperation in response to the challenges they faced in the Middle East.[90]

The upshot was that the EEC heads of government and state gathered in Copenhagen in mid-December 1973. This meeting was convened to discuss all aspects of the Middle East crisis, not simply the oil issue, thus underlining very publicly that the Community was now increasingly willing to consider the Arab-Israeli conflict in terms of extraneous factors, especially as the meeting was attended by four Arab foreign ministers who had been deputised by the recent Algiers summit to represent the Arab position on both oil and the Arab-Israeli conflict.

The Community's Middle East declaration of early November and its decision to meet at Copenhagen were heralded as showing the way towards further cooperation in the political sphere. Addressing the Bundesrat less than a week after the November declaration, Brandt explained the EEC's new Middle East policy in terms of the need to find a compromise solution, arguing that it was the price that had to be paid for Community cohesion.[91] Similarly, Jobert, who by this time was comparing his own visits to Washington to 'Daniel entering the lion's den',[92] also presented the Community's Middle East declaration as evidence that the Community could take common action.[93] His British counterpart, Douglas-Home, speaking before the Press Association in late November 1973, was even more optimistic: 'The EEC has found an identity in the political field…It has published a common policy on the Middle East… The world has yet to accustom itself to hearing Europe speak with one voice but as it does it will recognise the authentic note and true values which alone constitute peace'.[94]

Subsequently, Heath would note that while the oil crisis was 'a tremendous test for the Community…the very possibility of a united position on the Middle East situation revealed how far we had come'.[95] There was definitely some truth in this. The 'modification of [European] views',[96] as one Arab observer politely described it at the time, may well have been a consequence of the panic over oil that had plunged Europe into a recession. It may also have shown the world the extent of Europe's dependence on the oil sheikhdoms of the Gulf. But it also brought home a greater truth: the Community had no hope of increasing its international influence without increasing cooperation in the foreign policy sphere, and developing a new, extensive, relationship with the Arab world would be an important component of this.

Jobert would recall, in typically immodest style, how in the 'economic, political and psychological confusion [of the oil crisis] only France realised the reality before the other Western countries'.[97] Whether this was true or not, few disagreed that the challenge now was to overcome diverse national interests and US pressure in order to convince the Arab world that a newly-united Community was no longer willing to take a back seat in the region and no longer willing, in the words of Pompidou, to 'serve as ushers at the US-Soviet marriage'.[98]

3

DIALOGUE OF THE DEAF

'I have always heard politicians use the word "Europe" when they were making requests to other powers which they did not dare formulate in the name of their own country.'

Otto von Bismarck

'A genuinely political Europe seems about to be born',[1] was how one anonymous European official, writing in the leading US policy journal *Foreign Affairs*, summed up thinking inside the Community in early 1974. A well-known British commentator was no less optimistic. If the Community could 'achieve a united policy on the Middle East', he speculated, it would be 'in a strong position to hold the balance both in the United Nations and elsewhere…the Community may even be able to assume the role of "honest broker" from which both superpowers are debarred'.[2] Speaking at a press conference in the same month, President Pompidou expressed himself in similar terms, emphasising the great opportunity that Europe, with France at the lead, now had to play a significant role in resolving the Middle East conflict.[3]

It appeared that the Community had learned the primary lesson of the preceding months—that it could no longer simply look to remove itself from any significant practical role in the Middle East or leave matters to the superpowers alone. 'Evasive tactics and policies',[4] as one American Middle East expert put it, would no longer suffice.

The Copenhagen Summit had for the most part been a failure. France and Britain had vetoed the calls from the Dutch, Danes and West Germans for joint Community action on oil; a meeting of EEC foreign ministers three days later was no more productive. The Summit did, however, provide the opportunity for European leaders to agree to 'meet more frequently', to 'speak with one voice in important world affairs' and to 'decide on the means by which a common position should be worked out quickly in times of crisis'.[5] Copenhagen also saw discussions on the convening of a joint Euro-Arab conference, possibly at summit level, something that the Arab representatives attending the meeting in the Danish capital had pushed for repeatedly.

Arab policy makers and diplomats, as well as their supporters in Europe, saw all this as providing a tremendous opportunity for increased cooperation between Europe and the Arab world. In January 1974, voices emanating from close to King Faisal of Saudi Arabia were hopeful that after the turmoil of the recent past mutual ties would now improve rapidly.[6] But almost immediately European plans and Arab hopes faced a major setback when the Nixon administration announced that it was convening a conference in Washington for all the major oil consuming countries.

There was scepticism across the Community over whether the US goal of an agreement between those nations reliant on Arab oil was achievable in this period of instability in the international system. Nevertheless, it was difficult to reject the American invitation given the fact that Europe's overriding economic and political priority was stable energy supplies at affordable prices. The majority of EEC states, led by Britain and West Germany, agreed to attend but France did not. Adamant that the best way forward was direct negotiations between Europe and the oil-producing countries free of US involvement, Jobert attacked the US proposal as a 'provocation' and forecast that the Washington conference would be a 'total failure'.[7] A compromise whereby France agreed to attend in return for an American promise that there would be no move to establish a new US-led international oil institution did not materialise. This allowed Paris to rule itself out of the Washington meeting, much to the dismay of the rest of the Community.

The belief that 1974 would mark the beginning of a new era in joint EEC action evaporated almost overnight. If the acute crisis of late 1973 could not bring joint action, what would it take? As Brandt warned Pompidou, cooperation on energy must be the immediate priority because 'if the Community cannot agree on this, it is nothing'.[8]

This explains the unusual decision taken by the Commission to publish a statement on the eve of the Washington conference acknowledging 'a crisis of confidence, a crisis of will and a crisis of lucidity' in Europe. It also explains why West Germany's Finance Minister Helmut Schmidt, who had recently confided to a journalist that 'for some years now our economic policy has been simultaneously our foreign policy',[9] accused France of attempting to divorce Europe from the US. In reply, Jobert accused Germany of betraying Europe by siding with the US.[10]

As Kissinger would later note, Jobert lost no opportunity to 'stoke the Gaullist fires'.[11] But his public spat with Schmidt had little to do with grandstanding for a domestic audience. Jobert knew better than most that, as *Le Monde* put it, the disagreement over attending the Washington conference was a 'grievous experience' for the Community'.[12] So he insisted that neither he nor his government had 'sabotaged'[13] the conference attended by France's EEC partners, the US, Canada, Japan and Norway. But French anger could hardly be contained when the West German delegation at the Washington meeting pushed its partners to defy France by signing a communiqué calling for cooperation with the US in the energy field and establishing a framework for senior officials to coordinate action.[14]

Paris was extremely relieved when this communiqué, rather than a conclusive agreement, was all that came out of the Washington talks. This allowed France to fill the vacuum by insisting that the Community now convene a mechanism, named the Euro-Arab Dialogue (EAD), that would allow Europe to deal directly with the Arab world. The short-term objective of this new framework was 'stable oil supplies at fair prices',[15] as Christopher Mayhew explained. Mayhew, a veteran British Arabist and parliamentarian, became the first joint-chairman of the newly-established Parliamentary Association for Euro-Arab Co-operation in early 1974.

In March 1974, within weeks of the Community adopting the French call for the establishment of the EAD, the Arab oil producing states meeting in Vienna agreed (against the wishes of Libya and Syria) to ease their oil restrictions on Italy and West Germany, which were added to the list of 'friendly' nations. The embargo against the Netherlands remained in place, as did the special limitations on exports to Denmark.

By this time the continuing oil restrictions had no real impact even on the Dutch or the Danes. The Community, which in April 1974 had failed to agree on a French proposal for future discussions between oil consumers and producers, could take little credit for this. Rather, it was due to the fact that by now the oil available on international markets exceeded demand to the extent that European ports were finding it hard to accommodate all arriving oil tankers.

It was only in September 1974, almost one full year after the beginning of the crisis, that the EEC concluded its first substantive agreement to work towards a joint energy policy. But even this plan was a long way from the French goal of seeking a dialogue and concertation with the producer countries. It was limited to reducing petroleum dependence from a projected 60 per cent to 40 per cent of total consumption and only gained grudging acceptance because of the desperate need to address the rising cost of oil.[16] The European Parliament for one was not impressed. In early 1975 it issued a resolution expressing its 'dismay' that the 'governments of certain member states appear to have lost the will to achieve a common energy policy, thus weakening considerably their own advocation of European Union'.[17]

The immediate preoccupation with oil not withstanding, the overriding objective of Community policy-makers was that the EAD framework would lead the Arabs to have a 'kindlier view' of Europe, or at least 'make the Arabs think twice, if not three times, before taking discriminatory action against us'.[18] It was hoped that this could be achieved by using the EAD to build up Euro-Arab economic and cultural ties. As a French memorandum on the EAD put it, 'economic cooperation will be the principal theme [of the EAD]'.[19] Thus, the official objectives of the framework excluded politics and focused solely on developing economic, technical and cultural cooperation with the Arab world, especially in the areas of agriculture, rural development, industrialisation, trade, basic infrastructure, finance, science and technology.[20] James Callaghan, Foreign Secretary in the new Labour government in Britain, hoped that this framework could enable Western Europe to 'construct a triangle of interests' with the 'newly rich Arab oil countries' that would see Arab wealth joined to West European know-how and technology.[21]

During the summer of 1974, the EAD began to take shape. In June the Community delivered an *aide-mémoire* to all Arab states framing the EAD in terms of the request by Arab representatives at Copenhagen for a new relationship. At the inaugural discussions in Paris a committee system was established and a General Committee, charged with formulating the theoretical framework of the EAD, was approved. In September, a preparatory meeting of Arab and EEC parliamentarians in

Damascus was organised by the Parliamentary Association for Euro-Arab Cooperation, a cross-party group of European parliamentarians committed to persuading Europe's 'political leaders of the importance of establishing a partnership between Europe and Arabs'.[22] At a more senior level, in the same month, EEC foreign ministers attending the annual UN General Assembly meeting in New York hosted a lunch for their Arab counterparts. By November 1974, the permanent EAD working groups and the EAD General Commission were in place.

Twenty-one Arab states took part in the EAD under the auspices of the Arab League. Though very aware, in the words of the high-profile Arab League and UN official Lakhdar Brahimi, that the 'energy crisis' had been the 'decisive factor' influencing the Community's decision to establish the EAD,[23] many Arab governments were still interested in using the framework to promote the development of economic relations. Since its launch in the late 1950s, the EEC had succeeded in building constructive economic relations with North America and East Asia. However, neither geographical proximity nor historical ties had facilitated the development of mutually beneficial economic cooperation between the Arabs and Europe over this same period. In 1964 the Arab Common Market (ACM) was established. Five states—Egypt, Jordan, Syria, Iraq and Kuwait—joined. President Nasser, who had been the driving force behind the ACM, admitted that it was modelled on the Treaty of Rome, and following its establishment some Community tariffs on Arab goods were either reduced or eliminated, but the benefits to the Arab states were marginal.

The Community's Global Mediterranean Policy (GMP) was introduced in 1972. It resulted in the conclusion of a series of trade agreements between the EEC and Syria, Iraq, Lebanon and Jordan. But these agreements too had little positive impact on economic development in the Arab world. The preferential treatment and access for manufactured goods into EEC markets that they offered played no role in either developing the Arab industrial or agricultural sectors or increasing the value of Euro-Arab trade. In fact, the limited scope of the financial and technical assistance protocols attached to these trade agreements actually hindered Arab economic development.[24]

The North African nations of Algeria, Tunisia and Morocco, with their long-time ties to France, were enthusiastic over the potential that the EAD provided for increasing trade with Europe. They also saw this as a way of promoting the vision of the Mediterranean as a 'lake of collaboration and peace' between Europe and the Arabs, as the Algerian President Houari Boumedienne eloquently summed it up. French officials were equally optimistic. According to British diplomats stationed in Algiers, during a January 1975 visit the veteran French official Claude Cheysson got 'carried away' by future thoughts of cooperation with former French possessions under the EAD framework.[25]

Other Arab states also saw the economic opportunities in a formal mechanism promoting Euro-Arab economic relations. Contemporary diplomatic reports noted 'a great deal of enthusiasm' for the economic potential of the EAD across the oil-rich Gulf.[26] The same was true of Lebanon, with its deep cultural and economic links to France and, as yet, free of the bloody civil war that would soon plague it for almost two decades. Since the early 1970s, Iraq had been aggressively pursuing trade ties with EEC member states, most notably France and West Germany. Senior officials including Saddam Hussein immediately embraced the idea of the EAD. Once the framework got underway Saddam would consistently reject pressure from other Arab leaders to withdraw from the process for political reasons, arguing instead for due consideration to be given to the economic benefits of the EAD and for a 'calculated Arab reaction'.[27]

This plea did not go unheeded. In mid-1975, the day after the formal opening of the first substantive EAD meeting in Cairo, 19 Arab countries presented the EEC with a 'shopping list' of what they wanted to gain from economic cooperation under the new framework.[28] The Arab League followed this up with a request for the signing of a comprehensive trade convention between the Community and the Arab world under the auspices of the EAD.[29] In September 1976, 250 Arab and 800 European officials met at Montreux, where the organisers from both sides made a special point of emphasising that the meeting would 'refrain from dealing with any kind of political issues'.[30]

But, as EEC diplomats acknowledged, the overriding reality was that the Arab world was sharply divided between a minority who 'wish to discuss the practical business of co-operation' and a majority 'who wish to make political points'.[31] Those who adopted a political approach argued that while Europe had little influence over Israel compared to the US and could in no way match the Soviets in regard to economic and military aid to the Arab nations, it still had a key role to play in the politics of the

Arab-Israeli conflict. In particular, there was hope that via the EAD a united Community led by Britain and France could be convinced to exert significant influence on future US policy in the Middle East. As the Baghdad newspaper *Al Thawra* put it in May 1975, one Arab objective of the EAD was to make the EEC states 'use pressure on the USA to stop helping the Zionist entity'.[32]

In a late 1974 meeting in Cairo with the French foreign minister Jean Sauvagnargues, the Arab League Secretary-General, Mahmoud Riad, explained that the Arabs 'attached great importance to the Dialogue'. But as Sauvagnargues reported back to a meeting of EEC foreign ministers, Riad also warned that the Arabs 'could not make a distinction between the political problem and the economic issues'. He was also clear that in return for the 'lifting of the oil embargo against the Dutch and the Danes' the Arab world 'now expected some reciprocal political gesture from the European side'.[33]

One month later Riad entertained a senior EEC delegation, which included Klaus Meyer of the Commission and an official representing the Irish EEC Presidency. Once again Riad made it clear that the Arabs 'could not separate the political problems from the economic issues'. He added that while the Arabs had 'welcomed' the November 1973 declaration on the Middle East, since that time the Community had 'not moved any further forward in their comprehension of the Arab position'.[34] It was becoming very clear that for the Arabs the EAD was 'not just a question of finding means to expand trade and economic exchange with the European group; they consider it part of their means of struggle in recovering their usurped rights'.[35]

This tension was apparent for all to see in the first ever press conference held under the EAD framework in Paris in September 1974. Speaking as representative of France as current holder of the EEC presidency, Sauvagnargues felt the need to intercede with his Kuwaiti counterpart, Sheikh Sabah al-Ahmad, to put it on the record that discussions on the politics of the Middle East conflict would be out of place in meetings of the EAD.[36]

It was public statements like this, emanating from senior French figures like Sauvagnargues, that led British officials to assert with confidence in early 1975 that 'the position of all the Nine, including the French' was that the EAD 'should not, repeat not, concern itself with political issues involved in the search for Middle East settlement'.[37]

British optimism in this regard was somewhat misplaced. Those French policymakers who had initiated the idea of the EAD, from President Pompidou down the ranks, very much hoped that the framework would be political, in so far as it would contribute to the consolidation of a united European foreign policy. The French representative at an early meeting of the Community's EAD Co-ordinating Group, in Paris in December 1974, described the dialogue as 'one of the most significant exercises in political cooperation which the nine has undertaken'.[38] France also viewed the EAD framework as an opportunity to set out a Middle East policy that was not only different, but visibly different, from that pursued by the US in the region.

The French reluctance to use the EAD mechanism in the pursuit of these goals in its early stages was due to a number of practical realities that even Paris, with its distaste for 'Atlanticism', could not ignore. As Jobert acknowledged, the Middle East was 'fragile terrain'.[39] When it came to finding a consensus on the role that politics should play in the EAD, the Community was on no firmer ground. As one commentator eloquently put it at the time, it was not a Dialogue but 'a consort of very disparate musical instruments'.[40]

Certainly Harold Wilson, who had led the British Labour party back to power in early 1974, had no intention of dancing to the French tune. In his previous spell as prime minister between 1964 and 1970 Wilson had been an unusually dedicated supporter of Israel. As Opposition leader at the time of the 1973 war, he was said to have telephoned the Israeli embassy in London every day to offer support and promised to do what he could to get the Conservative government to lift the arms embargo on Israel.[41] On his becoming prime minister for the second time his relationship with Israel caused enough concern in the Arab world for President Anwar Sadat of Egypt to write to him that Arab leaders 'regard with some unease and apprehension the possibility of British policy deviating from the constructive line the United Kingdom has taken in the past few years'.[42]

Wilson's long-time confidante, Marcia Falkender, would later argue that Israel was 'exceptionally fortunate' that he was prime minister 'at such a crucial time'.[43] There is no doubt that throughout his time as British premier Wilson was very protective of Israeli interests inside the Community. On one occasion he even confided in a group of Israeli visitors that one of the strongest arguments against any attempt to reach a unified

EEC foreign policy on the Middle East was that several members of the Community did not share his own government's attitude to the conflict.[44] Once settled into Downing Street, Wilson agreed to drop any 'remaining reservations' he held about the November 1973 EEC declaration on the Middle East, but only because this would make his government 'better placed to ward off premature initiatives by the Nine'.[45]

Therefore, it was hardly surprising that Wilson was deeply opposed to the EAD becoming an overtly political mechanism. At a meeting of EEC foreign ministers in Luxembourg in April 1974, the British threatened to block French proposals for the EAD unless they agreed to a parallel British request for closer consultation with the US on the Middle East.[46] It was only in June 1974 that the Wilson government gave explicit support for the EAD, and then only on condition of agreement that the framework would not interfere with American peace-making efforts in the region.

This caused a certain amount of resentment in French political and diplomatic circles. In early 1975, the British Ambassador in Paris reported home that it was 'significant' that in a recent briefing to EEC ambassadors, although the French foreign minister 'spoke otherwise only in French, the two words, "lagging behind", were spoken in English while he looked squarely (but with a smile) at me'.[47] The Labour government did not bend in the face of such subtle reprimands. Throughout the regular meetings of the Community's EAD Co-ordinating group in the first half of 1975, the British delegation repeatedly made its position clear: 'Any compromise should be designed to ensure that the Arabs cannot make political capital embarrassing to the Community or its members'.[48] This point was made even more forcefully in private, with Foreign Office officials informing the British Ambassador in Brussels, 'We are determined to keep politics out of the dialogue as far as we can'.[49]

The Wilson government was not alone in the Community in seeking to ensure that the EAD limited itself to economic and cultural matters. At an early EAD Coordinating Group meeting in Paris in December 1974, the Dutch representative was clear: 'The Netherlands attached importance to a dialogue about economic and technical co-operation; but the Nine had always said political matters would be excluded'.[50] In the same month a majority of EEC leaders meeting in Paris echoed this sentiment. As Wilson remembered the scene in his memoirs:

We lunched at the Elysée and then adjourned to a drawing room, where he [the French President, Valéry Giscard d'Estaing] launched a discussion on Israel and her neighbours, clearly having prepared the ground with Chancellor Helmut Schmidt of Germany. Both of them took a strong anti-Israeli line, which provoked me to argue the contrary case. All our colleagues joined in and, as we left for the afternoon formal session, I checked with the Prime Ministers of Belgium and Luxembourg. My calculation was that the Giscard-Schmidt thesis had been opposed by 5 to 4, but my colleagues reckoned it was 6 to 3.[51]

The most serious political obstacle to the success of the EAD was the Arab demand that the PLO play a central role in the nascent framework. In the years prior to the 1973 war and oil crisis, the greatest diplomatic achievement that the PLO could claim in Europe was Yasser Arafat's appearance as the East German government's guest of honour at its tenth World Youth Rally in August 1973.[52] But the Palestinian cause was gaining ground across Western Europe. An incisive editorial in *The Times* of London in September 1970 under the headline 'A State in Palestine' clearly captured the mood of the time: 'They have made their point…by hijacking, by shooting and being shot at, the Palestinians have impressed on the world's conscience that there are 2.5 million peopled without a country prepared to take desperate measures to get one…the Palestinian problem has become transformed into the problem of the Palestinians'.[53]

In 1971–72, the PLO opened offices in London, Paris, Rome and Geneva as part of its attempt to promote its image as the diplomatic representative of the Palestinian people, as well as a revolutionary guerrilla organisation struggling for the liberation of its homeland. This led the Palestinian poet and PLO official Mahmoud Darwish to note on the eve of the 1973 war: 'Now Palestine enters by the front door rather than sneaking in through a secret window or through diplomatic pouches'.[54]

The November 1973 Middle East declaration had been the Community's most wide-ranging statement on Palestinian rights up to that point. The PLO also benefited from the fact that at their summit meeting in Algiers, in November 1973, Arab leaders had declared the PLO the 'only legitimate representative of the Palestinian people'. As an editorial in *Le Monde* noted, this decision meant that for the first time Yasser Arafat had been 'accorded equal status with the heads of [Arab] states'.[55]

From this point on, Arab diplomats in Community capitals would use any opportunity to further the legitimacy of PLO representatives based in Europe. For example, in May 1981, a decade after the PLO opened its first office in London, its representative, Nabil Ramlawi, was made Dean of Arab Ambassadors despite the fact that he was not the longest serving

Arab representative in London and did not hold ambassadorial rank. As PLO sources admitted, this move was intended to insert the PLO into discussions with the Foreign Office over Britain's Middle East policy.[56]

In November 1974, the same month that the EAD General Commission was established, the Arab leaders at their summit in Rabat endorsed the PLO as the 'sole legitimate representative of the Palestinian people' and authorised it to set up an 'independent national authority' on any liberated Palestinian territory.[57] In the words of a *Times* editorial, this decision of the Arab states to line up 'behind the flag of the militant Palestinian guerrilla movement'[58] fundamentally influenced the situation in the Middle East by establishing the PLO as a 'leading formal actor' in the region.[59]

The Rabat decision gave a boost to the PLO's efforts to increase awareness of its cause across Europe. It also provided the group with international legitimacy as France's foreign minister Sauvagnargues was dispatched to Beirut to breakfast with Arafat immediately following the meeting's conclusion.[60] By this time even Harold Wilson, the Community leader most sympathetic to Israel, was acknowledging that a 'just and lasting settlement in the Middle East…would also have to offer the Palestinians a stake in the future'.[61]

In their 1974 book *La Politique Arabe de La France: de Gaulle à Pompidou*, Paul Balta and Claudine Rulleau argued that under de Gaulle and Pompidou France had come nearer than any European country to responding effectively to the need for close ties with the Arab world.[62] Thus it is hardly surprising that following Pompidou's death in April 1974, there was some trepidation in the Arab world that his successor as president, Valéry Giscard d'Estaing, might not follow suit. Giscard d'Estaing may well have been, in the words of a well-known commentator of the era, a 'bloodless, upper class economist, looking vaguely like a Protestant bishop'.[63] But he was no less committed than his two immediate predecessors to promoting the Palestinian cause and consolidating France's pro-Arab position.

Early in his presidency he was the main moving force behind the French decision to grant the PLO official representation in Paris. Giscard d'Estaing also played a key role in the French strategy of promoting its Palestine policy at the UN, where by late 1974 the Palestine question had emerged as an independent agenda item in its own right at the General Assembly. On 14 October 1974, a Syrian-sponsored draft resolution calling for PLO participation in UN plenary meetings on the Palestine problem was adopted by 105 to 4 (with 20 abstaining).

Israel dismissed this vote as 'illegal and not binding...in any way' and the majority of EEC nations either voted against (the Netherlands, Denmark, Belgium and Luxembourg) or abstained (the United Kingdom and West Germany). France, Ireland and Italy voted in favour. In response, an Israeli foreign ministry statement expressed 'astonishment' that these three EEC member states had 'sided with the approach of the most extremist Arab states'.[64] The diverging attitudes within Community ranks over this vote on PLO participation at the UN highlighted clearly that even if the Palestine issue was central to Community efforts to build a common foreign policy, there was still little unanimity over the status of the PLO. It also underlined that France was still unable to dictate the Community's Middle East policy.

Nevertheless, France did have some success in moving its partners nearer to its position on the matter. For example, in October 1974 both Britain and West Germany had planned to vote against the Syrian-sponsored draft resolution, but ultimately decided to abstain instead so that the Community would not appear even more divided and France even more isolated. The following month only France chose to abstain, rather than vote against, two November 1974 UN General Assembly draft resolutions, 3236 (XXIX) and 3237 (XXIX). These resolutions ratified the inalienable rights of the Palestinian people to self-determination, independence and the sovereignty of Palestine without even mentioning the existence of Israel. They also called for observer status at the UN for the PLO on the grounds that this was equivalent to granting the PLO 'legal recognition'.[65]

At the same time, Giscard d'Estaing went much further than any other European leader up to that point when he claimed, during a news conference at the UN, that the international community had recognised that the Palestinians constituted 'an entity, a reality, a people; it must be assumed that they have the aspiration of a homeland [*patrie*]'.[66] As the British embassy in Paris reported, the French President's position was not negotiable: 'any lasting settlement would have to recognise the Palestinian right to a "patrie"'.[67]

In an interview in the Arab media, the well-known French author and commentator Jean Lacouture explained the new willingness of the Community to address the Palestinian issue in terms of the French lead:

What d'Estaing has done is this: he has picked up what has always been too hot to hold. He has smashed the taboo and broken the conspiracy of silence that surrounded the Palestine problem in the west...And because Giscard has opened a gap in the forest, because he has created a precedent in the West, it is now easier ...to talk of the Palestinian state and the rights of the Palestinian people.[68]

Despite France's pro-Palestinian record, the EEC was still one of the least anti-Israel blocs at the UN in the mid-1970s. As one newspaper summed up in late 1974, the demands of the PLO went 'far beyond the demand[s]'[69] of the Community. At the time, the majority of UN members (made up of pro-Soviet, Non-Aligned and Third World countries) favoured according official status to the PLO, an organisation whose publicly stated objective was the destruction of one of the UN's own members (Israel). There was certainly little appetite for this in the Community. Not even Giscard d'Estaing, who now spoke regularly of a homeland (*patrie*) for the Palestinians, was willing to concede a PLO state with juridical standing and rights and duties in international law.

The EEC's relative moderation regarding Israel was apparent in 1975 when, as Bernard Lewis noted, the entire Community 'with impressive unanimity'[70] voted against the General Assembly resolution stating that 'Zionism is a Form of Racism and Racial Discrimination'.[71] In response, at a meeting in Abu Dhabi in November 1975, the Arab League condemned the EEC's refusal to support this anti-Israel UN resolution. But this aside, the Community's evolving support for the PLO at the UN, including its ringing endorsement of Yasser Arafat's appearance before the General Assembly in November 1974, the first such appearance by someone who was not a head of state, undoubtedly added to the legitimisation of the PLO in Europe. Khaled al Hassan, a founder of Fatah and a long-time adviser of Yasser Arafat, would later recall that Community support for the PLO at the UN was vital in moving European public opinion 'away from the generally pro-Israeli feelings'.[72]

Shortly after the Arab success at the UN in New York in November 1974, the Arab governments (with the exception of Jordan) were adamant that the PLO must play a role in the EAD framework. The Arab League's Mahmoud Riad informed an EEC delegation visiting Cairo that the 'Palestinians must have the right to attend any meeting in the framework of the Dialogue...[there can be]... no retreat by the Arab states on the Palestine issue'.[73] It was quickly dawning on the Community that, in the words of one of its own diplomats, PLO participation was the 'only political issue which they [the Arabs] are interested in discussing'.[74] Growing support inside the EEC for the view, championed by France, that the key to a durable peace settlement in the Middle East demanded a PLO role in the political process did not translate at this time into majority support for a formal role for the PLO in the EAD. As a result the first plenary meeting of the EAD's General Commission, originally scheduled to take place at ambassadorial level on 26 November 1974, was indefinitely postponed.

While France and a number of the other EEC member states that had been most sympathetic to PLO demands at the UN—Italy, Ireland and increasingly other smaller members such as Luxembourg and Belgium— were open to the idea of some PLO role in the EAD, the British, Dutch, Danes and West Germans were far less flexible and were 'not prepared to make political concessions to the Arabs in this context'.[75]

At the outset of communal discussions on the EAD, the Dutch, bruised but unbowed by their recent boycott experience, were adamant that even a 'minimal PLO presence' in the EAD would be 'too much' to accept.[76] The Danes saw the EAD less as an opportunity to build on the PLO's diplomatic gains at the UN than as a way of providing a 'cooling-off-period' that could halt the PLO's recent momentum. The British, for their part, were determined that the EAD must not lead to 'an enhancement of the PLO's status'.[77] Thus they favoured a strategy that would allow them to 'side-step the problem' of the PLO for as long as possible.[78]

There was also another key reason for the Community's reluctance to allow the PLO to play a central role in the EAD. By the summer of 1974 the US administration had been engaged for eight months in a highly ambitious and ultimately successful attempt to cement its position as the predominant external party of influence in the Middle East. This was seen most clearly in the 'unprecedented intensity'[79] of Kissinger's role in the disengagement process between Israel, Egypt and Syria following the 1973 war. In January 1974, he spent ten days shuttling back and forward to Cairo. He spent a further week in the region in early March, and for the entire month of May he travelled numerous times between Jerusalem and Damascus.

Prior to the November 1974 decision by Arab leaders at Rabat to insert the PLO into the heart of the political process, the US had been open to pursuing a 'West Bank First' approach to Middle East peacemaking by facilitating negotiations between Israel, Jordan and non-PLO Palestinians. But after the legitimisation of the PLO at Rabat the US was no longer either willing or able to pursue this path. Israel refused categorically to accept any PLO involvement in negotiations.[80] At the same time the PLO's new status meant that King Hussein of Jordan could no longer claim to speak on behalf of the West Bank, all the more so when pro-PLO candidates triumphed over pro-Jordanian candidates in local elections in the territory in 1976. Kissinger now therefore 'concentrated his efforts',[81] as an internal memorandum circulated among EEC foreign ministries explained, on building on Sinai I, the first Israeli-Egyptian disengagement agreement of January 1974. Kissinger hoped that this would provide the framework for a final settlement between Israel and Egypt that would see Israel hand back Sinai in return for recognition and normalisation from Egypt.

On 5 March 1974, the day after the Community agreed to establish the EAD, a US State Department spokesman claimed that the US 'was not consulted on that particular activity and was only informed of the decision after it became public'.[82] In a speech in Chicago soon afterwards, President Nixon accused Europe of 'ganging up' on the US.[83] A few days later, at a press conference in Houston, he followed this up by saying that 'we can at least expect from our European allies that they will consult with us and not work actively against us in the political field or the economic field'.[84] Few European commentators or policy-makers went as far in response as an editorial in *Le Monde* which accused the US of the 'anti-European manoeuvre' of pressuring Saudi Arabia to refuse to normalise oil supplies with the Community as a way 'to hinder' the EAD.[85] However, there was sympathy for the less conspiratorial argument that the US had convened the Washington oil conference in early 1974 as part of an attempt to counter a European move towards a mechanism along the lines of the EAD.

In fairness to the Nixon administration, it had pressed its European partners on the need for a common approach to energy (the goal of the Washington conference) as far back as 1969 and continued to do so formally throughout 1971. In October 1972 the US administration even called on the Community to develop an oil strategy for the future regardless of whether it entailed joint cooperation with Washington.[86] By July 1974, the same month when a high-level Arab delegation travelled to Paris to discuss the EAD, the US was increasingly concerned that the nascent dialogue could pose a real danger to, or at the very least complicate, American efforts to broker an Egyptian-Israeli settlement.

Like Nixon, Kissinger criticised Europe for developing the EAD without consulting the US, and he regularly warned EEC leaders to keep politics out of the framework.[87] In a January 1975 discussion on the EAD with the British Foreign Secretary Callaghan, Kissinger 'accepted, with regret' that the Dialogue would take place. But he was also adamant that Europe would be dragged down a 'slippery slope' and he doubted whether the Community could prevent the Arabs from turning the EAD into a 'political forum'.[88] In a meeting with Chancellor Schmidt and foreign minister Hans-Dietrich Genscher of West Germany the following month, Kissinger commented that 'the PLO seemed to be a European obsession', adding that the US 'had nothing to discuss with the PLO until the PLO accepted Israel's right to exist'.[89] Some years later Kissinger would further expound on his discussions with State Department colleagues over the role of the PLO at this time. 'Once we recognise the PLO', he had argued with a number of career diplomats who were far more sympathetic to engaging the group than he was, 'we have lost all our leverage over them…of course it is possible that, after recognition, they would be more serious negotiators, but I think they would probably just be more cocky and arrogant'.[90]

Kissinger's opposition to a PLO role in the EAD found formal expression in a February 1975 US démarche to the Irish government, which at the time held the rotating EEC presidency. This diplomatic censure was forthright in its view that the presence of the PLO in the EAD 'cannot help but inject a political dimension into it'.[91] There was real American concern that although the EAD was ostensibly created to address economic issues, and many Community members were reluctant to stray from economic matters, it would nonetheless ultimately end up addressing the politics of the Palestine question and further legitimise the PLO's role in the political process.

This was an understandable concern. As Henri Simonet, vice-chairman of the European Commission in the mid-1970s, acknowledged in the same year, direct contacts between the EEC and the Arab countries via the EAD would always be political because they were 'bound up with the question as to whether Europe has a political identity of its own'.[92]

At a meeting between President Gerald Ford and European leaders in June 1975, the same month as the first major EAD meeting in Cairo, Kissinger explained that the EAD was so problematic from an American perspective because the 'issues were so complex and intangible that any new body would simply add another element to the confusion; if there were to be a new effort at a settlement, then the US and West Europe should not outbid each other'.[93]

The Community's sensitivity to Washington's 'immense and slightly hysterical interest'[94] in the EAD put it in a very difficult position. Torn between internal divisions over the legitimacy of the PLO, the maximalist demands of the Arab states and the minimalist expectations of the US, during late 1974 and 1975 the Community struggled to find an acceptable solution to the problem of the role of the PLO in the EAD. Klaus Meyer of the European Commission proposed that one way around the 'PLO problem' would be to use the EAD framework to address Community aid to UNRWA. This was rejected by the British, West Germans and others because 'hey presto, the Nine would be sliding down the slippery slope towards a political debate'.[95] Another proposal called for those attending EAD meetings to refrain from wearing name badges stating their nationality as, in the words of one bewildered observer of these discussions, this would mean that neither participants nor onlookers (the US and Israel) would be 'able to determine with any certainty whether the PLO is officially represented'.[96] This was rejected on the grounds that once the EAD met at a senior level, name-tags would not be needed to recognise delegates, whether they were European or Arab ministers or PLO leaders!

By the start of 1975, the French, who believed that it was 'imperative that the Nine take action on the Dialogue soon lest it collapse',[97] made a more plausible suggestion when they called for the convening of study groups consisting of experts chosen by the EEC and the Arab League who were not official representatives of governments, as this would allow for the inclusion of Palestinians in the Arab delegation.[98] Community ministers meeting in Dublin in February 1975 endorsed this proposal for the creation of 'non-governmental expert groups'[99] on condition that it was made 'quite clear' to the Arabs that the EEC 'would not regard the presence at the meeting…of PLO experts as implying European recognition of the PLO's claims'.[100] For their part, the British viewed this as a possible 'temporary solution' but also acknowledged that it was nothing more than a 'device that would simply gain time…postpone a rupture'.[101]

The entire Community, including the French, who under Giscard d'Estaing had sought to improve relations with Washington, were keen to present this proposal as complementary to US efforts. As the political director of the French foreign ministry explained, the EAD should be presented as a useful 'safety net' underneath Kissinger's diplomatic efforts in the region.[102] With this in mind it was also agreed that there would be no approach to the Arab League with the proposal for PLO participation in the EAD until after Kissinger had concluded his visit to several European capitals in late February 1975.

Such gestures did little to reduce Kissinger's 'rather scornful' view of this compromise over PLO inclusion in a unified Arab delegation. At the end of January he told Callaghan that he did not expect this 'subterfuge' to last more than a few months.[103] The PLO did its best to end it much quicker than that. On 7 February, on Radio Cairo's Voice of Palestine, the head of the PLO's political department announced that the PLO had agreed to participate in upcoming EAD talks as part of a single Arab delegation.[104]

Once in place, the 'Dublin Formula', as this compromise agreement was known, allowed for the convening of the first EAD plenary session in Cairo in June 1975. During this meeting, members of the PLO's finance department, the Palestine National Fund, participated as part of the Arab delegation. To further blur the affiliations of those attending, all delegates were identified, if at all, by function rather than nationality.

At the conclusion of the Cairo meeting a memorandum issued by both sides described the EAD as the 'product of a joint political will that emerged at the highest level, with a view to establishing a special relationship between the two groups'.[105] Developing this 'joint political will' became a goal of subsequent EAD working group meetings in Rome in July and in Abu Dhabi in November 1975.[106]

Despite these repeated expressions of 'joint political will', from its first meeting the EAD found itself a hostage to relentless attempts to force the normalisation of relations between the Community and the PLO onto the agenda. This stalemate was significantly worsened by the signing in May 1975 of a trade agreement between Israel and the EEC. The culmination of almost three years of negotiations, this was the first agreement of its type between the Community and a non-member Mediterranean state. It concentrated on the development of a free trade area for industrial goods with significant tariff reductions for 85 per cent of Israel's agricultural imports into Europe.[107]

At the time of British entry into the Community in 1973, Britain was Israel's third largest trading partner and an important market for Israeli agricultural produce. This meant that the first enlargement significantly increased Israel's trade with the EEC. By 1974 trade with the Community accounted for half of Israel's imports (c. US\$2 billion) and a third of its exports (c. US\$700 million). Not surprisingly, Yitzhak Rabin, Israel's new premier, who succeeded Golda Meir in 1974, assured the Knesset in his first speech as Prime Minister, that 'increased co-operation between us and…the Common market in particular will now be one of the central objectives of the new government'.[108] The following year Israel's foreign minister Yigal Allon characterised the EEC-Israel agreement as a 'great and even spectacular' opportunity for future relations with a European trading bloc that occupied 'pride of place in Israel's foreign trade'.[109]

The Arab world was furious with the Community for signing this trade agreement with Israel. Coming as it did just one month before the first EAD meeting in Cairo, this 'flurry of criticism'[110] from Arab governments focused on two points: first, that the agreement was 'not in accord' with the Community's November 1973 Middle East declaration, and secondly, as the official Algerian newspaper *El-Moudjahid* put it, by signing the agreement the Community had 'endangered' the EAD. Egypt's state-controlled newspaper *Al-Ahram* made a similar argument and concluded that it was 'hard to believe that the EEC countries are serious in their wish to activate Arab-European dialogue'.[111]

The Algerian and Libyan governments called on the Arab League to postpone the Cairo meeting. This option was rejected, but the chairman of the Arab delegation in Cairo did use the occasion to condemn the EEC-Israel trade agreement as 'an action which goes contrary to the principles' of Euro-Arab relations and which contradicted the November 1973 Community declaration.[112] For its part, the PLO issued a statement through the Palestine News Agency that claimed that 'Zionists and those who harboured an imperialist mentality were cooperating to plot against the Dialogue'.[113]

Though acknowledging that the timing was unfortunate, the Community rejected the Arab argument that its trade agreement with Israel contravened the 1973 Middle East declaration. It explained that it was a technical rather than a political agreement that simply replaced an earlier bilateral document. Moreover, it was pointed out that it was balanced by the Community's economic cooperation with the Arabs under the EAD framework.[114] This did little to soothe Arab dissatisfaction. Garret Fitzgerald, the Irish foreign minister and president of the European

Council at this difficult time, faced several attacks in Arab capitals during a tour of the region in mid-1975. At one meeting in Cairo with the Arab League Secretary-General Riad, Fitzgerald gave an assurance that the EEC-Israel trade agreement did not apply to territories occupied by Israel. However, he was clear that he was speaking on behalf of Ireland rather than the Community. As this would not satisfy his Arab League hosts he agreed to put in writing his conviction that the new agreement did not cover any of the territories occupied since 1967.[115] On his return to Europe he informed a meeting of EEC foreign ministers in Dublin of the 'clarifications' he had given to the Arab states on the matter and argued that he had acted as he did in order to get Europe 'out of a fix' and to clear up 'serious misunderstandings'.[116] He went further by arguing that he now felt that there was 'scope for Europe to take a political initiative in the Middle East' and that if the Europeans did nothing, there was a risk that events would pass them by.[117]

Fitzgerald's analysis of the situation was greeted positively by the French foreign minister Sauvagnargues. But others were less impressed. Roy Hattersley, a junior minister at the British Foreign Office who was standing in at the meeting for Foreign Secretary Callaghan, protested against Fitzgerald's action and accused him of being unable to 'divorce' his role as Irish foreign minister from that of EEC president.[118] But while the British were furious that Fitzgerald had 'deliberately played a lone hand' by presenting the Community with a *fait accompli*, they refrained from going public with their dissatisfaction, as this would prompt a 'major row' and might even 'strengthen' the radical Arabs.[119]

In subsequent years a harsh critic of Euro-Arab relations would argue that the EAD marked a 'decisive shift' in Europe's relationship with the Arab Middle East as it provided for a 'formidable political and legal superstructure that encompasses the entire Euro-Arab relationship' and 'established the conditions for a genuine Euro-Arab symbiosis'.[120] But the reality was very different. While EEC diplomats dealing directly with the EAD acknowledged that a 'threshold had been crossed'[121] with the establishment of the framework, the EAD had hardly established the 'conditions for genuine Euro-Arab symbiosis'. In fact, all it had really done was cover up some deep cracks in Europe's relationship with both the Arab world and the US. These cracks would resurface very soon.

4

GET CARTER

'Egypt is one big pebble on an Arab beach, but not the only one.'
British Foreign Office Memorandum

By the time President Jimmy Carter was sworn into office in January 1977, the US had established itself as the paramount external power in the Middle East. In little over three years since the end of the 1973 war, Kissinger's pro-active 'step-by-step approach'[1] had won over Egypt and had eliminated Soviet influence on this pivotal regional state by showing President Sadat the potential rewards of moving towards a gradual *modus vivendi* with Israel. As the charismatic Israeli soldier-statesman Moshe Dayan summed up in his memoirs, Sadat recognised that the 'Arabs could get arms from the Soviet Union, but the key to a political solution lay with the United States'.[2]

At the same time as Kissinger was consolidating and extending US influence in the region and building the platform for the Carter administration's mediation of an Israeli-Egyptian peace, senior European officials were championing the EAD. Klaus Meyer, the Commission's Director-General for Development, argued that the EAD proved that the Community was able 'to deal efficiently and harmoniously in one single delegation with matters which affected community business, political cooperation and other matters'.[3]

But in reality, the Community was struggling to develop the EAD into a viable framework. Looking back at this period a few years later Michel Jobert, who had preceded Sauvagnargues as French foreign minister, was in no doubt—the Palestine issue had 'poisoned' the EAD.[4] Certainly the Community's failure to reach an agreement with its Arab partners on the role of the PLO in the framework until mid-1975 made a mockery of the claim in early 1974 by one EEC commissioner, Ralf Dahrendorf, that Europe was successfully moving towards 'transforming' its relationship with the US 'into relations between partners in principle equal'.[5]

The gap between European and American influence in the region was clear for all the Arab world to see. In January 1974 at the time of the signing of Sinai I, Sadat had described the deal as a '[disengagement] from the US, not from Israel…The headquarters is America'.[6] This explained why, during visits to Paris in 1975 and 1977, Sadat was unwilling to agree to a request from President Giscard d'Estaing to allow France, or France at the head of the Community, to play a role as 'guarantor' of a Middle East peace.[7]

The vehemently anti-American George Habash, the head of the PFLP, shared Sadat's reading of the situation. 'On the imperialistic level', this Marxist theoretician explained in August 1974, 'the prominent achievement of American imperialism… is the return of American influence in the area, and the continuous expansion of this influence politically, economically and morally'.[8]

US dominance of the region was further consolidated with the signing of Sinai II in September 1975. This second interim agreement between Israel and Egypt not only marked the beginning of the end of pan-Arab solidarity on the Palestine issue but also further complicated the Community's relationship with the US. As Kissinger would later recall, the 'purpose' of Sinai II, 'had been to keep the PLO out of the West Bank, not to turn the territory over to it'.[9] When Egypt and Israel signed up to the agreement, the Ford administration made a commitment not to deal with the PLO until it recognised Israel's right to exist and accepted UN Security Council Resolutions 242 and 338 as the basis for a negotiated settlement of the conflict.[10]

Despite its exclusion from US peace efforts in the region during the Ford presidency, the PLO continued to make gains in Europe. The group's Beirut-based Research Centre produced books, magazines and bulletins in French, English and German and distributed them across the Community. The European Co-ordinating Committee of Friendship Societies with the Arab World, founded in Paris in 1972 to promote closer relations between Europe and the Arabs, established offices in London, Paris and the West German town of Aachen. In 1975, it began publishing a new quarterly in French, English and German entitled *Eurabia*.

Even more significant was the increasing success of Palestinian and Arab representatives in presenting their case before the European media. As one person present at a May 1976 Colloquium on Palestine held in Brussels noted, 'there was a time not so long ago when foreign sympathisers with the Palestinian cause longed for the day when the Arabs could match the Zionists in debate. This day has now arrived'.[11]

By the summer of 1976 the European media were noting that the Arabs 'appeared confident' that the EAD would gradually move towards embracing the PLO and that the political aspect of the EAD was finally coming to the fore.[12] It was a gradual process. 'Anodine' was how *The Times* described the final communiqué of the May 1976 Luxembourg EAD meeting.[13] A view endorsed by one participant at the meeting who described the joint declaration as 'long, friendly and full of good ideas, but on points where precision was needed, it was noticeably vague'.[14]

At the Tunis EAD meeting in February 1977, the Community agreed to discuss political issues with the Arab delegation for the first time, though the final communiqué differed little from its predecessors. Both sides explained their views on the Middle East problem 'including the question of Palestine' and 'reaffirmed that a solution to the question of Palestine based on the recognition of the legitimate rights of the Palestinian people is a crucial factor in achieving a just and lasting peace'. The European delegation also 'took note' of the proposal put forward by the Arabs to establish a committee for political consultations between the two sides.[15]

The polite deceptions of Euro-Arab diplomacy could only go so far. Ismael Khelil, the Tunisian delegate at this meeting, warned the Community that there could be no progress towards greater economic cooperation between Europe and the Arabs if there was no progress on political questions, adding that some Western powers encouraged Israel's occupation of Arab lands while others kept silent about it.[16]

The third meeting of the EAD General Committee, in Brussels in late October 1977, also failed to produce any breakthrough in the political sphere. This led the PLO's senior participant in the EAD, Ahmad Sidqi al-Dajani, to tell a press conference that the Europeans needed to go further in addressing Arab political concerns; he hinted that the framework might be abandoned if this did not take place. Al-Dajani, a professor of history in Beirut, also demanded that the EEC provide an explanation of precisely what it envisaged by a 'homeland for the Palestinian people' and called on it to expound on what it understood by the phrase 'legitimate rights of the Palestinian people'.[17]

The text of the final communiqué of the October meeting in Brussels underlined this impasse. For the first time the Arab delegation insisted on explicitly using the EAD to call on the Community to endorse the principle of Palestinian statehood. In response, senior EEC officials such as the Belgian foreign minister Simonet and the Commission's Klaus Meyer explained that the EAD could only function with the full backing of all EEC members, and because of this any attempt to address political issues through the EAD must both be very gradual and have the approval of all member states.[18] Nothing could have highlighted more clearly the validity of Kissinger's comment during a speech in London in 1975, that the challenge of dealing with Europe was due to the fact that it was almost impossible for the Community to renegotiate its position once it had arrived at a difficult compromise.

On matters related to the Middle East, Kissinger acted as 'an extension of the president'[19] and could claim to draw on the authority of that office in making decisions. Community officials had very little authority to expand on the foreign policy positions of member states that had been agreed at the European Council, the forum for heads of member state governments that met a few times a year. From the start, European representatives at the EAD were powerless to develop a joint political platform with their Arab counterparts. They also had to take into account the internal weaknesses of Community institutions, described in 1976 by one astute observer as 'an ambitious but gun-shy Commission, an embryonic unrepresentative Assembly and a cautious calculating Council'.[20] The reality was that as long as there were revolving EU presidencies, national foreign ministries and attempts by the Commission to extend its competence, there would always be division, distrust and disunity in the formulation of foreign policy on such a sensitive issue as the Middle East. On top of this, despite calling for the strengthening of EEC institutions, and arguing that a collective approach was key, national governments had little appetite for ceding power to European institutions in matters of foreign policy.

Despite Arab frustrations over the failure to gain explicit EEC endorsement of the PLO and a Palestinian state through the EAD mechanism, the framework did have its benefits. It provided the Arabs with the prestige of having a special relationship with Europe, which was denied to Israel, while the strategy of placing the PLO at the heart of official meetings between Community and Arab representatives meant that the Palestine issue was always at the top of the Euro-Arab agenda. For example, at both the Luxembourg and Tunis meetings in May 1976 and February 1977 respectively, the PLO representatives in the Arab delegation had the honour of drafting the Arab communiqué. At the Brussels EAD meeting in October 1977, according to a British Foreign Office report, al-Dajani 'did most of the talking on the Arab side'[21] and 'launched into a plea for European recognition of the PLO'.[22]

Similarly, the EAD provided PLO officials with numerous opportunities to attend inter-parliamentary meetings and unofficial Euro-Arab conferences alongside senior Arab officials and, more importantly, current and former senior European figures attending these events in a personal capacity. During the widely publicised Euro-Arab conference in Florence in April 1977, PLO representatives mingled with, among others, Dr Rinaldo Ossola, the Italian Minister for Foreign Trade, the former British Chancellor of the Exchequer Reginald Maudling, and Maurice Couve de Murville, who had served as both prime minister and foreign minister of France under de Gaulle.

As al-Dajani later explained, inserting the PLO as a 'major element' in the EAD improved the group's standing inside the Community. He recalled how PLO delegates to the EAD were able to travel regularly to West Germany, ostensibly on EAD business, during which time they succeeded in gaining political acceptance.[23] Al-Dajani himself benefited from such opportunities. In the summer of 1976, he met West German foreign ministry officials at the invitation of Bonn's EAD representative.[24] Al-Dajani also used EAD meetings to lobby European officials 'privately' and to persuade them that the 'time was ripe for a move', as one victim of this targeted diplomacy reported home.[25] Recognising the cumulative value of these efforts, the thirteenth session of the PNC, meeting in Cairo in 1977 welcomed the 'effective role' played by al-Dajani at the EAD and promoted him to the PNC executive, which now took direct control of EAD strategy.[26]

As far back as mid-1975, in a meeting with the British foreign secretary Callaghan, Israel's foreign minister Yigal Allon had described the EAD as a 'dangerous procedure'.[27] By the time of the Tunis meeting in early 1977, Allon was arguing that the Dialogue should not seek to 'deal with the problem of the Israel-Arab conflict in the absence of Israel'. He also warned that the EAD 'might become a politically dangerous tool which would diminish not enhance, the role of Europe in the Middle East in various ways'.[28] Allon's concerns were compounded by the official gains the PLO was making outside the EAD at the same time. For example, on 29–30 June 1977 the Community published a London communiqué whose longest section addressed the 'legitimate right of the Palestinian people to give effective expression to its national identity'. It also expressed the view that a solution to the conflict had to include an end to Israel's occupation and a 'homeland for the Palestinian people'. There was also an implicit reference to the PLO when the communiqué demanded that the 'representatives of the parties to the conflict including the Palestinian people must participate in the negotiations in an appropriate manner'.[29]

The June 1977 statement on Palestine must be viewed as part of the ongoing attempt by the Community to consolidate political cooperation in matters of foreign policy. The previous January, Giscard d'Estaing had called on his Community partners to use the European Council to 'make the voice of Europe heard'.[30] This request by the French President was endorsed at the London meeting in June, during which the Palestine statement was presented by participants as the practical expression of a new assertiveness in international affairs.

But the June statement was also, in part, an attempt by the EEC to create good will in the Arab world, where it was welcomed as a significant advance on the Community's previous position. As a British diplomat in Brussels reported home, 'on the whole the Arabs are feeling pretty well-disposed to the EEC at the moment, thanks almost entirely to the June statement'.[31] In order to maximise the benefit of this move, the European co-chairman's opening statement at the third meeting of the EAD General Committee in Brussels in October 1977 began with reference to the London declaration and an explanation that it was issued because it was 'incumbent' on the EEC to 'assist the endeavours to reach a negotiated settlement'.[32] For its part, the Arab delegation at the meeting insisted on including the full text of the June statement in the final communiqué.[33]

The June 1977 statement had been released at a time of deadlock in the tentative US-sponsored Egyptian-Israeli peace talks. It was therefore viewed by Jerusalem as a serious setback to the Israeli attempt to persuade the Community to support its negotiations with Egypt and endorse the preferred Israeli option of Palestinian autonomy (rather than statehood) in the occupied territories.

Upon taking office, President Carter had been by no means averse to a move towards a Palestinian homeland and a Palestinian role in any future peace settlement. Zbigniew Brzezinski, Carter's choice for national security adviser, had publicly endorsed the idea of a Palestinian state and had signed the controversial Brookings report, published in 1975, which called for a comprehensive approach to the Arab-Israeli conflict.[34] Cyrus Vance, Carter's secretary of state, also supported bringing the Palestinians into the peace process consistently, and even considered creating a model similar to the EAD, whereby the US could negotiate with the Palestinians by means of PLO representatives participating in a single Arab delegation. At the same time Vice President Walter Mondale had expressed the view that trading territory for peace meant establishing some form of Palestinian entity separate to, or in connection with, Jordan.

In February 1977, the Policy Review Committee of the National Security Council recommended that the Middle East be dealt with as a matter of priority by the new administration.[35] The following month, in a speech in Clinton, Massachusetts, Carter himself publicly called for the establishment of a 'Palestinian homeland'. In a meeting with President Hafez al-Assad of Syria the following May he restated his support for a 'resolution of the Palestine problem and a homeland for the Palestinians'.[36] Carter followed this up later in the same month by telling an audience at Notre Dame University that it was the 'most propitious time for a genuine settlement'.[37] In June, just two days before the EEC's London statement, the US administration issued its own statement acknowledging the Palestinian right to a homeland. The following October, Carter endorsed a joint US-Soviet statement that called for any future peace settlement to take into account the 'legitimate rights of the Palestinian people'.[38]

Not surprisingly, within weeks of Carter's election victory in November 1976, two PLO representatives, Sabri Jiryis and Issam Sartawi, visited the US to discuss the process of American acceptance of PLO participation in the political process. During their trip they met intermediaries of State Department officials. By the summer of 1977, there were rumours that a PLO information office would soon be opened in Washington and that the Carter administration was preparing to upgrade relations with Arafat's organisation.

But just then, on 19 November 1977, President Sadat of Egypt made his momentous visit to Jerusalem. His motive, he explained, was to 'overcome the psychological problems' that were posing obstacles to progress in the peace negotiations.[39] For Israel his move, in the words of Abba Eban, was a 'breach in the walls of Arab rejection and Israeli suspicion'.[40] It also completely changed the dynamic in the stalled Egyptian-Israeli peace talks, which had made little progress since Menachem Begin, leader of the Likud Bloc, became Israeli Prime Minister in June 1977.

William Quandt, a Middle East expert close to the Carter administration, noted how Sadat's visit to Jerusalem marked 'a sharp departure'[41] from the administration's earlier support for possible substantive concessions to the Palestinians. From this point on the Carter administration, often reluctantly, looked to build on the strategy of the previous administration by focusing primarily on the Egypt-Israel front instead of adopting a comprehensive approach addressing all issues, including the Palestinian one. This approach offered (in Kissinger's own words) the best chance of 'keeping the political initiative in American hands, of preventing the coalescence of radical Arab and Communist pressures, of forestalling Soviet mischief, and of deferring the most contentions and painful issues until a more propitious moment'.[42]

European leaders endorsed the French Prime Minister Raymond Barre's public description of Sadat's historic journey to Jerusalem as 'very noble'.[43] Community foreign ministers issued a declaration that hailed it as 'courageous'. But the same declaration also shifted the focus away from the bilateral Egyptian-Israeli relationship by expressing the hope that this 'unprecedented dialogue…will open the way to a global negotiation leading to a just and durable overall settlement…for all peoples of the region…including the Palestinian people'.[44] By this time even West Germany, traditionally the Community member most sensitive to Israeli concerns, appeared ready to accept the PLO as the representative of the Palestinian people on the condition that it renounced violence.[45] As senior West German officials explained during a mid-1975 meeting with their British counterparts 'the one area' where there was 'scope for a political initiative by the EEC was the Middle East' and the Arabs were waiting for the EEC to 'play a more active role'.[46]

The British government under both Wilson and Callaghan had been the Community's most outspoken critic of the PLO. Publicly it maintained a strenuous anti-PLO position. In December 1977 Callaghan told

Parliament that 'while [the PLO] fails to recognise the existence of Israel ... I do not see how we can have dealings with it'.[47] But the Labour government was also becoming increasingly open to PLO involvement in negotiations and had started to urge Israel in private to consider promoting moderate elements within the group.[48]

In June 1978, the Community issued a statement on the Middle East which called for representatives of the Palestinians to participate in negotiations and for Israel to grant 'effective expression' to Palestinian national identity and to 'recognise the legitimate rights of the Palestinian people' in the context of an overall settlement of the conflict.[49] The following September Carter, Begin and Sadat and their negotiating teams travelled to the Camp David presidential retreat in Maryland for an unprecedented 12 days of substantive peace discussions.

The fact that Carter had succeeded in bringing Sadat and Begin together at all was viewed by some in Europe as a 'success',[50] and the Community welcomed the meeting as 'a further major step towards...settlement', and offered 'strong support' for the process.[51] All the more so as European officials still held out hope that Sadat would fulfil his promise that Egypt would not agree to Israel's plans for limited Palestinian autonomy in Gaza and the West Bank, and would seek to link the normalisation of ties with Israel, especially the exchange of ambassadors, to the establishment of a self-governing authority in the West Bank and Gaza.[52]

The Carter administration, which in early 1978 had a very public and sharp exchange with Israel over the building of new settlements in occupied territory, shared this objective. It wanted the issue of interim self-government for the Palestinians to be considered in parallel to negotiations on an Egyptian-Israeli settlement. Carter also hoped that an agreement by Israel on the principle of a Palestinian self-governing authority would lead, after a five-year transitional period, to Palestinian self-determination.

The trouble was that by this time the Camp David discussions primarily focused on achieving full Israeli withdrawal from Sinai in return for Egyptian recognition of Israel and a normalisation of bilateral relations. Prime Minister Begin had no interest in linking self-determination or even autonomy in the West Bank and Gaza with a bilateral agreement with Egypt. Neither, in the final account, did Sadat. Despite his consistent attempts to promote the Palestinian position, his priority was regaining territory rather than immersing himself in 'West Bank haggling'.[53]

Ultimately Sadat was even willing to forego a date for the beginning of Palestinian autonomy in the occupied territories in order to secure the return of his prized Sinai.[54]

As one Arab commentator put it, Sadat's unilateral initiative 'demolished'[55] Carter's plans for a comprehensive peace. Moreover, from February 1979 onwards US thinking on the Camp David process was also influenced greatly by events in Iran. The overthrow of the pro-US Shah made it vital for Carter to facilitate an Egyptian-Israeli agreement both for strategic reasons and in order to boost his flagging domestic popularity. It was no coincidence that Carter invited Begin and Sadat to restart talks in Washington only days after the birth of the Islamic Republic of Iran in early February 1979.

On 26 March 1979, Carter hosted Begin and Sadat on the north lawn of the White House to celebrate the signing of the Egyptian-Israeli peace treaty. Celebration of this defining moment in the history of the modern Middle East was tempered by one overriding reality. As the *Financial Times* noted, this treaty offered 'peace without agreement' precisely because the concept of Palestinian autonomy as set out was not defined or integrated into a comprehensive framework.[56]

There was little that Carter could do about it except play up the success of the bilateral agreement and marginalise the PLO. In April 1979, the head of the PLO's Beirut office, Shafiq al-Hout, visited the US at the invitation of the Chicago Council on Foreign Relations. He was allowed into the country but was prevented from publicising his ideas. After the trip he questioned whether 'giving a Palestinian a visa for two or three weeks [is] to be considered a change in the US position? If so, God only knows how we are going to reach a day when they recognise our rights and the existence of the PLO'.[57]

The PLO viewed Camp David as 'a wholly retrograde move'[58] and dismissed Carter's role in it as 'nothing more than a manoeuvre'.[59] As PLO official Mohammed Zuhdi Nashashibi explained in September 1980, the idea of self-rule as envisaged in the Camp David proposals and endorsed by Washington was '[a] denial of the very existence of the Palestinian people. It was nothing but an attempt to legalise the occupation of Arab territories, justify the Israeli settlements and put a final stop to any hope that the Palestinians, who under duress had been compelled to leave their country, could ever return there'.[60]

The Carter administration called on the EEC to support the Camp David deal. European ambassadors in Washington were briefed on the agreement and were requested to ask their governments to refrain from sabotaging the treaty.[61] Some were more obliging than others. Certainly, France made no secret of its distaste for what its foreign minister Jean François-Poncet dismissed as 'the bilateral peace treaty'.[62] The communiqué issued by the French Council of Ministers on 29 March noted that the peace deal failed to address a number of key issues concerning a comprehensive peace.[63] The Élysée Palace told Washington that while it would continue bilateral technical aid to Egypt it would not do so through the Camp David framework. The West German government was less openly hostile to the agreement, but Chancellor Schmidt was unwilling to give explicit backing or to provide financial support to Egypt under the Camp David framework unless it was part of an international aid effort, so as to avoid being seen as pro-Camp David by Arab opponents of the treaty.[64]

As British Foreign Secretary between 1974 and 1976, James Callaghan had played a constructive role in nurturing Israeli-Egyptian relations. Throughout the entire post-1973 period he had consistently supported Washington's efforts at mediation. Speaking in the House of Commons in 1975, he had been insistent that the 'American contribution was indispensable' for Middle East peace and that 'Europe must work to find the maximum agreement with America and build on that…that was bedrock policy'.[65] Roy Hattersley, Callaghan's deputy at the Foreign Office, followed suit, telling European colleagues that while the Middle East was of prime importance to the Community, the British view was that 'a political settlement in the Middle East was best left to the US'.[66]

Callaghan had close ties with Sadat who, in 1975, made the first visit to Britain by an Egyptian head of state. Sadat would telephone Callaghan in the middle of meetings with US officials to brief him.[67] A lifelong socialist, Callaghan also had strong ties to socialist leaders in Israel, most notably Golda Meir. This common bond ended when Menachem Begin became Israeli Prime Minister in 1977. Begin was the first right-wing prime minister in Israel's history. He had also been the commander of the extremist Jewish underground group, the Irgun, during the final years of British mandatory rule in Palestine during the 1940s. Three decades later many in the British media, political and foreign policy elites still considered him to be an anti-British terrorist. On a previous visit to London in 1972, as leader of the main Israeli opposition party, the Gahal bloc (an alliance of the right wing Herut Party and the Liberals), he had been forced to cancel two pre-arranged official events owing to anonymous bomb threats. During the same trip the ambassadors of eight Arab governments in London took advice on the possibility of having him extradited for alleged war crimes and even considered having him tried in a London court.

Begin's rising political fortunes did little to improve the negative attitude towards him. An uncompromising profile of the new Israeli leader in *The Times* in May 1977 appeared under the headline 'Israel's founding father reaps the rewards of terrorism'.[68] This was an obvious impediment to Anglo-Israeli relations, and following his election Begin 'lashed out' at the British media for labelling him a terrorist during the election campaign.[69] The Callaghan government tried to cool passions. The foreign secretary, David Owen, explained that 'they [Likud] are a new government, democratically elected and they must be given the benefit of any doubt or anxieties that people may have about the future position over a negotiated peace settlement'.[70]

In October 1977, the British government invited Begin on an official visit the following December. As *The Times'* diplomatic correspondent David Spanier noted, by issuing this invitation Callaghan 'intends to put Mr Begin's past behind him in their talks, and to start fresh'.[71] On his return home from meeting Callaghan and Owen, Begin informed the Knesset that both men had 'expressed their favourable assessment' of peace negotiations and that Callaghan thought it was a 'very constructive plan'.[72]

Thus Callaghan was more openly supportive of the Camp David Accords than his counterparts in Bonn or Paris. He described the agreement as 'a great risk' but also a 'legitimate risk'.[73] However, even Callaghan, who had contributed as much as anybody to propping up the Egyptian-Israeli track, was in favour of a far more substantial role for the PLO in the political process than was envisaged by Camp David. At the March 1979 summit in Paris that was convened to formulate a Community response to the Camp David agreement, the British suggested drawing up a statement calling for the PLO to have a role in decisions on the future status of the West Bank and Gaza.

Britain also endorsed the final declaration agreed at this meeting and published on 26 March 1979. It stressed that Europe was 'appreciative of the will for peace' that had led Carter to play a key role in negotiations, as well as the 'efforts made by President Sadat and Prime Minister Begin'. The statement also expressed the view that 'just and lasting peace....must translate into the right of the Palestinian people to a homeland…this is not a separate peace, but as a first step in the direction of a comprehensive settlement….including representatives of the Palestinian people'. To achieve this it called on President Carter to 'engage himself personally in the negotiations' for a 'comprehensive agreement, in which all the parties, including representatives of the Palestinian people' would participate.[74] The next EEC statement on the matter, issued in June 1979, failed to address or even acknowledge the Egyptian-Israeli peace agreement and called on peace to be comprehensive and on the basis of UN Security Council Resolutions 242 and 338.[75]

On 5 November 1978, the Arab states held a summit meeting in Baghdad highly critical of the Camp David process. Egypt was not invited to the Baghdad meeting, and when an Arab League delegation was sent to Cairo to discuss the issue Sadat refused to meet it. Instead, he explained before the People's Assembly that 'they came from Baghdad thinking I was like Hafiz Assad, who can be bought with cheques…or [King] Hussein, who also is bought with cheques…our ears are closed to the hissing vipers and we stand aloof from the antics of dwarves'.[76]

At a further meeting of Arab leaders in Baghdad, in March 1979, the Arab states agreed to break diplomatic ties with Egypt as punishment for Sadat's decision to make a separate peace deal with Israel without gaining a commitment on the Palestinian issue acceptable to the majority of the Arab world. Egypt's state-controlled media refuted this charge. Egyptian Radio called on the Arab world 'not to outbid us and [to] raise themselves to a level of responsibility'.[77] *Al Ahram* was less diplomatic in describing Arab opponents of Camp David as 'false leaders who are enemies of the Arab people' who were 'playing children's games' with the region. It also railed against the PLO's claim that Egypt's separate peace with Israel was 'apostasy against the dearest and most scared goals of our people'.[78]

After the signing of the Camp David treaty Sadat himself publicly dismissed his Arab critics as 'cowards'.[79] He was particularly critical of Syrian opposition to the peace deal. At the time of the signing of Sinai II, President Assad of Syria had accused Sadat of 'sacrificing the blood of thousands of martyrs' and 'turning his back' on Arab unity.[80] Once the Camp David process got under way Assad continued to attack Sadat's efforts as 'a painful blow to the Arab nation, a violation of the Arab will'.[81]

Sadat always rejected these accusations. He compared Begin and Israel favourably with Assad and Syria. 'The difference between the Syrians and the Israelis', he said, 'was very great—like the difference between igno-rance and knowledge, clowning and seriousness'.[82] On his third and final visit to Israel in September 1979 he dismissed Assad as a man who 'couldn't understand or does not want to understand' before asking his audience of journalists to look at what 'Egypt is achieving every day... [Israeli] withdrawal...negotiations...for the full autonomy of the Pales-tinians...what is in the other camp?'[83]

Isolated in the Arab world, Egypt now looked to Europe to support its deal with Israel. Speaking in Strasbourg in October 1979, Egypt's foreign minister Boutros Boutros-Ghali called on the EEC to exert influ-ence on the Arab states so that they would adopt a more understanding view of Egypt's peace strategy.[84] Israeli leaders, with the foreign minister Moshe Dayan in the lead, made similar pleas to the Community. 'It had', Dayan explained, 'been our hope and expectation that the European Community would give its full support to the historic achievement of the Israel-Egypt Peace', but instead its position had been 'injurious to the entire negotiations'.[85] In a subsequent speech before the Council of Europe in October 1979 Dayan expressed 'disappointment' with the Community, adding that it was 'saddening and surprising to find out that a large number of European governments did not welcome the peace treaty'. He also warned that this 'position can only weaken the hands of those who support the peace process' before concluding with the plea 'we beg you—give a helping hand to peace'.[86]

Like Egypt and Israel, those Arab states opposed to a separate Egyp-tian-Israeli peace agreement under US auspices also looked to Europe for support. At the Damascus meeting of the EAD in late 1978, the Arab delegation had urged the EEC to take a firm stand against Camp David. The following year Syria's Deputy Prime Minister Abdel Halim Khaddam warned that it was not 'in Europe's interest to defy the Arabs...let them leave the role of ingrate to the Americans'.[87]

From the day the Camp David agreement was signed, Europe's cor-ridors of power were rife with predictions of its imminent collapse. But fearful of the US reaction, neither the Commission nor any member state government was willing to break explicitly with it. France vetoed a March 1979 proposal that the Community issue a statement calling for a PLO role in future negotiations, because it might upset the Carter administra-tion's attempts to rejuvenate the Camp David negotiations. The following July, even as he was dismissing the Camp David agreement and playing up the future role of the PLO, François-Poncet of France was telling senior PLO officials that Arafat could not visit Paris until the US had reviewed the Palestinian aspect of the Camp David process at the end of 1979.[88]

For his part, Britain's new foreign secretary Lord Carrington believed that the Egyptian-Israeli peace was fundamentally flawed because the PLO was 'going to have to play a part in settling the problems'.[89] Having been secretary for defence in the Heath government of the early 1970s, the blue-blooded Carrington, who had taken up his hereditary title and place in the House of Lords on his twenty-first birthday in 1940, became Foreign Secretary when the Conservatives returned to power under Margaret Thatcher in late 1979. But even this outspoken proponent of a comprehensive peace felt obliged for the sake of transatlantic relations to put a positive spin on Camp David when he announced in late 1979 that it was something he 'greatly welcome[d]'.[90]

Of course, none of this amounted to outright support for the US-sponsored peace. As the understated Abba Eban noted at the time, there was a general 'restraint on enthusiasm' in Europe in the wake of the Camp David agreement, an outlook he termed the EEC's 'primary fallacy'.[91] The Community's unenviable position of having to navigate a course that took US interests into account was made worse by the fear of alienating Arab opponents of the Israeli-Egyptian peace, which perhaps explains why no Community statement ever called on the Arab world to embrace Camp David. This concern was influenced by the fact that by 1977 Europe was dependent on the Arab world for five-sixths of its oil. It would be a number of years before the efforts undertaken in the wake of the 1973 oil crisis to moderate demand and develop new sources of energy (most notably the French re-focus on nuclear power) paid off. In the intervening period oil dependency continued as the Arab states became increasingly expert in linking the oil weapon to the Palestine issue when dealing with both individual European states and the EEC as a single entity.

In 1977 a PLO representative, speaking at an unofficial EAD conference in Italy, warned of the likelihood of a second oil embargo that would cripple Europe unless the West's Middle East policy changed.[92] Saudi Arabia's minister responsible for oil, Ahmed Zaki Yamani, admitted in a 1979 interview that he would not be surprised if Palestinian frustrations with Western policies led them to sink 'one or two supertankers in the Strait of Hormuz' blocking the flow of oil to the West and making previous oil crises 'seem like child's play'.[93] Later in the year, in a newspaper interview he linked an 'overall solution for the Middle East Crisis' with Saudi Arabia taking positive action by increasing oil production.[94]

In a speech broadcast live on Italian television during an EAD meeting in Rimini, Mana Said al-Oteia, the United Arab Emirates oil minister, speaking in his capacity as OPEC president, explained that there could be no effective dialogue between the EEC and oil-producing countries unless Europe decided to recognise the PLO as the only legitimate representative of the Palestinian people. Dismissing the accusation that such talk constituted 'oil blackmail', he said it was an issue of justice: 'therefore we Arabs wish to hear from our European friends a word of justice'. Al-Oteia concluded, echoing Yamani, with the warning that 'hungry for justice, frustrated in their decades old national aspirations, the Palestinians may one day set fire to the wells. If the oil catches fire, there will be none either for [us] or you'.[95]

By 1979 over 60 per cent of West European oil imports came from the Persian Gulf. When the oil producing states cut back the oil supplied to major international oil companies to 44 per cent from 78 per cent in 1974, this increased their influence further by reducing the amount of oil that international oil companies were able to provide to third parties.[96]

Concerns over oil aside, the EEC's reluctance to embrace Camp David also came at a time of unprecedented public sympathy for the Palestinian cause in Europe. In 1979, a senior US State Department official described 'the pace of the turnaround in opinion' in Europe in favour of the Palestinians as 'amazing'.[97] Speaking at the UN in same year, King Hussein of Jordan also drew attention to what the *New York Times* called 'the slow erosion of Israel's support in Western Europe'. Hussein told his UN audience that 'Western Europe is overcoming the effects of Zionist control both in the mass media and in national parliaments…the European mind has been opened to the realities in the Middle East and to the aspirations and suffering of the Palestinian people'.[98]

King Hussein made his statement on the same day in September 1979 as the Irish foreign minister Michael O'Kennedy, speaking at the UN on behalf of the Community, called for the 'representatives' of the Palestinians to 'play a full part in the negotiations of a comprehensive settlement'.[99] This statement was heralded by Arab commentators as the 'first time that the EEC mentioned the need for the PLO to have a role in the peace process'.[100] As one participant noted at the time, 'virtually every word of his statement [was] argued over at innumerable meetings'.[101] West Germany's foreign minister Genscher in particular took much convincing before he endorsed the final text. But this provided little solace for Israel. Speaking in a question and answer session with European officials following O'Kennedy's UN speech, Dayan suggested that Europe should not go about making 'cynical' statements, and on his return to Israel he expressed the view that Europe was becoming more and more pro-Palestinian.[102] The ageing ex-general also argued repeatedly that the European stance was 'injurious to the entire process of negotiations' with Egypt and morally wrong as 'no country can or should be expected to negotiate with a party [the PLO] which denies its very existence, aims at its destruction, and uses terror against its civilian population'.[103]

Such arguments had little impact on the Community. In the months following the Camp David agreement there was a significant increase in direct contacts between senior European figures and PLO leaders. In July 1979, following a meeting between France's foreign minister François-Poncet and the head of the PLO's political bureau, Farouk Kaddoumi, French officials acknowledged that Paris now took the PLO 'increasingly seriously'.[104] This coincided with a West German decision to send a close political ally of Genscher to meet Arafat in Beirut. In October, Belgium's foreign minister Simonet, who had previously met Kaddoumi in Brussels, stated that, 'it seems to us that the PLO is, at present time, the means by which the wishes of the Palestinian people are being expressed'.[105] Later in the same month, Kaddoumi was the guest of the Italian foreign minister, Franco Maria Malfatti, in Rome. Following the meeting Italy became the first EEC member state to grant formal recognition to the PLO. All this led the *New York Times*, in an article entitled 'PLO gains in Western Europe', to speculate as to 'which of the common market countries will be the first to receive Yasir Arafat...on an official visit'.[106]

One significant reason why the *New York Times* was so confident in predicting the PLO's move to official status in Europe in the short term was the relentless efforts by Austria's charismatic chancellor, Bruno Kreisky, to legitimise the organisation. Though Austria was not yet a member of the EEC, the outspoken Kreisky was vice-chairman of the Socialist International and was arguably Europe's most prominent Jewish politician of the era. Relations between Kreisky, an ardent non-Zionist, and Israel had been bad since the premiership of Golda Meir. In 1973 she had been openly critical of the Austrian leader when he agreed to close an Austrian transit camp for Jewish refugees on the way to Israel, in return for the release of hostages being held by terrorists.[107] But relations reached a nadir in 1978 when Kreisky was quoted in the Dutch media as calling Israel a 'police state', Begin a 'political grocer' and Israeli diplomats 'the most hated in the business'.[108]

In July 1979 Arafat held his first meeting with a European head of government when Kreisky received him in Vienna. This was the 'opening shot'[109] in the PLO's strategy of building a broad consensus against Camp David in Europe and of using growing diplomatic legitimacy on the continent to influence the US attitude towards the PLO. Its timing was also important as the Arafat-Kreisky meeting coincided with the fourth round of Israeli-Egyptian autonomy talks under the Camp David framework in Alexandria. As Christopher Hitchens noted at the time, Austria's move greatly increased 'awareness' in Europe of the need to legitimise the PLO.[110] Al-Dajani, who had accompanied Arafat to Vienna, now confidently predicted that 'this year is the year of the West European states' recognition of the PLO'.[111] For its part the PLO Central Committee adopted a resolution authorising Arafat to continue his European initiatives.

Hugely troubled by the Austrian Chancellor's effort to normalise the PLO's position across Europe, Israel withdrew its ambassador from Vienna. Begin called Kreisky's efforts 'a calumny' and the Labour leader Shimon Peres bemoaned the fact that his actions were a 'threat to the process of peace, and serves to encourage international terrorism'.[112] Unfazed by these criticisms, Kreisky told *Le Monde* that it was 'completely absurd to believe that the PLO is seeking to destroy the state of Israel'.[113] He followed this up with a speech at the UN General Assembly that set out his plan to recognise the PLO as the representative of the Palestinian people. During an official visit to the Middle East the following January he met Arafat in Saudi Arabia. In March 1980, Austria became the first Western state to accord the PLO official recognition with the same diplomatic standing as nation-states. Kreisky explained his decision to extend a 'new form of diplomatic recognition' to the PLO as representatives of a stateless and government-less people on the grounds that 'someone had to do it first'.[114] Now, as one Spanish government official acknowledged, the 'intellectual race'[115] was on to see which EEC country would follow Kreisky's lead.

5

BET IN VENICE

'The Camel laboured and gave birth to a mouse.'

Arab Proverb

Writing in late 1979, Theo Sommer, the publisher of Hamburg's *Die Zeit*, enthused that the EPC framework had achieved a 'formerly unknown cohesion and profile' for the Community, due 'first and foremost in its support for Palestinian self-determination'.[1] Certainly, the recent diplomatic embrace of the PLO was partly an attempt to capitalise on American vulnerability and isolation in the wider Arab world following Camp David. While some in Europe argued that 'we should support Sadat in his search for peace',[2] the majority view identified more with the argument of the celebrated Palestinian-American academic Hisham Shirabi, that the time was ripe for Europe to 'build bridges' with those Arab states that rejected Camp David.[3]

From a Community perspective, this window of opportunity was likely to be brief. European ambassadors in Washington were warning that if Carter won re-election in 1980 he would make a comprehensive peace in the Middle East, a peace that included the Palestinians, a priority of his second term.[4] Already in the summer of 1979, his administration had attempted to regain some of its standing in the region by backing an Arab initiative calling for a new UN Security Council Resolution that added an extra section on Palestinian self-determination to Resolutions 242 and 338.[5] The following September, the same month that both the *New York Times* and the *Washington Post* published columns calling for the US government to deal with the PLO, the National Security Adviser, Zbigniew Brzezinski, called on Israel 'to accept legitimate Palestinian rights and to interpret the Camp David accords on the West Bank and Gaza both generously and with wise attention to the needs of an enduring peace with the Palestinian people'.[6]

Italy's decision to become the first EEC state to recognise the PLO officially, in October 1979, raised the question of whether Rome would have made this move without consulting Washington and its EEC partners. Speculation was fuelled by President Carter's unexpected appearance at a long meeting between the Italian foreign minister Malfatti and Secretary of State Vance two weeks prior to the announcement.[7]

If the Camp David process had damaged US relations with most of the Arab world, it had also significantly undermined the EAD framework. No Egyptian representatives attended the fourth EAD General Committee in Damascus in early December 1978. Worse, on 31 March 1979, nineteen Arab League members (including a Palestinian delegation) ejected Egypt from the League for signing a separate peace with Israel. This put an end to French efforts during its 1979 EEC presidency to boost the EAD by offering to convene a meeting of the EAD framework at ministerial level, something that the Arabs had been lobbying for since late 1974 and that France itself had been 'pushing' since 1975.[8]

On top of this, after expelling Egypt, the Arab League transferred its headquarters from Cairo to Tunis. This forced the Community to ignore requests from both the rump Cairo office and the new Tunis office for EAD documentation, lest it be seen to be taking sides. In April 1979, the new Tunis headquarters informed the Community that EAD meetings at all levels would be suspended until the Arab League reorganised itself fully in the wake of Camp David.[9]

By the end of 1979, the EAD had ceased to function without having officially been disbanded. Talks in February 1980 on reviving it came to naught in the face of Arab demands that the Community should now address politics as a priority and use the EAD to speak out against Camp David in more explicit terms.[10] A further meeting under the framework in Rome in early March 1980 made no more progress and led one Arab delegate to denounce the EAD as 'nothing but a hoax' that was now 'at a complete standstill'.[11]

The PLO's Ahmad al-Dajani, who led the Arab League delegation at this meeting, was no less emphatic. The Community, he argued, had to 'cease to pretend that there are two Arab Leagues, one consisting of Sadat's Egypt and on the other side the rest of the Arab states'. It also had to agree to make the EAD 'global', to include political issues and to accept that any future EAD meetings must be held at head of government or foreign minister level.[12]

In early March 1980, at exactly the same time as these discussions were taking place, President Valéry Giscard d'Estaing took advantage of a visit to Kuwait to set out officially France's support for Palestinian self-determination 'within the framework of a just and lasting peace'. Less than one week later he went further and called for the inclusion of the PLO in peace negotiations.[13] French officials explained the timing of Giscard d'Estaing's statement in terms of a desire to preempt similar moves by other EEC members.[14] In particular, there was real concern in Paris that the British government was now looking to outmanoeuvre France on the Palestine issue by sponsoring a draft resolution at the UN Security Council recognising Palestinian political rights and accepting the PLO as the sole representative of the Palestinian people.

This suspicion was aroused primarily by the stance of Lord Carrington. One French official would later recall how Carrington had 'a greater awareness than his predecessors of Great Britain's interest in a more active and dynamic presence in the Arab Middle East'.[15] The US secretary of state, Alexander Haig, was more blunt: Carrington, he said, 'appeared to be devoted to the idea of bringing the PLO into the peace process'.[16] In particular, Carrington was known to be in favour of amending UN Security Council Resolution 242 in favour of a greater commitment to Palestinian rights and the PLO. In the weeks after Giscard d'Estaing's pronouncement in Kuwait, Carrington even told the House of Lords that 'I do not think that the PLO, as such, is a terrorist organisation...it would be a great mistake to assume that it is possible to get a settlement in the area without taking into account the PLO'.[17] Douglas Hurd, a junior minister at the British Foreign Office who would later become foreign secretary, shared Carrington's view. At the beginning of 1980, Hurd was adamant that 'no one should doubt that the PLO will have to be involved in the peace process'.[18] On 5 March, in the course of an interview with the BBC Arabic Service, he went further. He admitted that the British government, along with some of its EEC partners, was 'considering... whether there is some helpful way in which the countries of Europe can improve the chances for a fair settlement', before adding that the Palestinians 'have rights which go well beyond' those addressed in UN Security Council Resolution 242 and 'we consider that there is a case for the Security Council to recognise those rights'.[19]

Giscard d'Estaing's March call for Palestinian self-determination was widely interpreted as highly innovative and responsible for the speedy embrace of a similar position across the Community. Arafat welcomed it as the first time a major Western European country had called on the PLO to join negotiations.[20] In a June 1980 interview Eban explained the 'shower of European statements in favour of Palestinian "self-determination"' as a direct consequence of the efforts of 'President Giscard d'Estaing in Kuwait'.[21] During a full-scale parliamentary attack on the French President in the same month, James Callaghan berated Mrs Thatcher's government for 'going along with a process that President Giscard d'Estaing initiated'.[22]

In reality, however, the Community was not 'following the French lead' as was widely claimed.[23] Giscard d'Estaing was following the lead of some smaller EEC members. In July 1979, during a visit to Baghdad, Belgium's foreign minister Henri Simonet issued a joint communiqué with his Iraqi counterpart which called for '[the]…implementation of the national right of the Palestinian people… [the] right to self determination'.[24] The following October Simonet went further. 'It seems to us', he told a press conference, 'that the PLO is, at present time, the means by which the wishes of the Palestinian people are being expressed'.[25]

In his speech on behalf of the Community at the UN General Assembly in late September 1979, Ireland's foreign minister O'Kennedy supported the 'right of the Palestinians to determine their own future as a people'.[26] In February 1980, in the course of a state visit to Bahrain, Brian Lenihan, O'Kennedy's successor as foreign minister, and his Bahraini counterpart, Sheikh Muhammed bin Mubarak al-Khalifa, issued a joint communiqué calling for Palestinian self-determination and a role for the PLO in the political process. It also saw Ireland become the first Community member to use the word 'state' in relation to Palestinian rights.[27]

The Bahrain Declaration was heralded in the Arab world as 'Ireland's definitive commitment to an independent Palestine'.[28] In Israel it was widely condemned.[29] Shlomo Argov, Israel's ambassador to Britain and Ireland, forwarded an official protest to Dublin that preceded similar diplomatic protests to France and other EEC member states on the issue.[30] Begin, who believed that there was 'nothing graver' than Europe's attempt to legitimise the PLO,[31] went onto Irish radio to appeal for a renunciation of the Bahrain Declaration.[32]

Although the Arab world warmly welcomed the statements by both Simonet and Lenihan, Giscard d'Estaing's Kuwait statement was greeted with far less enthusiasm. This was primarily because the French President had refused to go as far as either the Irish or Belgian governments in calling for the establishment of a Palestinian state or in welcoming the PLO fully into the political process. *Tishrin*, the Syrian daily, explained that the French initiative 'suffers from an intrinsic defect'. It concluded its critique by raising the 'great question that faces the planners of the new French initiative': 'Is Europe ready to make the necessary sacrifices and to exceed the limits set by America for the sake of a just initiative that deals with the roots of the problem, or does it still want to lean on its American ally, the US, to leave the decision to it?'[33]

Similar sentiments were expressed by the Fatah-dominated PLO. Yasser Arafat was of the view that 'France must be more explicit and recognise that self-determination means the establishment of a Palestinian state'.[34] Another senior PLO official, Faisal Hurani, went further. He compared Giscard d'Estaing's statements to the valueless 'coloured glass beads' that colonialists would offer tribal chiefs in exchange for vast concessions. He also advised that to win over the Arab world France would have to 'go beyond these loosely-worded expressions' by calling for a Palestinian state to prove that this was not simply 'another chapter in the Camp David process'.[35] *Filastin al-Thawra*, the PLO weekly published in Beirut, wondered if Giscard d'Estaing's statement had 'been cooked up by America for Europe to serve?' before concluding with the question: 'to what extent is the European stand capable of achieving anything at the practical level?'[36]

A similar view was expressed by Palestinian splinter groups that rarely endorsed the Fatah position. The PFLP dismissed Giscard d'Estaing's statements as 'no more than the smallest of advances on what the Camp David agreements have to say about "self-governing authority"'.[37] The Democratic Front for the Liberation of Palestine (DFLP) saw it as evidence of the 'limited effectiveness of Western Europe in the Middle East' and argued that the French statement was intended to 'secure a European consensus and international cover for the American settlement'.[38]

Determined to capitalise on this negative Arab response to Giscard d'Estaing's Kuwait statement, France's main competitors in the Community now entered the debate. West German foreign ministry officials reminded the media that during his tour of the Arab world in 1979, Genscher had supported the principle of self-determination. They also took the unusual step of compiling and circulating a collection of German official statements in support of Palestinian self-determination dating back to November 1974. On 6 March 1980, just three days after Giscard d'Estaing's call for Palestinian self-determination, both West German and British representatives at the UN Security Council gave speeches in support of self-determination for the Palestinian people. This resulted in the representatives of both countries being summoned to the Israeli foreign ministry in Jerusalem to explain the positions of their governments.

The following month, the Council of Europe unanimously adopted a resolution very critical of Camp David. It called for the rephrasing of UN Security Council Resolution 242 to support Palestinian self-determination and demanded mutual recognition between Israel and the PLO.[39] The Israeli foreign ministry, whose observer at the Council of Europe was denied the right to intervene in the debate, described the resolution as 'one of several steps taken recently which actually militate against the present ongoing peace process'.[40] Israel's Europe-based ambassadors also met in London to discuss how best to counter the European attempt to introduce the concept of Palestinian self-determination into the political debate.[41]

The unanimous passing of such a pro-Palestinian resolution at the Council of Europe highlighted a massive shift in European attitudes on the Palestine issue by 1980. This was especially true for the Socialist bloc in the European Parliament. Less than two decades earlier this prominent pan-European grouping had been Israel's staunchest Western ally. But in the decades since the 1967 war and the occupation of the West Bank and Gaza, it had come to sympathise overwhelmingly with the Palestinian cause.

This high level and very public European support for Palestinian self-determination also had a practical impact. It directly challenged the Israeli attempt to use the Camp David process to institutionalise Palestinian autonomy rather than statehood in the occupied territories. In an interview with French-speaking journalists in March 1980, Begin stated bluntly that the term 'self-determination' 'means a state—that phrase self-determination does not appear in the Camp David agreement. In the Camp David agreement, we decided about autonomy, which is not a state.

A Palestinian state…[is a] mortal danger to Israel…Europe should be very careful in making statements like these'.[42]

The foreign minister, Dayan, was adamant that 'autonomy is not a state. If the administrative autonomy declares itself a state, the autonomy becomes null and void'.[43] On succeeding Dayan as foreign minister in March 1980, Yitzhak Shamir looked to downplay the practical implications of European calls for self-determination on the grounds that the Arabs 'cannot gain much from the declarations of European statesmen'.[44] Dismissive as he was, Shamir was still concerned enough to visit a number of European capitals to try to gain support for Israel's position on autonomy. He had little success.

In January 1980, Egypt rejected the proposed Israeli model for self-governing authority as agreed upon at Camp David. Israel, in turn, rejected the Egyptian model which, it argued, contained many points contradicting the Camp David agreement and which, if accepted, would form the basis for a Palestinian state.

By the spring of 1980 Camp David was widely viewed across Europe to be 'dead as a doornail'.[45] The earlier European reluctance to take a stand against the US by challenging the bilateral Egyptian-Israeli peace was fading. In part this was because the European view was now increasingly shared by senior US State Department officials, one of whom admitted in April 1980 that if things failed to improve on the Palestinian front 'we're not going to have an agreement worth talking about'.[46] At a meeting in Luxemburg on 28 April 1980, the European Council issued a statement declaring that 'Conscious that Europe may in due course have a role to play', it had 'instructed the foreign ministers to submit a report on this problem on the occasion of its next session at Venice'. By the first week of May 1980 it was an open secret that the Community was preparing to make a major statement on the Middle East in order to keep up 'momentum' in the peace process following the inevitable collapse of Camp David.[47]

On 10 May 1980, European predictions of Camp David's demise appeared to be coming true. The Egyptian-Israeli autonomy negotiations for the West Bank and Gaza failed to meet the agreed May deadline for conclusion. Sadat broke off discussions and, on 15 May, Egypt formally announced that it was suspending autonomy talks on the grounds that the Knesset was in the process of debating a bill to make Jerusalem the capital of Israel.

At the same time a group of pro-Arab British MPs wrote to Begin to tell him that the 'Camp David formula...is not accepted as a basis for peace by all who are fundamentally involved'.[48] On the eve of the Venice meeting, the Parliamentary Association of Euro-Arab Cooperation, which represented 350 MPs from European parliaments, sent an open letter to President Carter informing him that the 'Camp David formula, in so far as it sought to address the central problem of devising an acceptable modus vivendi for Israel and the Palestinians is dead'. It concluded that:

it should be possible for US and European 'Nine' to work out a new more widely acceptable formula for peace, discarding those features of the Camp David Accords which experiences has shown to be detrimental or misconceived...we feel sure [the EEC] would prefer to act in concert with the US in developing a truly even handed policy for bringing peace to the Middle East, rather than pursuing an independent European initiative which set Europe and America on divergent paths.[49]

Europe's seemingly inevitable break with the Carter administration over Camp David appeared, at least from an American perspective, to give credibility to Kissinger's analysis at the time that there was a 'Soviet-Arab-European coalition regarding Middle East issues'.[50] In numerous meetings with their EEC counterparts US officials still insisted that Camp David was the only viable framework for peace. Edmund Muskie's first major task on becoming secretary of state in early May 1980 was to convince EEC leaders not to put forward a European initiative on the Middle East at the forthcoming summit in Venice in June. In a meeting with the French foreign minister François-Poncet, Muskie was adamant that despite the suspension of the autonomy talks between Israel and Egypt, the US administration considered Camp David to be alive, and that any European initiative would damage US efforts.[51] Muskie also intervened personally with West Germany to thwart any attempt by EEC member states to extend *de jure* recognition to the PLO under any new initiative.[52]

Muskie received assurances from senior European officials, including the European Council President Emilio Colombo, that the Community was not opposed to Camp David and that it was only trying to help.[53] But at the same time the Arab world was lobbying the Community hard to support its call for the UN to provide a framework for a comprehensive settlement, since, in the words of one Syrian official, the 'circumstances' were more 'favourable' there.[54] In April 1980 Khaled al Hassan, the head of a PLO delegation visiting Strasbourg, outlined the role that he wanted the EEC to play once Camp David had officially collapsed. Europe, he explained, should refer the issue back to the UN Security Council, which would then vote to force Israel to make a complete withdrawal from all occupied territories. This in turn would be followed by the birth of a Palestinian state.[55] There was growing European interest in backing an amendment to UN Resolution 242 along these lines as an alternative to Camp David, so that the landmark resolution no longer referred to the Palestine question as a 'refugee problem' and instead made reference to 'legitimate national rights'.[56]

Speaking in a television interview at the end of May, President Carter was clear: 'We are asking the European allies not to get involved in the negotiations for the time being…my predication is that without very much delay we will be back at the negotiating table, making progress'.[57] He also warned that, if necessary, he would not hesitate to veto any draft resolution submitted by the EEC to the UN Security Council in order 'to prevent this Camp David process being destroyed or subverted'.[58] In early June, Carter again threatened to veto any European attempt to push through a Security Council draft resolution on Palestinian self-determination.

In taking this stand, Carter was reaffirming the promise, known as the 'Kissinger Clause', that had been included in a letter to Israel at the time of the Sinai deal in 1975. This had committed the US to veto any change that was incompatible with UN Security Council Resolution 242's original intention. Carter's stance on this issue was a relief to Prime Minister Begin who was 'happy' to reassure the Knesset that 'if a certain [EEC sponsored] motion is presented to the Security Council, averting the basis upon which the Camp David agreements are founded, the US will cast a veto'.[59] Carter's multiple threats to veto any draft resolution on Palestinian self-determination were enough to deter the EEC from opting for the UN route.[60] It even led a nervous Community to send Emilio Colombo to Washington to reassure the administration that any European proposal should not be misconstrued as an 'alternative in contradiction with the Camp David formula'.[61]

However, the Community was still in favour of setting out a major new policy declaration on the Palestine issue at its June summit in Venice. For a number of months prior to this meeting the Arabic media had warned that in any new initiative Europe must 'not be a tool in the hands of

America and not bind herself to the wheels of Camp David'.[62] A resolution passed at the fourth Fatah congress in early June 1980 further illuminated the role that the Arab world, excluding Egypt, expected Europe to play:

The US is the leader of the enemies of our people and nation….we have no choice but to strengthen the international front against the US, wage war on its policies and strike out against US interests in the region. As for the position of Western Europe, the Common Market…political efforts will be made to utilise the support of democratic progressive forces there to reduce and eventually eliminate support for the Zionist entity, isolating it by obtaining the recognition of the PLO by these countries as the sole legitimate representative of the Palestinian people, and getting maximal political and material help for the Palestinian cause.[63]

The long-anticipated Venice Declaration was published on 13 June 1980. As André Fontaine, editor-in-chief of *Le Monde*, noted, 'most of the Nine had already said more or less the same thing, but each in its own way, and in less solemn circumstances'.[64] While acknowledging Israel's right to exist it contained outspoken criticism of Israeli 'territorial occupation' since 1967 and condemned settlements built outside pre-1967 borders as illegal under international law. In a reference to the political claims of the Palestinian people, it rejected the traditional view that the Palestinian problem was 'simply one of refugees' and it called for the Palestinian people to be allowed to 'exercise fully its right to self-determination'. Most controversially, it also called for the PLO to be 'associated with' future negotiations.[65] This broke new ground in so far as it was the first Community statement on the Middle East conflict to include explicit support for Palestinian 'self-determination' and a role for the PLO in future peace negotiations.

There had been consensus among participants at Venice that Camp David was dead. But there had been little unanimity and a lot of 'hard bargaining'[66] over whether to mention the PLO by name in any final communiqué. As Margaret Thatcher would later recall, 'almost every half-sentence was discussed and debated'[67] before a formula acceptable to all was found. Britain, France, Italy, Ireland and Luxembourg wanted explicit mention of the PLO; the Netherlands, West Germany and Denmark preferred limiting the statement to a call for a role for the Palestinian people.[68]

The final wording, calling for PLO association rather than participation, influenced the response of the US administration. Though privately it 'disliked' the document's content, as Carrington would later admit,[69] Washington greeted it in a relatively positive way. Muskie explained that he 'didn't see anything in it that challenges the Camp David process or seeks to divert the parties to the Camp David process from their work'. He also thanked the Community for showing a 'sense of restraint' in the way it expressed support for a PLO role in negotiations, though he did state that the US would refuse to deal with the PLO as long as it was 'bent on' Israel's destruction.[70]

Unconstrained by the niceties of transatlantic diplomacy, the American media were far more scathing. In a highly critical editorial entitled 'A minor-league Mideast game', the *New York Times* described the Venice Declaration as 'absurd'. It also added that any 'aware political amateur' could have summed up what Europe was trying to say at Venice: 'We need oil and Arab trade so badly we cannot wait any longer for America, Israel and Egypt to turn their partial peace into a broader settlement... so we hope that by granting the Palestinians a state....we will somehow persuade them to accept Israel. Even if this doesn't work, the Arabs will think better of Western Europe and treat it kindly'.[71]

The Venice Declaration also received a cool response from Arab opponents of Camp David. While acknowledging the Community's 'important political role', the PLO criticised the document for failing to 'recognise officially' either the organisation or an independent Palestinian state.[72] The PLO also dismissed the statement as a 'product of American blackmail', inspired by a European desire to rescue the struggling Camp David process. This left the European position 'short of our expectations because the European countries are still on the American line and still on the line of Camp David'.[73]

Speaking at the UN General Assembly in July 1980, Farouk Kaddoumi, by now widely acknowledged as the PLO foreign minister in waiting, described Venice as a hopeful beginning but one that was inadequate and unsatisfactory. Arafat was particularly dismissive in comparing the declaration to 'a piece of bone that they could throw to us and keep us busy', and he reminded the world that 'the Palestinian people are in no need of a political statement or initiative to determine its destiny'.[74] However, in a later meeting with Gaston Thorn, the Community's special representative in the region, he only went so far as to note some 'contradictions and ambiguities'[75] in the Venice statement.

For its part, the DFLP, the Palestinian splinter group, called it 'a small step in the right direction';[76] while George Habash, the head of the PFLP, got right to the point. Any support for the Palestinian cause in Europe, he argued, 'has not taken place because of the suaveness of PLO representatives in London, Paris or Rome, but thanks to the rifle'.[77]

The fact that the Palestinian response to Venice ranged from lukewarm to outright hostile was of little comfort to Israel. In the week before its publication Israel's Defence Minister, Ezer Weizman, told ABC News that 'we shouldn't encourage' a European initiative 'but should stick to the Camp David approach'. He added that if Begin and Sadat could agree on the matter of Palestinian autonomy, 'the European initiative will be stopped'.[78] But the initiative was not 'stopped', and in an interview in the French press the day following its publication, Begin characterised the Venice statement as 'a shame'.[79]

Following a cabinet meeting in which the Prime Minister attacked the 'hypocrisy and cynicism of the heads of the EEC countries',[80] the Israeli government issued a statement dismissing the document as 'a Munich-like surrender' and condemned the Community's endorsement of the 'Arab SS known as the PLO'.[81] Shamir, who had visited six European capitals on 9–10 June 1980 to try to organise European opposition to the forthcoming initiative, characterised the expression of support for dialogue with the PLO at Venice as 'really a shame and scandal for Europe'.[82] He also condemned the 'bad spirit that prevailed in Venice', considering that it was motivated by 'an attempt to demonstrate independence from the United States' as well as 'various economic pressures' that had resulted in it giving succour to the 'most radical elements [in the Arab world]'.[83]

The opposition Labour Party was equally forthright. Its leader, Shimon Peres, described the French position at Venice as more extreme than that of Egypt. Later, after he became foreign minister in a national unity government he dismissed the document as 'a piece of paper' that changed nothing on the ground.[84] Peres noted that the Venice Declaration had been issued just weeks after Fatah, the dominant constituent group within the PLO, had reiterated its objective of liquidating Israel. He also warned the Community not to adopt the PLO as a partner on the basis of 'smiles, promises and hopes' at the cost of ignoring the real PLO.[85] His veteran Labour colleague Abba Eban made the same point when he criticised Venice for giving the PLO access to the peace process without extracting any 'ideological or rhetorical concessions' in return.[86]

Decades earlier the *New York Times* had crowned Eban 'Israel's Chief Orator'.[87] Now he drew on all his debating skills to argue that Europe's position at Venice was motivated by its attempt to secure Arab oil. 'The West', he explained, 'breathes with one of its lungs, oil, outside of its body'.[88] Begin made a similar, if less eloquent, point, when he asked rhetorically, whether 'Western Europe, because of a barrel of oil, should support this?'[89] Shamir also explained the European position in terms of Arab 'oil and their capacity for extortion'.[90] Sergio Minerbi, the Israeli ambassador in Brussels, was more diplomatic. The Community, he explained in a somewhat resigned tone, had 'chosen the path of pro-Arab statements in hopes that they [are] conducive to secure her oil supplies'.[91]

In early 1981 Sadat addressed the European Parliament. His speech paid tribute to the Venice initiative, but he was careful not to overplay the EEC's future role in peace making or to undermine the Camp David framework.[92] Similarly, Egypt's vice-president Hosni Mubarak welcomed the Venice statement on the grounds that it did not conflict with Camp David.[93] But privately the Egyptians had pleaded with the Community to refrain from making the statement. During a visit to London on the eve of the Venice meeting, Mubarak and the Egyptian deputy foreign minister Osama El-Baz argued that a European initiative that lacked US support would do more harm than good. They also emphasised to their hosts that the Camp David process still provided the best way forward and that Egypt hoped the Community would drop its upcoming initiative all together.[94]

The Venice Declaration failed to provide a real alternative to Camp David because it refused to give formal recognition to the PLO or to express explicit support for the establishment of a Palestinian state. This left the Community with no more influence over the PLO after the document had been published than before. At the same time, the position adopted by the Community at Venice contributed to a significant worsening in Euro-Israeli relations. As an Israeli foreign ministry report written in the wake of Venice summed up, 'the political principles of the European Community are destructive and unacceptable and stand no chance of being considered viable by Israel'.[95]

On the other hand, the Venice statement did achieve some short-term positive results for the Community. The energy crisis triggered by the overthrow of the pro-Western Shah of Iran in February 1979 had fuelled inflation, a huge balance of payments deficit and recession across Europe. This had left the Community very vulnerable to the Arab world, which increasingly linked the oil weapon and petrodollars to the politics of the

Palestine issue. Mana Said al-Oteia, the oil minister of the United Arab Emirates and OPEC president, calmly summed this reality up at the time of the Shah's fall. The balance of power between Europe and the Arabs was all the time changing in favour of the latter, he argued, so that if 'yesterday we spoke English at these meetings, now we speak Arabic'.[96]

Saudi Arabia, in particular, had become a global economic powerhouse since the 1973 oil crisis. Between 1973 and 1981, its annual oil revenues increased from US$4.3 billion to $102 billion.[97] Much of this new found wealth was re-invested in Europe. In 1976 alone, Saudi Arabia agreed to finance a US$1 billion loan to Italy and a $300 million loan to Ireland.[98] This financial support was explicitly intended to move the Community towards open support of the Palestinian cause. As one Saudi official informed the *New York Times* in 1979, 'we no longer think of oil in terms of money alone'.[99]

Speaking in the House of Lords in the wake of Venice, Lord Carrington, a moving force behind the declaration, described oil 'as a major cause, not a symptom, of international tension, instability and distress'. He added that those who drew up the Venice statement were 'very conscious of the seriousness of those problems'.[100] But for Carrington the Venice Declaration was 'wholly right' for a number of other reasons.[101] It was an acknowledgement that 'the PLO enjoys considerable Palestinian support [and] …cannot be left out of account' and as such it attempted to place a 'proper appreciation of the Palestinian aspect'.[102] It was also, as Carrington later explained, a response to the 'political vacuum' in the Middle East when the Camp David process was 'in the doldrums',[103] and the US was 'having a sabbatical and moderate Arabs, in particular, needed to see that somebody, somewhere, was alive to the problem and wanted to help'.[104]

In these terms the Venice Declaration did succeed, as one Arab commentator explained, 'in keeping the Arab world from total alienation from the West'.[105] Despite its failings, it did mark a 'highpoint' in the EEC's attempt to develop a 'distinctive role' in the search for Middle East peace, as Carrington argued before the UN General Assembly in September 1981.[106] President Giscard d'Estaing of France made much the same point. The Venice Declaration, he declared was 'a clear text that does not evade the issues, but offers a just and balanced point of view'.[107] No less important, he felt that it was a major contribution to 'the emergence, or rather re-emergence, of a European presence, acting in its own way and for its own ends'.[108]

As a new decade dawned, the Venice Declaration served notice to the international community of Europe's intent it to use the EPC framework to compete with the US in extending its influence across the Middle East.

6

DUE SOUTH

'Yes, peace and freedom are certainly coming, but will Europe confine itself to the position of an observer, or will it proceed to participation and action?'

Yasser Arafat

'I do not fear anything my friend', was Prime Minister Begin's brusque response to a mid-1981 question from a journalist over whether he feared that his 'harsh attacks' on European leaders since the Venice Declaration would 'cause serious difficulties for Israel's relations with Europe?'[1]

Begin may not have thought so, but it was a pertinent question. In the previous months the Israeli premier had accused Chancellor Schmidt of West Germany of being 'driven by greed and avarice';[2] had described President Giscard d'Estaing of France as a man of 'no principles whatsoever';[3] had dismissed Britain's Foreign Secretary Lord Carrington, as 'no friend of Israel';[4] and had charged Carrington's Dutch counterpart, Christoph Van Der Klaauw, with shaking the hand of a man 'covered in the blood of Israeli children' after he had met Arafat on behalf of the Community.[5]

Such outspoken public attacks, described as 'slanderous' by one London-based Arabist publication and 'highly emotional' by the *Economist*,[6] were clear evidence of the ever-widening rift between Israel's Likud-led government and the EEC since the publication of the Venice Declaration. Some EEC leaders had done their best to reassure both Israel and the US on the matter. Speaking on the day of the announcement of the Declaration, Margaret Thatcher, the British Prime Minister, admitted that Venice addressed 'something that hasn't been dealt with before' and that it 'accepts that the PLO is one of the parties that must be associated in the talks'.[7] But she rejected the claim it had undermined Camp David, stressing that 'no-one here wants to tread on the America's toes, we just want to try to be helpful'.[8] Subsequently, Thatcher acknowledged that the Declaration had received a 'mixed reception' but restated the view that it was not intended to 'undermine Camp David, but to try to do something complementary to it'.[9] She emphasised this point several more times during a visit to Washington in February 1981. In a speech at the Washington Press Club she explained that the Venice initiative was 'not meant in any way to compete with American negotiations'.[10] In a lengthy interview on the ABC network, Thatcher expressed regret for the 'complete misunderstanding about the European initiative on the Middle East'. She also reassured viewers that the US was the 'single most important nation and what it does is the single most important thing in the Middle East. And we all understand that in Europe and we'd like our American friends to know that we understand that'.[11]

But Thatcher's efforts aside, the reality, as Yitzhak Shamir noted shortly after its publication, was that the Venice Declaration was an attempt by the EEC to 'play a more active role in what happens in the Middle East'.[12] In July 1980, Luxembourg's foreign minister Gaston Thorn, in his role as Europe's special envoy to the Middle East, met Chedli Klibi, Secretary-General of the Arab League, in Brussels. Thorn gained Klibi's agreement that the EAD would restart immediately and that a political meeting of the framework would be held in Luxembourg in November 1980. This opened the way for a major announcement at the November meeting that a Euro-Arab summit would be convened in the summer of 1981. Postponed twice, this never took place, because of ongoing divisions within the Arab world after Camp David and the outbreak of the Iran-Iraq war in September 1980.

Stilted efforts to build ties with the Arab world aside, Europe's desire to increase its involvement in Middle East politics in the wake of Venice necessitated a more explicit stand on both the PLO and Palestinian rights. Within a month of the publication of the Venice statement all nine EEC member states agreed to abstain, rather than vote against, a UN General Assembly draft resolution that called for PLO 'participation' on an equal footing with Israel in future UN debates and demanded that the Palestinians be permitted to 'establish their own independent sovereign state'.[13]

In August 1980, during a visit to Beirut, Thorn became the first representative of the European Council of Ministers to meet Arafat. Even those traditionally most supportive of Israel inside the Community—the British, West Germans, Danes and Dutch—now moved closer to the Palestinian position. By mid-1981 Chancellor Schmidt was acknowledging that European foreign ministers favoured the participation of the PLO in any future meetings of the EAD, adding that 'the Israelis must realise one day that the Palestinians have the right to determine their own fate and who should represent them'.[14] In July 1982, Thatcher authorised Douglas Hurd to meet the PLO's Farouk Kaddoumi. Admittedly, as Hurd would later acknowledge, this concession had to be 'dragged out of a reluctant prime minister'. But it was 'a shift in policy' nonetheless, and nine months later Thatcher herself met Kaddoumi as part of a delegation led by King Hussein of Jordan.[15]

In the months before Venice the Dutch foreign minister Christoph Van Der Klaauw, whom Begin would castigate the following year for meeting Arafat, held talks with senior PLO officials in Beirut. Following Venice a majority of the Dutch second chamber voted to move the Dutch embassy from contested Jerusalem to Tel Aviv, and a member of the cabinet attended a lunch in The Hague in honour of Khaled al-Hassan, a close associate of Yasser Arafat.[16] Israel explained this shift in the Dutch position in terms of 'cynical pressures...brought to bear... by certain Arab states'.[17] But tensions between Dutch troops serving with the UN in Lebanon and pro-Israeli Christian militias had also soured relations. More important, with Dutch public opinion increasingly sympathetic to the Palestinian cause, politicians were now more inclined than ever before to fall into line with the majority position inside the Community.

The entry of Greece into the EEC in 1981 also had a significant impact on the Community's evolving approach to the Palestine conflict. In 1981 Andreas Papandreou's socialist PASOK party came to power. The new prime minister was one of the most outspoken supporters of the PLO in the international arena. Prior to its election defeat by PASOK, Greece's conservative government had allowed the PLO to set up an office in Athens, but had kept the group 'at arms length' and publicly stated that it would not grant full recognition to any organisation, only to sovereign states.[18] However, on his first day in power in October 1981, Papandreou invited Yasser Arafat to Greece at his 'earliest convenience' in order to discuss co-operation and the upgrading of the PLO office in Athens. Soon afterwards, the PLO was granted full diplomatic status.[19]

In response, Israel's diplomatic representative in Athens took the unusual step of issuing a public statement expressing his country's 'shock' over Papandreou's dual decision to invite Arafat to Athens and to recognise the PLO as the legitimate representative of the Palestinian people.[20] Despite this protest, Arafat arrived in the Greek capital in December 1981. During their meeting Papandreou promised the PLO leader that 'we shall assume, to the best of our ability, the role of a bridge between your struggle in the Middle East and Europe'.[21] The PASOK government constantly advocated enhanced European support for the Palestinian cause and engagement with the PLO. While leader of the opposition in parliament, Papandreou had been a harsh critic of the Israeli-Egyptian peace and had been adamant that once in office he would never sign any EEC statement that directly or indirectly accepted Camp David.[22] In accordance with this, one of his first practical efforts on behalf of the PLO inside the EEC, much to Arafat's delight, was to veto Community actions or statements that could be viewed as endorsing the Camp David framework.

The Israeli-Egyptian treaty had agreed to set up a multinational force to monitor security arrangements in Sinai prior to Israel's full withdrawal from the area in 1982. In January 1981 Britain, France, the Netherlands and Italy agreed to participate in the Sinai Multinational Force and Observers (MFO) on the grounds that to refuse to do so would go against the EEC's commitment, set out at Venice, to play a role in a resolution of the conflict.[23] Israel made European acceptance of the Camp David process a condition of participation in this force and insisted that there would not be 'any reference to the Venice Declaration' in the European explanation for sending troops to Sinai.[24] When the matter came up for debate at the EEC ministerial meeting in late 1981 Greece, true to Papandreou's word, staunchly opposed any EEC contribution to a Sinai force within the Camp David framework.

For the first time since the establishment of the EEC in the late 1950s, a Community statement on a foreign policy issue failed to gain the signature of all member states. Instead, a compromise was found whereby two separate statements on the matter were issued. The first, favouring participation in the multinational force, was adopted by Britain, France, Italy, and the Netherlands. The second statement, which refrained from mentioning the Camp David process, was signed by the remaining EEC member states.[25] This divide within the Community, brought about first and foremost by the Greek position (with unofficial support from Lord Carrington[26]), signalled that there were EEC members prepared to take a practical stand against Camp David at the Community level. It also signalled that Greece was more than willing to challenge its longer serving, larger, and more influential partners in the promotion of Palestinian interests.

Greek efforts at this time were especially significant because of the victory of the Socialist candidate François Mitterrand over Giscard d'Estaing in the French presidential elections of March 1981. Mitterrand, who would serve as president of the French Republic between 1981 and 1995,[27] was a long-time supporter of Israel. He had been a member of the 1950s French administration that had laid the foundations for the Franco-Israeli strategic relationship, sitting in the cabinet that, in 1957, approved the construction of Israel's nuclear reactor at Dimona. In 1974, the prominent French commentator Jean Lacouture summed up the general view that 'Mitterrand's relations with Israel are good and his reputation in the Arab world is not good'.[28] Mitterrand visited Israel several times in a private capacity over the course of his career and was the only European political leader to attend the Israeli Labour Party Congress in Jerusalem in 1980. During the election campaign the following year he criticised the pro-Arab policy of Giscard d'Estaing and promised that if he won he would be the first French president to visit the Jewish state.[29] Following his victory he endorsed the Camp David framework as the only viable approach to a settlement of the Arab-Israeli conflict and expressed doubts over the terms of the Venice Declaration.[30]

In 1979, Begin expressed the hope that Israel's 'many friends in France' would 'succeed in influencing a change in her negative policies which render harm to both our nations'.[31] Mitterrand's victory seemed to answer his call as he considered the new French president a 'true friend of Israel'.[32] In an interview on French television, he spoke in hugely positive terms about the new president in comparison with the Giscard d'Estaing era, which he described as the worst time in Israeli-French relations.[33]

There was significant speculation across Europe over whether Mitterrand would break with France's Middle East policy since 1967 by adopting a more pro-Israeli position, especially as he was succeeding three presidents—de Gaulle, Pompidou and Giscard d'Estaing—who had championed the Palestinian cause.[34] In a January 1982 interview with Per Gahrton, a former member of the Swedish parliament, Arafat was asked: 'The French have been a disappointment to you?' He answered bluntly: 'Yes, completely. We were dealing with the French as long as they were following the policy of President de Gaulle. But now it will sooner or later affect their relations with the whole Arab area'.[35] In the same month Arafat asked Papandreou, his staunchest Community ally, to mediate between the PLO and the French government in order to overcome obstacles to the relationship since Mitterrand took office.[36]

In practice, despite his past record and some symbolic moves in the early months of his presidency—such as rescinding a notorious 1977 government directive that bowed to the Arab boycott of Israel—Mitterrand did little to earn his reputation in some parts of the Arab world as 'France's Jewish president'.[37] French Middle East policy would alter very little during the decade and a half that Mitterrand occupied the Élysée Palace.[38] This was evidenced by his appointment of the 'quixotic super-Gaullist'[39] and veteran Arabist Michel Jobert as Minister for External Trade and of Claude Cheysson as foreign minister. Cheysson liked to talk about 'a continuity that goes beyond majorities'[40] in French foreign policy. On taking office he wasted no time in applying this theory to French interests in the Middle East by expressing his view that 'it is the right[s] of the Palestinian people that is being denied, trampled upon…this right must be accepted and recognised as quickly as possible'.[41] He also met Arafat, praising the PLO leader as a 'very great personage' and even comparing him to de Gaulle.[42]

Mitterrand, for his part, did keep his pre-election pledge and visited Israel in early 1982. During his trip he spoke positively about Camp David's achievements and praised his hosts as 'a noble and proud people',[43] an obvious contrast to de Gaulle's 1967 description of Israelis as an 'elite …and overbearing people'. However, his first presidential visit outside Europe was to Saudi Arabia, by now a major market for French arms.[44] And while in Israel he was uncompromising in his support for Palestinian rights and a role for the PLO in the political process. In his speech before the Knesset, subsequently described by Hubert Védrine as a 'masterpiece of Mitterrandian farsightedness, tact and courage',[45] he called for a homeland for the Palestinians, which 'can at the appropriate time mean a state'.[46] During the same visit he sent Cheysson to meet West Bank mayors linked to the PLO while he met Israeli dignitaries. He was also careful not to fly over any territories occupied by Israel in 1967.

On 7 June 1981, Israel destroyed the French-built nuclear reactor at Osirak in Iraq, in an air raid that resulted in the death of a French technician working there.[47] The Israeli operation, condemned by France as 'unacceptable and very grave',[48] led to the first sign of discord in Franco-Israeli relations since Mitterrand took office. Almost one year later to the day, any suspicions that France's Middle East policy under Mitterrand had changed substantively from that of his predecessors evaporated. On 2 June 1982, Shlomo Argov, Israel's Ambassador to Britain and Ireland, was shot in the head as he left an official reception at London's Dorchester Hotel. Abu Nidal's Black June group claimed responsibility for the assassination attempt. In response, the Israeli cabinet authorised retaliatory strikes against Palestinian bases in Lebanon, which resulted in the PLO opening fire on Galilee in Northern Israel.

By the first weekend of June over 500 shells had landed in northern Israel. Ariel Sharon, Israel's minister of defence, and Rafael Eitan, chief of staff of the Israel Defence Forces (IDF), requested cabinet approval for an operation inside Lebanon that would place Israeli population centres in Galilee beyond the range of terrorist fire. Sharon estimated that the operation would only require a day or so and would extend no further than forty kilometres into Lebanon. On the evening of Saturday 5 June, a bitterly divided Israeli cabinet warily approved this operation, code-named Peace for Galilee.

Variously termed the 'war of desperation' or the 'war of choice', Israel's invasion and subsequent entanglement in Lebanon (which continued until the last of its troops were withdrawn in the summer of 2000) would have a profound impact on an Israeli society that immediately split over the merits of the war. It had a similar effect on Lebanese society, which was radicalised by the war, and on the PLO, whose leadership was forced to take refuge in Tunisia while its military infrastructure in Lebanon was destroyed.

Peace for Galilee also had a very negative impact on Euro-Israeli relations. Inside the Community, France, a country with deep historical ties to Lebanon, took the lead. During a fraught meeting with Yitzhak Shamir in Paris in the weeks following the invasion, and subsequently in a number of public statements, President Mitterrand let it be known that he felt personally betrayed by Begin who had misinformed him about Israel's 'limited aims' in entering Lebanon.[49] The French foreign minister, Cheysson, took charge of efforts to co-ordinate the EEC's response to the invasion. He was assisted by Papandreou's Greece and neutral Ireland, whose troop commitment to the UN peacekeeping force in Lebanon since 1978 was the single biggest operational task of its military. The Irish had a 750-strong battalion in Lebanon, and following the Israeli invasion these troops found themselves in a southern area of the country under the control of Israel and its Christian allies. Regular clashes between Irish peacekeepers and the IDF and local proxy groups angered political and public opinion back in Ireland and motivated the Irish government to take a lead role in condemning the invasion at the UN Security Council, where Ireland had recently been elected to a two-year temporary seat.

If the actions of Israel and its Christian allies in Lebanon provided a major boost for the Palestinian cause in Ireland, the PLO's own response to the United Nations Interim Force in Lebanon (UNIFIL) deployment earned it further sympathy in Ireland, as well as in Italy and the Netherlands, the two other EEC member states with peacekeepers in Lebanon at the time of the invasion. Yasser Arafat had welcomed the establishment of UNIFIL in 1978, both as a way of pressuring Israel to halt its operation to crush PLO forces in southern Lebanon and also as an opportunity to draw the international community (in particular EEC troop contributing nations) into the Israeli-Palestinian conflict and place the international spotlight on the Palestinian cause. This was a prescient strategy and Arafat was prepared to go to major lengths in order to appear supportive of the UNIFIL role. In March 1978 he met the UNIFIL commander, Emmanuel Erskine, in Beirut and agreed to order a PLO ceasefire in clashes with Israel in border areas. His desire to make a good impression on the UN force, and hence on the contributing nations and the UN Security Council, meant that this was the first time that Arafat had committed himself to a ceasefire to which Israel was a party; the symbolism of this caused several senior Fatah officers to challenge his decision (all of these were removed from their positions of influence or forced out of Lebanon).[50]

Following the Israeli invasion of Lebanon, the Greek government, for its part, instructed its delegation at the UN to call for the convening of an emergency meeting of the Security Council in order to condemn Israel's actions and to formulate a UN position regarding the 'withdrawal of foreign [Israeli] troops from Lebanon'.[51] When the Security Council convened on 5 June, a draft resolution was introduced that called for a practical way to force Israel to comply with demands for its withdrawal from Lebanon. France and Ireland voted in favour of this draft resolution, though Britain abstained on the grounds that the draft implied that Israel should be evicted from Lebanon by force. This draft failed to pass but was followed up by a less controversial resolution that called for an immediate cease-fire.[52]

On 6 June 1982, the Israeli government admitted publicly that its objective on entering Lebanon was not only to secure Israel's northern border towns from shelling but to 'purge it of terrorist concentrations emplaced there'.[53] In response, the Irish government sponsored a draft resolution addressing the 'massive invasion' and the 'extremely grave' situation.[54] This resolution was adopted unanimously by the Security Council. However, it antagonised Israel by failing to make any specific reference critical of the PLO. Instead it only drew attention to the need for 'strict territorial integrity' and demanded that Israel withdraw all its military forces 'forthwith and unconditionally' to international borders.[55]

France, with the backing of Ireland, put forward its own Security Council draft resolution in late June, calling for an Israeli cease-fire and an 'initial disengagement of forces'—a key PLO demand at a time when Arafat's Beirut headquarters was coming under increasing threat.[56] It was vetoed by the US and ignored by Israel, whose cabinet had already demanded that the PLO hand over its weapons to the Lebanese army and that all PLO members 'without any exception' leave Beirut.[57] In late July, France again submitted a joint draft resolution with Egypt to the Security Council, linking the siege of Beirut to a solution to the Palestinian problem.[58]

On 1 August 1982, Israel mounted a large-scale offensive against PLO targets in Beirut. Thus Lebanon continued to dominate the Security Council agenda during a month that saw Ireland take its presidency. Noel Dorr, the Irish Ambassador, was instrumental in coordinating the Security Council's condemnation of Israel, which even saw the US vote in favour of a resolution that demanded an Israeli cease-fire and called for an end to the blockade of Beirut and cooperation with the UN.[59]

Outside the UN, the efforts of Greece, Ireland and France shaped the Community's official response to the invasion. At a two-day summit in late June, these three lobbied their Community partners to recognise the PLO formally as a way of guaranteeing the survival of the 'heroic and proud' organisation.[60] They were opposed most vocally by West Germany, Denmark and the Netherlands. The meeting's final statement did address the Lebanon war in terms of the need for Palestinian 'self-determination' and for the PLO to be 'associated with negotiations', and argued that Israel would only achieve security by 'satisfying the legitimate aspirations of the Palestinian people'.[61] On the other hand, it included a compromise by which the Community agreed to a watered-down position on the role of the PLO in any peace process, and also included a criticism of PLO attacks on Israel from Lebanese territory prior to the invasion.[62]

By mid-August Israel had succeeded in destroying the PLO's capacity to wage war from Lebanon and had overseen the evacuation of the first groups of PLO fighters to Cyprus, Jordan and Iraq. Arafat left Beirut permanently in September and by December 1983 over four thousand PLO fighters had been expelled from Lebanon.[63] Although it was a victory for Israel, the long-term cost of Operation Peace for Galilee was to prove extremely high, not only in terms of the lives of its own soldiers and growing opposition within Israel to the war, but also in terms of its international standing and its relationship with the EEC.

In the words of Greece's UN Ambassador, there was 'shock and revulsion' across Europe over the 'appalling massacre'[64] of several hundred Palestinian civilians at the Sabra and Shatila refugee camps by Christian Phalangist allies of Israel. There was also a general consensus, as the then Irish foreign minister put it, that 'Israel must accordingly carry considerable responsibility' for the tragedy.[65] Condemnation of Israel for its role in the Sabra and Shatila massacre aside, the most notable aspect of the Community's response to the Lebanon crisis was the extent that it was motivated by the goal of protecting both the physical and political integrity of the PLO, which Mitterrand was now referring to publicly as a 'combat' rather than a terror organisation.[66]

In the summer of 1982 both Mitterrand and Cheysson, who had visited Arafat in Beirut the previous year, met Kaddoumi in Paris. French soldiers participated in the PLO evacuation of Beirut in the summer of 1982 and the Tripoli evacuation in December 1983. After his early distrust of the new French president, Arafat was now informing Mitterrand: 'From the rank of a friend, France has now become a brother'.[67] Begin was far less happy and was now openly accusing the French government of embracing anti-Israeli policies.[68]

Athens was Arafat's first stop following his flight from Beirut in September 1982, after which he travelled to Rome to meet the Italian president, while Kaddoumi flew to the UN in New York and held talks with the Danish foreign minister who represented the Community.[69]

In September 1982, the US administration put forward a proposal, the Reagan Plan, in response to the Lebanon crisis. Drawing on the Camp David Accords, it called for Arab recognition of Israel and a confederation between the West Bank, Gaza and Jordan in exchange for an Israeli commitment to forego sovereignty over Palestinian territories. It fizzled out in the face of Israeli and Arab rejection and the further deterioration of the situation inside Lebanon. This was a relief to the EEC, which had been completely excluded from any role under the Reagan Plan. It was far more enthusiastic about concurrent Arab proposals for peace. In recognition of the Community's commitment to the PLO during the turbulent months following the Israeli invasion, the Arab League sent a high-level delegation to European capitals to canvass support for an Arab peace plan first put forward at an Arab summit at Fez in Morocco in September 1982. The Fez Declaration, as it was known, called for a total Israeli withdrawal from the occupied territories and the establishment of a Palestinian state, though there was implicit recognition of Israel's right to exist.[70]

The Fez Declaration was widely welcomed across the EEC. It indicated a 'readiness for peace' at a time when Europe was 'deeply disturbed by the continued lack of progress'. In March 1983, Community leaders promised to use their 'influence' to further political negotiations on the basis of the Fez proposal.[71] At the same time, the EEC restated its desire for the PLO to be 'associated' with future negotiations. West Germany's foreign minister Genscher called for a 'mutual gesture of recognition' from Israel and the PLO, and the Dutch government approved a motion calling on it to enter into discussions with the PLO information office in The Hague.[72]

Greece took over the rotating presidency of the Community for the first time in mid-1983. Elie Salem, Lebanon's then foreign minister, later recalled that Arab leaders had asked Papandreou 'to play a leading role in the European Community to help us' during the Greek presidency.[73] Papandreou actively attempted to influence his EEC partners to adopt a more critical response to Israel's involvement in Lebanon and to recognise more formally the necessity of PLO participation in negotiations.[74] But although Israel expressed grave concerns over the damage that the Greek presidency was doing to Euro-Israeli relations, Greek efforts on behalf of the PLO during its presidency and thereafter were unsuccessful. This was due in part to the unwillingness of successive Greek delegations to invest any serious time or thought in preparing the Arab case or in consulting Community partners.

More importantly, Greece's refusal to be a 'team player' on the Middle East, and its reputation as a foreign policy troublemaker in general, explains why on taking the EEC presidency Papandreou's government suffered from what was described at the time as a 'credibility gap'.[75] It also explains why the proposal by the Greek foreign minister, Yannis Charalambopoulas, to lead a fact-finding mission to the Middle East during the Greek presidency, as his British, Dutch and Belgian predecessors had done previously, was vetoed.[76]

Despite these efforts at damage limitation, involvement in the EPC framework was a consequence and corollary of entry into the EEC. This provided smaller member states like Greece with a role in policy formulation far greater than their size or power permitted in other contexts. As a result Greece's commitment to the PLO notably reduced the capacity of the Community to present a unified front on the Middle East at a time when it was looking to develop a common position on major foreign policy questions. The failure of the Athens EEC summit of December 1983 to produce a joint statement, something standard for most other high-level community meetings, highlighted this shortcoming. The official explanation was that a statement on the Middle East was 'inappropriate' because leaders had been preoccupied with internal matters. The real reason was that the Dutch and West Germans had vetoed any Middle East statement on the grounds that, having been prepared by Greek officials, it would be too pro-Palestinian. The EAD's General Committee, which had rarely been convened since Camp David, also met in Athens during the Greek presidency. The hosts were unable to bridge the gap between the two delegations and proceedings were concluded without any agreement to reconvene the forum.[77]

Over subsequent years the Papandreou government continued to cause its EEC partners significant aggravation on matters relating to the Palestine issue. West Germany protested to Athens that its approach to the conflict was retarding the great efforts to rebuild diplomatic relations with Israel since the Lebanon War.[78] Mrs Thatcher, answering a journalistic enquiry as to how the Community's policy could be 'credible' when Athens was constantly siding with the PLO, used the unusually succinct words, 'I cannot answer for Greece's policy on the PLO'.[79]

Greece's refusal to adopt the Community's compromise position was clear to see across international forums such as NATO and, especially, at the UN. The year of Greek entry into the EEC, 1981, was the first year that the Community voted together on Middle East draft resolutions at the UN less than 80 per cent of the time. By December 1983, during which month Greece voted separately from its EEC partners nine times on various paragraphs of two resolutions, this had fallen to 68 per cent.[80]

This ongoing disconnect inside the Community had an impact on the attitudes of Middle Eastern parties to the conflict. Between 1984 and 1988, a Likud-Labour National Unity Government ruled Israel and Yitzhak Shamir and Shimon Peres (the Likud and Labour leaders respectively) held the premiership, vice-premiership and foreign ministry on a rotating basis. Shamir had been Begin's foreign minister. Though more reserved in manner he was, in the words of Margaret Thatcher, 'a hard man'.[81] He was also just as adamant as his former leader that there could be no compromise on the PLO issue. Shimon Peres took an equally firm line. As both prime minister and foreign minister he consistently challenged Europe over its 'obsequious attitude towards the PLO' and called on the continent's leaders to see their 'great mistake' and 'cease closing their eyes…and refrain from an attitude of forgiveness' towards the PLO.[82] Yitzhak Rabin, minister of defence and Labour's other leading figure, was equally dismissive of Europe's PLO policy in these years. In the wake of the Palestinian attacks on Vienna and Rome airports that caused 20 fatalities in December 1985, he said that it was 'tragic-ironic' that the attacks took place in two countries whose governments had been very supportive of the PLO.[83]

There were occasions during the mid-1980s when it appeared that senior members of the Community might be reassessing their approach to the PLO in favour of the Israeli position. In 1985, the British government cancelled a visit to London by two senior Palestinian figures because they refused to sign a statement condemning violence prior to their arrival.[84] In the same year Israel welcomed a statement issued by the Élysée Palace that President Mitterrand was reconsidering his positive attitude towards the PLO; the following year an Israeli newspaper quoted the French prime minister, Jacques Chirac, as expressing opposition to a Palestinian state and support for exclusion of the PLO from future negotiations.[85]

However, the French foreign ministry quickly clarified on both occasions that Chirac and Mitterrand continued to believe that 'the PLO should be associated with the negotiation of a global settlement that would, in particular, permit the Palestinian people to exercise their right to self-determination'.[86] Thatcher took the occasion of a state dinner during a visit to Israel in 1986 to clarify her own government's position. 'We believe', she told her hosts, 'that you will only find the security you seek by recognising the legitimate rights of the Palestinian people and their just requirements'.[87]

Spain and Portugal's entry into the Community in 1986 concerned Israel for both economic and political reasons. At high-level meetings in Brussels in February 1983 and Luxembourg in October 1985, Shamir had asked the EEC to consider the impact of Spanish and Portuguese entry on the Israeli economy.[88] In a speech to the European Parliament on the eve of the Iberian accession, the Israeli President, Chaim Herzog, made the same argument, warning that without 'remedial' arrangements Israel's all-important agricultural sector would suffer.[89]

Gideon Rafael, Israel's Ambassador to Britain in the wake of the first EEC enlargement, recounted in his memoirs that a 'major objective' of Israeli foreign policy following the 1973 war was to normalise relations with European countries like Spain and Portugal who up to that point had not established diplomatic ties with the Jewish state.[90] Both countries had been long-time supporters of the Palestinian cause.[91] In September 1979, Arafat met the Portuguese President, prime minister and foreign minister in Lisbon before travelling to Madrid where he received a hero's welcome from Spanish Prime Minister, Adolfo Suárez. This three-day visit caused considerable controversy because Arafat had been invited in his capacity as head of the PLO at a time when Spain had not even recognised Israel on a *de facto* basis. Aware of the symbolic significance, Arafat had expressed the hope that in the light of its future membership of the EEC, Spain would use its influence to help secure further recognition of the PLO in Europe.[92]

Spanish and Portuguese support for the PLO, on top of the Greek efforts and those of Kreisky's Austria over the same period, influenced attitudes across the Community. In June 1980, for example, 41 British MPs signed a motion in the House of Commons calling on Prime Minister Thatcher to follow Austria, Spain, Greece and Portugal in according recognition to the PLO.[93]

In an attempt to contain this trend, Israel opened an office in Madrid in 1982 and El Al began flying there in 1985. But it was only in January 1986, after what Shamir described as 'many years of endeavours',[94] that Peres met a Spanish delegation in The Hague for talks where it was agreed to establish full diplomatic relations including the opening of embassies in Tel Aviv and Madrid.[95] The Spanish move was not due to a significant shift in political sympathies; during his meeting with Spanish representatives Peres was presented with a statement fully supportive of Palestinian rights. In mid-January 1986 it was followed by a public declaration by the González government restating Spain's commitment to the Palestinian cause and explaining the decision to commence diplomatic ties with Israel in terms of the necessities of EEC membership.[96]

Spain's upgrading of diplomatic ties following entry into the Community had a precedent in the case of Ireland following its own accession to the EEC in 1973. A small, neutral, nation on the margins of Europe, Ireland was now a member of an economic superpower that led the way in trade with both Israel and much of the Arab world. It was increasingly difficult for Ireland to claim an equal role in the formulation of foreign policy with other member states without having similar diplomatic ties. Like Spain a decade later, Ireland was influenced by these considerations, rather than a shift in political outlook, in deciding, almost thirteen years after granting *de jure* recognition, to formalise diplomatic ties with Israel in December 1974—especially as it took on its first presidency of the European Council in 1975, a factor that also led Ireland to commence or upgrade diplomatic relations with eight Arab states and Iran at the same time.[97]

It is widely assumed that a nation's entry into the Community with a track record of bad relations or under-developed diplomatic ties with Israel further fuels divisions between Europe and Israel. But the Irish and Spanish cases highlight that entry can also moderate the position of new members by bringing them closer to the Community norm.

On the eve of its first presidency of the Community in 1983 Greece studied the Irish decision to upgrade ties with Israel shortly before its own first presidency in 1975.[98] Though aware of the reasons for this move, Papandreou refused to follow the Irish precedent on the grounds that 'only the Greek government is competent to take decisions about its foreign policy',[99] and he ignored quite a few opportunities for granting *de jure* recognition to Israel during Greece's first EEC presidency.[100] However, as a gesture of goodwill Papandreou did end his veto of a US$50 million EEC aid package for Israel that Athens had blocked the previous year.[101] And while his government refused to allow Israel to open an embassy in Athens and did not recognise the Jewish state *de jure* until

1990, it did allow Israel to maintain a diplomatic mission staffed by officials below ambassadorial rank. In 1986, an Israeli government minister was also invited to visit Athens for the first time in 26 years.[102]

In part, this 'renewed diplomatic engagement'[103] on the part of the new Mediterranean members of the EEC explains why Shimon Peres acknowledged 'much closer'[104] relations between Israel and the EEC in 1987. But this more positive Israeli view of Europe was also due to the fact that for much of the first half of the 1980s the EEC had been, in the words of Michel Rocard, 'tragically absent' from the politics of the region.[105] Rocard, a senior French Socialist politician who would later serve as French Prime Minister, was not the only one to observe this. In mid-1985, a journalist for *Al-Ahram* asked Prime Minister Thatcher why Europe refused to 'exercise an accountable role in efforts aimed at solving the [Middle East] crisis'.[106] The following year the Lebanese paper *Al-Watan* condemned the 'European retreat'[107] from the region. Mattityahu (Matti) Peled, a decorated Israeli general and a vocal member of the Israeli peace camp, was no less critical. Europe, Peled argued, had a 'choice': it could either 'continue to watch passively…or to go back to the Venice Declaration'.[108]

In February 1985, King Hussein of Jordan and Yasser Arafat announced a joint Jordanian-Palestinian agreement on a peace framework. This called for the convening of an international conference attended by the five permanent members of the UN Security Council and all local parties to the Arab-Israeli conflict. The PLO would represent the Palestinians but would attend the meeting as part of a joint Jordanian-Palestinian contingent.

When this proposal was shelved in early 1986, owing to King Hussein's deteriorating relationship with Arafat who was unable to control growing rejectionism inside the PLO, the Community looked once more to find a way to play a role in Middle East peacemaking and to promote ties with the Arab world. With both goals in mind the Dutch foreign minister, Hans van den Broek, met Arafat and the Arab League Secretary-General Chedli Klibi in Tunis. Apart from trying to get Klibi to agree to restart the EAD, which had now been in a 'coma'[109] for a number of years, van den Broek also restated the EEC's view that 'the PLO is a key element and cannot be ignored'.[110] Soon afterwards, following his own meeting with PLO officials, the French foreign minister Jean-Bernard Raimond was no less clear: 'the PLO should be associated with the negotiation of a global settlement that would, in particular, permit the Palestinian people to exercise their right to self-determination'.[111]

In a move that was welcomed as evidence that the Community had 'broken its seven-year silence',[112] in February 1987 EEC foreign ministers meeting in Brussels called for a UN-sponsored international conference on the Middle East.[113] This was motivated in part by a desire to underline its own foreign policy independence following America's economic sanctions and air raid against Libya the previous year. It also came in the midst of the Iran-Contra affair, and resulted in a further deterioration in the already tense relations between the EEC and the Reagan White House.

The EEC proposal for an international conference attended by the five permanent members of the UN Security Council had been endorsed at the UN General Assembly as far back as December 1983. Now senior international statesman such as Egypt's President Hosni Mubarak, King Hussein of Jordan and the Soviet president, Mikhail Gorbachev, endorsed the European plan. At first Leo Tindemans, Belgian foreign minister and EEC council president, was 'extremely encouraged' by this international endorsement of the Community's efforts. But by the summer of 1987 Tindemans was far less positive. He acknowledged that the idea of an international conference on the Middle East was 'still alive' but said the Community was 'pausing for reflection'. Privately, other officials were admitting that they were 'extremely disappointed' in the failure to get the conference off the ground.[114]

Efforts to bring about an international conference did little to improve relations with Israel. Yitzhak Shamir, prime minister and leader of the Likud bloc within the government, wanted all future peace talks to follow the Camp David framework, leading to a transitional period of autonomy for the Palestinians and negotiations that would conclude with a final settlement of the conflict. Shamir rejected the Community's call for an international conference as 'perverse and criminal'.[115] His spokesman offered a more measured rebuttal:

We say yes to peace; yes to negotiations; yes to cooperation; yes to practical arrangements with Jordan within the framework of the peace process; yes to the participation of agreed upon Palestinian representatives in the Jordanian delegation…no to an international conference of the UN….no to a framework whose objective is to exercise pressure on Israel and no to inviting the PLO.[116]

Disagreement intensified over the best way to move forward because of the Intifada, the popular Palestinian uprising, which began in the West Bank and Gaza in December 1987. Even those EEC members most supportive of Israel took a tough line on its security response to the crisis. At an emergency foreign ministers' meeting in February 1988, the Dutch, British, West Germans and Danes all condemned Israel's 'repressive measures' and 'deeply deplored' ongoing 'violations of international law and human rights'.[117] Not surprisingly, those more traditionally antagonistic towards Israel went even further. Claude Cheysson called the Israeli response 'shameful' and Greece announced that it was indefinitely suspending any decision to upgrade diplomatic ties with Israel.[118]

Hopeful that the upcoming US presidential election would distract Washington from Middle East affairs for the rest of the year, in early 1988 West Germany's foreign minister Genscher once more attempted to promote a European peace plan linked to an international conference. The Arab states were responsive to this and rewarded Genscher's efforts with a Euro-Arab meeting in Bonn in June 1988, where they promised a 'swift reactivation' of the EAD.[119] Concurrently the US Secretary of State, George Shultz, launched his own initiative, travelling to the Middle East three times between February and June. His proposal, like the PLO-Jordanian agreement of 1985, called for new negotiations hosted by the five permanent members of the Security Council, attended by Israel and the Arabs including a joint Jordan-Palestinian delegation. In order to appeal to Israel it also called for parallel bilateral discussions and promised that the hosts would have no power of veto or enforcement.

The election of George H.W. Bush in November 1988 put an end to Shultz's peace efforts, but not before it had distracted attention from, and then sidelined, the Community's own proposals.[120] It appeared that the decade would end as it began, with EEC initiatives being overshadowed by US proposals. Yet it did not prevent Yasser Arafat from travelling to Strasbourg in September 1988 at the invitation of the Socialist group in the European Parliament. During his trip, viewed all round as a diplomatic triumph, the PLO leader met Lord Plumb, President of the European parliament, France's foreign minister Roland Dumas, and his Greek counterpart Carolos Papoulias.

Speaking before the parliament, Arafat raised the idea of sending a European force with a UN mandate to the occupied territories. He also made it clear that although he did not expect a guarantee of formal recognition from European governments, such a move would be just and would help the PLO leadership win over sceptics within the Palestinian movement. He ended his speech with the following question: 'Will

Europe confine itself to the position of an observer, or will it proceed to participation and action?'[121] The parliamentarians from the EEC's 12 member states sitting before him, as well as their governments back home and Commission officials in Brussels, had been grappling with this question for much of the previous two decades. Soon, as the Cold War ended and the Community looked to translate its economic power into political influence in the New World Order, they would have no choice but to look harder than ever for an answer.

7

THE BOSNIA COMPLEX

*'Only the United States could save us from annihilation: if they do not come there will
soon be no Muslims left. The Europeans will debate until we are all dead.'*

President Alija Izetbegović of Bosnia

In the early hours of 15 November 1988, to the sound of a band playing
the Palestinian national anthem and with the Palestinian flag flying over-
head, the PNC, the PLO's governing body, meeting in Algiers, declared
an independent Palestinian state without defined borders but with Jerusalem as its capital. At the same time the PNC called for the convening
of an international peace conference under the auspices of the UN Security Council and on the basis of Security Council Resolutions 242 and
338. It also renounced terrorism with a significant caveat that exempted
those fighting foreign occupation.[1]

The Algiers Declaration, as it came to be known, was the first time that
the PNC had verbally endorsed a settlement of the conflict along the
lines set out in UN Security Council Resolutions 242 and 338. The EEC
rejected the Israeli claim that the statement was a 'deceptive propaganda
exercise intended to create an impression of moderation'.[2] Instead, it
noted the 'particular importance' of the declaration as an implicit 'acceptance of the right of existence and of security for all states of the region,
including Israel'. It also expressed 'satisfaction that the PNC has explicitly
condemned' terrorism.[3]

In mid-1988, the Greek Prime Minister Papandreou had characterised
his government's efforts on behalf of the PLO as a 'justification [for] the

Greek foreign policy in the Middle East'.[4] Therefore, Greece welcomed the Algiers statement as a huge boost to the key objective of its second EEC presidency in the latter half of 1988—convincing the Community to upgrade its relationship with the PLO. The foreign minister, Carolos Papoulias, called for Arafat to be invited to explain the PNC's move before a specially convened meeting of EEC foreign ministers.[5] He failed to get support for this proposal, but a few days later Farouk Kaddoumi met EEC diplomats representing Britain, Greece, Spain Portugal, France, Belgium, Italy, West Germany and the Netherlands in Tunis.

The PNC's announcement that an independent Palestinian state had been created was largely symbolic. And despite the best efforts of the Greek presidency, the Community refrained from following the move of the 55 Muslim, Third World and Non-Aligned nations who in the weeks immediately following the declaration recognised explicitly the PLO's proclamation of statehood.

While Greece had support from Spain, Ireland, France and Italy for a Community statement specifically addressing this matter, the remaining member states were opposed to any wording that could be construed as EEC support for statehood. Seven members (Denmark, Belgium, the Netherlands, Britain, Portugal, West Germany and Luxemburg) even opposed any reference to UN Resolution 181 of 1947 (which called for the establishment of Arab and Jewish states in Palestine) for fear that it would be viewed as an endorsement of a new Palestinian state's borders.[6] In its official response to the Algiers Declaration, the Community once again settled for a compromise by simply reiterating its support for 'the right of self-determination of the Palestinian people with all that this implies'.[7]

By mid-December 1988, Greek officials were conceding that any European recognition of a Palestinian state was 'extremely remote'. Arafat found this out for himself during an end of year tour of European capitals. Not even the Greek government, though it openly acknowledged its preference for formal recognition of an independent Palestinian state, was willing to go it alone and break with the rest of the Community on this issue.[8] Instead, all followed France's lead when its foreign minister Roland Dumas explained that it had 'no difficulty of principle' in recognising a Palestinian state and was 'gladdened' by the PLO's move, but added that it was impossible to recognise a 'state that does not dispose of a defined territory'.[9]

During his European trip, Arafat thanked the EEC for its support and expressed his faith in the Community's 'political responsibility and moral responsibility'.[10] But by the beginning of 1989 the Community was still unable to meet the key Palestinian demands—acceptance of the PLO as the official representative of the Palestinians at an international peace conference, and recognition of a Palestinian state without defined borders but with Jerusalem as its capital, as proclaimed at Algiers.

The European failure to capitalise on the Algiers Declaration by responding with substantive concessions to the PLO was widely condemned inside the Community. Jacques Delors, President of the European Commission, summed up this inability to make a 'real gesture' with the words 'we've failed'.[11] The Spanish foreign minister, Francisco Fernández Ordóñez, reiterated this pessimistic sentiment when he told the Spanish parliament in January 1989 that the EEC had missed the opportunity to give full backing to the Palestinian cause because of the ongoing reluctance of some Community partners (he named Britain and the Netherlands) to take a stand against either Israel or the US.[12]

Fernández Ordóñez used the Spanish EEC presidency in the first half of 1989 to propose the convening of an international conference attended by Israel, the PLO, the US and the EEC.[13] In late January he also hosted Arafat's first official talks with an EEC Troika that also included the foreign ministers of France and Greece. Following this meeting, Fernández Ordóñez attempted to muster further enthusiasm when he promised that 'there is support in the European Community to speed up as much as possible the calling of a peace conference'.[14]

In April, Mitterrand hosted Arafat in the Elysée Palace on his first official visit to France, during which he declared in a television interview that the PLO's charter was '*caduc*' (null and void).[15] The French government used this as evidence of its influence over the PLO and of France's international standing. In reality, Arafat's statement had little to do with French prestige or influence, and was not aimed at French television viewers; its intended audience was the US administration. Since 1986 the PLO had stated that it would 'only accept' Resolutions 242 and 338 'in return for ironclad guarantees from the US for direct involvement in a suggested international peace conference and American recognition of the Palestinian people's national rights including its right for self-determination'.[16] The main goal of the Algiers Declaration had been to convince Washington to engage with the PLO, but the Reagan administration had not viewed the move as going far enough, and called on Arafat to be more explicit in stating his willingness to abandon the armed struggle. This resulted in a series of meetings between the PLO leader and a delegation of Jewish peace activists from the US in Sweden at the beginning of December, where he gave assurances of his peaceful intentions. On 12–13 December 1988, while attending a UN meeting in Geneva, Arafat went further in expressing his commitment to renounce terror, recognise Israel's right to exist and accept UN Resolutions when he read from a statement whose wording had been agreed in advance with the US.[17]

Bassam Abu Sharif, a veteran adviser to Arafat, would subsequently describe Arafat's speech and press conference in Geneva as the 'most important [of]…his career' precisely because they set the stage for US recognition of the PLO which would bring the Palestinians 'that much closer to achieving…[a] sovereign state'.[18] Soon after Arafat's Geneva statements, Robert H. Pelletreau, the US Ambassador to Tunisia, telephoned PLO headquarters to arrange for the PLO's first formal contact with the US in 13 years. The PLO was 'elated', with one senior official, Mohammed Milhem, explaining that 'the battle with Israel now will be in the United States'.[19]

There was praise for Washington's decision in the EEC. Prime Minister Thatcher described it as 'a very considerable step forward' and President Mitterrand declared it a 'real step forward', while the Bonn government welcomed it as a 'step that would contribute to the peace process'.[20] But public endorsements aside, nothing could hide the fact that despite the Community's championing of the organisation for almost two decades, the PLO's primary objective was still US recognition. Publicly Arafat still praised the Community as a model of peaceful reconciliation,[21] but all knew that diplomatic engagement with the US was a far more valuable prize than anything that the Community could offer.

At this time, the Community's relationship with Israel was also at an all time low. In January 1989, Israeli Prime Minister Shamir had informed the President of the European Parliament that it was difficult to see the EEC as a participant in any future peace process because it was so pro-Palestinian, without regard for Israel's fundamental needs.[22] In June 1990, Shamir formed a government without Labour participation but with the support of Right and Centre Right parties. He now no longer had to share power with Shimon Peres and could ignore the recent calls by the

Labour leader for an international peace conference and a rethinking of the Israeli approach to dealing with the PLO.

Shamir was no less distrustful of both the Soviet Union and the EEC now that he was at the head of a Likud, rather than a national unity, government, and he continued to oppose an international conference. He hoped to build on the Camp David formula of bilateral negotiations and opposed a multilateral process in which Israel had to deal with all the Arab states and the PLO as one. He ruled out negotiations with the PLO, preferring negotiations with the Arab states (in particular Jordan and Egypt) and elected local Palestinian leaders in the West Bank and Gaza.

The Shamir government was also fully committed to the rapid growth in Jewish settlements in the occupied territories. When Likud came to power for the first time in 1977, there were an estimated 20,000 Jews living in 31 settlements. By 1991, there were more than 100,000 settlers in over 100 settlement communities in the West Bank alone.[23] This exasperated the EEC, leading to explicit criticism of Israel's settlement policy in numerous Community declarations, including the conclusions of the European Council's 1990 meeting in Dublin.[24]

In June of that year, the PLO representative in Brussels called on the Community to increase its involvement in the Middle East peace process, arguing that 'Europe must assume a more effective role'.[25] Before it could answer the call, it found itself preoccupied with events in another part of the Middle East. On 2 August 1990, Iraq invaded Kuwait, its smaller but far wealthier neighbour. Saddam Hussein's invasion and annexation of Kuwait, and the subsequent war between Iraq and an American-led international coalition that included Arab states, destroyed any lingering illusions that pan-Arabism was a relevant factor in regional considerations. It also opened a new chapter in the European attempt to insert itself into the politics of the Israel-Palestinian conflict.

By the late 1980s, Iraq had developed into a major trading partner of a number of EEC states, for example in beef (Ireland), arms (France), and construction (West Germany). The economic sanctions imposed on Iraq by the UN at the start of the crisis had a severe impact on these trade ties. Over 6,500 EEC citizens based in Kuwait and Iraq were among those from 21 Western nations who were for some time refused permission to leave by the Iraqi authorities once the crisis began.[26]

The Community issued a statement condemning the invasion on the day it occurred. This was followed up on 4 August with a decision to approve a partial embargo on the sale or supply of arms to, and the import of oil from Iraq. In September this embargo was extended. The European Council, meeting in Rome in October, dedicated significant discussion to Iraq's 'prolonged and destructive occupation of Kuwait' and demanded Iraq's 'unconditional withdrawal' from the Gulf emirate.[27]

Saddam Hussein was motivated to invade Kuwait by a desire to incorporate the kingdom's massive oil wealth into Iraq at a time when the Iraqi economy was in turmoil following eight years of war with Iran.[28] Once he realised that the international community was not prepared to accept his invasion as a *fait accompli* he attempted to link his action in Kuwait to the Israeli occupation of Arab territory. In mid-August 1990, Saddam demanded Israel's withdrawal from occupied Arab land in the West Bank and Gaza (as well as south Lebanon) as a precondition before Iraq would enter into discussions over the future of Kuwait. From this time onward, Saddam and his senior officials, notably the foreign minister Tariq Aziz, 'repeated like a gramophone'[29] the claim that Iraq had invaded Kuwait in order to liberate Palestine. This was only a stalling tactic intended to win support for the invasion of Kuwait on the 'Arab street' and to delay any international military response long enough for his army to complete its pillage of Kuwaiti wealth, its eradication of Kuwaiti opposition and its integration of the kingdom as a province of Iraq.

Arab leaders from Nasser to Assad had always claimed to act on behalf of the Palestinian cause in their efforts to exert regional influence. But the Iraqi claim that the 'restoration of Kuwait to the motherland' was the first step towards 'the liberation of Jerusalem' was categorically rejected by governments in Cairo, Damascus, Beirut and Rabat, all of whom viewed linkage as 'Saddamspeak for disguising defeat in Kuwait as victory in Palestine'.[30] Syria's President Hafez al-Assad was particularly dismissive and his state-controlled media mocked the claim that an Israeli withdrawal from Arab land could be achieved by invading another Arab state.[31]

However, Saddam's attempt at linkage did gain support from Yasser Arafat, who could not resist this opportunity to draw Iraq into the Israeli-Palestinian conflict. This had the full support of Palestinians in the West Bank and Gaza who hailed Saddam as the 'Knight of Arabism' and the 'Second Saladin' preparing to take on the modern-day Crusaders by making their cause his own.[32] King Hussein of Jordan, whose kingdom bordered Iraq and included a significant Palestinian population, also felt obliged to back Saddam in the face of domestic pressure and economic dependence on his much larger neighbour.[33]

Saddam's claims gained sympathy from senior international figures such as the Soviet foreign minister, Eduard Shevardnadze. In early September 1990 he stated the view that the convening of an international conference on Palestine could have a 'positive influence' on the Gulf crisis.[34]

Following the invasion of Kuwait, France had expressed a preference for a solution to be found 'within the Arab community' with the external parties playing only a minor role.[35] Once this failed to materialise, both President Mitterrand and his foreign minister Dumas sought to entice Saddam out of Kuwait by making promises over Palestine. In a speech at the UN General Assembly in late September, Mitterrand expressly linked Iraq's unconditional withdrawal from Kuwait to a resolution of the Israel-Palestine conflict by promising that 'if Iraq would declare its determination to withdraw from Kuwait and free hostages, then everything is possible'.[36] To follow this up, Mitterrand put forward a four-stage plan beginning with Iraq's withdrawal from Kuwait and ending in a global agreement on the key issues affecting the Middle East.

Until December 1990 the Community, excluding France, refrained from calling for its own negotiations with Iraq, in order to avoid the perception of a divide between Europe and the US. In the run-up to the UN's 15 January 1991 deadline for Iraq to withdraw from Kuwait, the EEC's diplomatic unity fell apart. In early January Luxembourg's foreign minister Jacques Poos, whose country had just taken over the Community's rotating presidency, let it be known that he was looking to travel to Baghdad on behalf of the Community.[37] Soon afterwards Dumas called for EEC foreign ministers to meet their Iraqi counterpart, Tariq Aziz, and for the Community to back the French linkage proposal.

This led to some heated discussions. At one point in proceedings the Dutch foreign minister, Hans van den Broek, was so strident in his objections to any EEC role independent of the US that Dumas retorted, 'if the EC had majority voting on foreign policy you would be outvoted'. This led the British foreign secretary Douglas Hurd to reply that this was 'exactly why Britain wants to maintain unanimity'.[38] Although the British and Dutch vetoed the call for the Community to adopt linkage, Dumas did gain support for his plan to invite Aziz to Luxembourg following the Iraqi foreign minister's upcoming Geneva meeting with the US Secretary of State, James Baker. Almost immediately the Iraqi foreign minister rebuffed the European invitation, a slight that forced the Community to acknowledge that further collective diplomacy was pointless, as the Italian Prime Minister Giulio Andreotti explained to a senior aide of Arafat who had travelled to Rome in January to urge the Community to send a delegation to Iraq in a last-ditch effort to prevent war.[39]

France's unwillingness to cooperate with its partners was demonstrated by Dumas' refusal to attend the EEC discussions that agreed to abandon crisis mediation in the Gulf. On 9 January 1991, Baker's meeting with Aziz in Geneva made no progress because the Iraqi foreign minister had only been willing to discuss one issue: linkage. The next day Mitterrand convened a press conference where he was adamant that France reserved the right to launch its own peace initiative if US efforts failed.[40] Less than a week later this was followed by French sponsorship of a Security Council draft resolution stating that once a 'peaceful settlement' to the Kuwait crisis had been reached the Security Council would undertake 'active participation' to achieve a settlement of the Palestinian problem by convening an international conference.[41] Mitterrand accompanied this diplomatic initiative with a controversial UN speech where he once more linked the invasion of Kuwait to the Israel-Palestine conflict.

Britain's new prime minister John Major had been lunching with Mitterrand only hours before, but the French President had kept the details of his imminent speech confidential. Nor did he inform the Bush administration, the Arab leaders participating in the anti-Saddam coalition, or any of his other EEC partners. This lack of consultation irritated many within the Community. The Danish foreign minister, Uffe Elleman-Jensen, publicly attacked the French approach; the Commission President, Jacques Delors, warned senior French officials that Mitterrand's unilateralism could only damage Community cohesion.[42]

Mitterrand's efforts failed to avert a military conflict over Kuwait and did nothing to increase French influence in the region. Gilles Kepel would subsequently argue that the 1990–91 Gulf conflict marked the end of France's 'Arab policy' as conceived by de Gaulle and implemented by his successors.[43] In mid-September 1990, the day after Iraqi troops raided the French Embassy in Kuwait and took French diplomats hostage, Mitterrand had signalled a practical commitment to participate in any military coalition against Saddam if war was unavoidable. Thus it was inevitable that Mitterrand would join the US-led international coalition against Saddam following his failure to broker a peace deal. However, his agreement to surrender operational control of French forces to US command did result in a certain backlash at home, notably the resignation of the Defence Minister, Jean-Pierre Chevènement. It also undermined the argument that France could pursue a policy in the region independent of Washington.

At the start of the war, in February 1991, Serge July, editor of the French daily *Libération*, mocked as 'pretension' any remaining French aspirations to emerge from the crisis as a major political force.[44] The following month, as Saddam's routed army returned home, Dumas seemed to admit as much. In a widely-publicised interview, which the neo-Gaullist opposition greeted with silence, he downplayed France's longtime Arab policy as a 'myth' that was in no way a priority of French foreign policy.[45]

Events in the Gulf between August 1990 and March 1991 highlighted very clearly the growing disparity between the economic weight of the Community, which following German reunification was an even more potent global economic force, and its weakness as a political and military player. In his seminal 1991 essay 'The Unipolar Moment', Charles Krauthammer argued that the 'disarray and disjointed national responses' of Europe to the Gulf crisis showed that the notion that economic power 'inevitably translates into geopolitical influence' was a 'materialist illusion'.[46] During a high profile speech in London less than a week after the end of hostilities in Kuwait, Delors admitted as much. The Gulf crisis, he acknowledged, 'provided an object lesson…on the limitations of the European Community'.[47]

Like the oil crisis of 1973–74 and the lengthy Egyptian-Israeli moves towards peace later in the same decade, events in the Gulf also underlined the real differences between the European and American capacities to act in the region.[48] In response to the invasion of Kuwait, the Bush administration successfully assembled an unprecedented international coalition under its command. Over the same months, the EEC failed to build a common diplomatic front even among its own members. By January 1991, the three leading EEC states of Britain, France and Germany were all pursuing distinct national policies. Throughout the crisis there was no mention of any role for the Community. Member state participating in the coalition—the British, Spanish, Italians, French and Dutch—spoke only in terms of their national contributions. Mitterrand did not even mention Europe in his first post-war television broadcast in early March. As one perceptive commentator noted in the wake of the war, 'the key to European participation in the Gulf crisis was not the degree of coordination among European states or the lack thereof, but the enduring links of the individual countries with the United States'.[49]

Despite the efforts of Secretary of State James Baker to address the Israel-Palestine conflict in May and October 1989, the Bush administration had shown little desire to engage in Middle East peacemaking in its first year in office. However, during the months of drawn-out pre-war diplomacy over Kuwait it had increasingly warmed to the idea of convening of an international conference on the Middle East once Saddam had been defeated. In late December 1990, the US endorsed a statement read out by the then Yemeni President of the UN Security Council, which called for a 'properly structured' Middle East conference at the 'appropriate time'.[50] Following the expulsion of Iraq's devastated army from Kuwait in March 1991, the US began to capitalise on its predominant international position in the post-Cold War era and its post-Gulf War prestige in the Middle East to bring the major regional parties to the conference table.[51] Speaking before a joint session of Congress on 6 March, President Bush explained that the principle of exchanging territory for peace was at the centre of his administration's plans for the region and a lasting peace based on that formula was now possible.[52]

With presidential backing, Baker now invested much time and political capital and applied significant financial pressure on the Arab states, the PLO and Israel in a course of 'shuttle diplomacy' in the region between March and October 1991.[53] The EEC endorsed Baker's post-war diplomacy and welcomed his 'painstaking efforts' in persuading Israel, Syria and a joint Jordanian-Palestinian delegation to attend the Madrid international peace conference that opened on 31 October 1991.

Baker's success in convening this unprecedented meeting was due to America's global predominance, as well as vital domestic considerations that made it unwise for any of the local parties to say no to the US at this time. For example, Israel's Prime Minister Yitzhak Shamir agreed to attend Madrid despite long time opposition to an international conference because he felt that Israel was increasingly secure in the region following the disintegration of the Soviet Union and the defeat of Iraq in Kuwait. Israel was also enjoying improved standing in the international arena because of its decision not to respond militarily to Iraqi SCUD missile attacks and thus jeopardise the fragile US-led anti-Saddam coalition. Israel also agreed to attend Madrid because the cost of absorbing the hundreds of thousands of new Soviet Jewish immigrants made it increasingly dependent financially on the US.

However, Shamir's Likud government was unbending in its refusal to negotiate with the PLO. A compromise was found whereby 'non-PLO' Palestinian representatives from the occupied territories (though not from Jerusalem or the Palestinian Diaspora community) would participate at Madrid as part of the joint Jordanian-Palestinian delegation. The PLO leadership was in no position to dispute this arrangement. The Intifada had highlighted to both Israel and the international community that there existed a viable Palestinian leadership inside the occupied territories that had the potential to represent the Palestinians of West Bank and Gaza as well as, if not far better than, the Tunis-based PLO. At the same time, the PLO's prized dialogue with the US collapsed because of Arafat's refusal to expel a Palestinian splinter group affiliated to the PLO from the organisation after it had undertaken an amphibious attack on an Israeli beach. Meanwhile the imminent collapse of the Soviet Union not only deprived the PLO of an important source of diplomatic support and military equipment and training, but left the US—a country which had refused to meet or recognise the group for almost its entire existence—as the only global superpower.

The PLO's decision to support the Iraqi invasion of Kuwait had been a major strategic miscalculation. In the wake of Kuwait's liberation, the Gulf States, led by Saudi Arabia and Kuwait itself, set about punishing the PLO for its stance during the war. One under-reported aspect of this response was the widespread slaughter of Palestinians living in Kuwait by the host population. Far more serious, at least from the perspective of the PLO leadership in Tunis, was the economic cost of siding with Iraq. Not only had the large Palestinian workforce in the Gulf been expelled en masse, thus vastly reducing the income funnelled from this constituency to the PLO, but the Gulf States had also cut off their financial support for Arafat's organisation and increased funding to Palestinian Islamist groups, notably Hamas.

Although the EEC froze high-level ministerial contacts with the PLO after the Gulf War, it still supported PLO attendance at Madrid. In a meeting with Bush in March 1991, Mitterrand made it clear that 'Arafat remains, to my knowledge, the leader of the PLO, and to my knowledge, the PLO remains the representative organisation'.[54] But the Community was well aware of the precarious state of the PLO at this time, and thus chose to play down the significance of the PLO's exclusion from the Madrid conference and to support the official Palestinian delegation on the grounds that it was 'broadly representative of the Palestinian people and is acceptable to the PLO'.[55]

Despite its exclusion from the Madrid conference, the PLO managed to exert its influence through Faisal Husseini, a resident of Jerusalem and a member of Arafat's Fatah organisation, who attended the meeting as head of an advisory team attached to the joint Palestinian-Jordanian delegation. Contrary to promises made by the US to the Israeli government, the Palestinian delegates at Madrid were allotted their own space at the conference table and allowed to address the conference independently of the joint Palestinian-Jordanian delegation.[56]

Besides indirectly legitimising the PLO at Madrid, this negotiating process also set a precedent for Israel entering into bilateral political discussions with delegations representing Jordan-Palestine, Syria and Lebanon. These talks took place under US supervision, which reminded all observers of the ongoing marginalisation of the Community in the politics of the Middle East. An unseemly internal spat between the European Council and the Commission on the eve of the conference over who would represent the Community at Madrid did not help matters. The Council, made up of the heads of state and government, won out over the Commission, the executive branch whose members are selected by national governments but independent of them.

Speaking at the conclusion of the Madrid conference on behalf of the Council, the Netherlands foreign minister van den Broek promised that the Community was 'fully prepared not only for a constructive partnership but also for a concrete partnership' and would 'stand ready to assist this cause for any party that calls on us and we will remain in close consultation with the co-sponsors'. He concluded, 'We feel that parallel to the bilateral negotiations also multilateral negotiations should be started up in due course; not at the expense of the political process [but] parallel with the political process'.[57]

The Community was granted a central role in the multilateral track discussions initiated at Madrid, and chaired the Regional Economic Development Working Group (REDWG). It also co-sponsored the working groups on water, the environment, and refugees and participated in the arms-control working group. This multilateral track was secondary to the political discussions, and Syria and Lebanon refused to enter into multilateral talks prior to the successful conclusion of political agreements with Israel; however it did provide a framework, under EEC supervision, for the parties to the conflict to discuss the wide-ranging challenges facing their region.

For this, as much as anything else, the Madrid Conference was of 'great significance' to the Community, as the Maastricht European Council of December 1991 acknowledged.[58] Subsequently, the European Commission argued that Madrid 'succeeded in triggering the mutual recognition and establishment of direct negotiations between Israel and the PLO'.[59] Though a notable achievement, Madrid failed to establish the Community as a key partner in the substantive political negotiations between Israel and the various Arab delegations, all of whom continued their discussions from December 1991 in Washington under the sole patronage of the US.

These talks did not get off to a promising start. Prime Minister Shamir had refused to allow the foreign minister, David Levy, to represent Israel at the Madrid conference, even though the Arab states were represented by their foreign ministers. Instead he went himself to ensure that the more moderate Levy made no concessions. Subsequently, he packed the Israeli delegation to the Washington talks with Madrid-sceptics. As Martin Indyk recalled, this unwilling group of negotiators turned up a week late in order to register its anger with the US over the timing and venue of the talks. When it did appear discussions with Lebanon got bogged down over the issue of Syrian troops in Lebanon; the Syrians would not agree to hold substantive discussions until Israel agreed to withdraw fully from the occupied territories, and Israel countered that it would not discuss withdrawal until Syria agreed in principle to a peace treaty. On top of this the Israeli-Jordanian talks also made little progress as Israel refused the Palestinian demand that there should be separate Jordanian and Palestinian delegations.[60] Less than a year after the Madrid meeting, it seemed that Baker's attempt to harness post-Cold War US global dominance to force a breakthrough in the Middle East was no match for the long-held positions of the local parties meeting in Washington.

In Israel, between 1977 and 1992, Labour's only taste of government had been in a national unity coalition with the Likud party between 1984 and 1990. Otherwise, Labour had been in opposition and many of its most senior figures, in particular Shimon Peres, had become increasingly dissatisfied with Likud's steadfast opposition to dealing with the PLO or attending an international conference. Then, across Europe, the Labour Party's success in the 1992 Israeli elections was viewed as having 'paved the way' for peace.[61] The Labour leader, Yitzhak Rabin, had promised to make the promotion of peace with the Palestinians his government's 'central goal' if victorious in the elections.[62] Shortly after taking power, the new Labour government repealed the law prohibiting unauthorised contact between the PLO and Israeli citizens. Very quickly Labour's leaders—who, with few exceptions, had been the architects of the settlement policy in the late 1960s—came to be widely perceived as the moderate anti-settlement party within Israel.

However, at no time during the election campaign did Rabin ever promise to negotiate with the Tunis-based PLO. Instead, he limited Labour's objective to 'negotiations with authorised and agreed on Palestinians from the territories occupied by Israel since 1967'. He also called for 'an agreement in a Jordanian-Palestinian framework…and not a separate Palestinian state west of the Jordan'.[63] Hence, during Labour's first year in power there was little progress in ongoing rounds of bilateral talks in Washington between Israeli and Palestinian representatives under the Madrid process. This ongoing stalemate in Washington coincided with the greatest challenge that the Community had faced since the end of the Cold War—the disintegration of Yugoslavia.

Europe had greeted the end of the Cold War with unbridled optimism. The collapse of the Soviet Union had ended the bipolar international order and instilled many with the belief that at long last the EEC would be free to turn its economic power into political influence on the world stage. As the French Prime Minister Michel Rocard explained in a speech in 1989, the *annus mirabilis* of the new Europe, the coming years would be a crossroads both at home and abroad and the Community needed to seize the moment.[64]

This euphoria, or 'Europhoria'[65] as some liked to call it, was also evident among commentators on international affairs on both sides of the Atlantic. One noted Washington foreign policy pundit spoke for many in expressing the view that Europe would soon have 'more influence … a more sustained and durable political, economic and cultural presence… than either the United States or the Soviet Union'.[66]

Confident of its new standing and opportunities on the global stage, the Community declared the fragmentation of Yugoslavia to be a European opportunity to assert its geopolitical influence in the New World Order. As Luxembourg's Jacques Poos famously stated in May 1991, this was 'the hour of Europe'. Jacques Delors was even more direct: 'We do not interfere in American affairs; we trust America will not interfere in European affairs'.[67] As the former British Foreign Secretary David Owen, co-chairman of the Conference on Former Yugoslavia and an early peace mediator, summed up, the crisis in Yugoslavia was quickly embraced as 'the virility symbol of the Euro-federalists' all of whom believed that it was now 'the time when Europe emerged with a single foreign policy'.[68]

Fighting in Yugoslavia began on a large scale in Croatia in the summer of 1991 between Serbs backed by the Yugoslav government in Belgrade and a Croat government that seceded from the federation in June. Early European involvement showed promise. Community foreign ministers made the trip to Belgrade on a continuous basis and by the end of July there were 50 EEC observers stationed across Yugoslavia. But an August 1991 emergency meeting in The Hague highlighted the internal divisions that would prevent an effective coordinated EEC response to the evolving crisis over the coming years. Britain called for a Conference for Security and Cooperation in Europe (CSCE) meeting at ministerial level to discuss the crisis. France demanded a UN meeting to discuss peacekeeping. The Dutch wanted Troika mediation. The Irish and Danes wanted military intervention led by the larger EEC states. For its part Germany demanded recognition of Slovenian and Croatian independence as a way to deter Serb aggression, only to be blocked by Spain and France.[69]

The disunity of the Hague meeting was a foretaste of things to come. A peace conference organised by the Community in early September 1991 under the chairmanship of the former British Foreign Secretary Lord Carrington, the first of a number of international peace mediators, highlighted further the deep divides within the Community.[70] Despite opposition from Carrington, the US administration and European ambassadors in Belgrade, Germany restated its support for immediate recognition of Slovenia and Croatia. As a compromise its EEC partners agreed to provide joint recognition to both on 15 January 1992. Germany pre-empted this and on 23 December 1991 unilaterally recognised both republics and called for their entry into the UN.

France, traditionally pro-Serb and still in favour of a federal Yugoslavia, was aghast at the German decision. Viewing it as evidence of a German-Croat alliance similar to the one that had existed during World War Two,

France now accused Germany of betraying the EEC and said Berlin had 'crushing responsibility for speeding up crisis'. Britain, like France, favoured a united Yugoslavia and believed that a strong Serbia was necessary for holding the country together, but it also followed the German line of the time in condemning Serb aggression.[71]

War broke out in Bosnia following its vote for independence in February 1992 and its secession from the federation in March. The declaration of a Serbian Republic in Bosnia in the same month further highlighted the impotence and divisions inside the Community. In April 1992, the EEC recognised Bosnia, and later in that month, following the Serbian-Montenegro declaration of a new Federal Republic of Yugoslavia, the EEC recalled its Belgrade ambassadors and looked to increase economic pressure on Serbia.[72]

The Community's attempt to prevent the disintegration of Federal Yugoslavia through financial incentives failed to prevent war in Bosnia, and by December 1992 the Serbs controlled 70 per cent of Bosnian territory. Once its strategy of financial inducements proved itself to be completely unsuitable for the Balkan challenge, the Community found itself at a loss over how to respond. There was no willingness to use military force to eject Serbia and there was growing concern that without decisive and immediate action the violence could spread across the Balkans. Europe's inability to address this crisis was all the more embarrassing because the Maastricht Treaty (formally the Treaty on European Union, TEU), which institutionalised Europe's Common Security and Foreign Policy (CSFP), was signed in February 1992 and entered into force in November 1993.

Far from providing an opportunity for Europe to demonstrate the capacity of the nascent CSFP to achieve its 'fundamental objectives', especially its mandate to 'strengthen the security of the Union' and to 'preserve peace and strengthen international security', the Yugoslav crisis almost killed it off.

Writing in 1993, the British Foreign Secretary Douglas Hurd tried to make the best of the debacle. He rejected the argument that the EEC's performance in Yugoslavia showed that the CSFP could never work. Instead, he made the case that 'ten years ago it would have been inconceivable that the Community should act together on a subject as sensitive and complex as Yugoslavia...The habit of working together is growing every day'.[73] This was dismissed by critics and considered the height of cynicism. By August 1993, all the Community could agree on was to 'value discretion over valour and leave the action in the hands of the UN',[74] as the well-known German commentator Josef Joffe said at the time. It was apparent that the Community, suffering from profound 'Yugowariness', was, in the words of EU Commissioner Leon Brittan, a 'paper tiger' in the Balkans, where its efforts had been '[a] spectacle…[a] shame'.[75] An editorial in *Le Monde* made much the same point. There had been some goodwill and much sacrifice, especially from the 209 soldiers serving the UN in Yugoslavia who lost their lives, but on a political level Europe's 'impotence' was 'clear for all to see', and the US-brokered peace agreement at Dayton, Ohio, in 1995 ended 'what can only be termed a European fiasco'. It was, in the paper's assessment, by all accounts a 'miserable outcome for a putative great power'.[76]

The Community's failure in Yugoslavia provided ammunition to US commentators seeking to poke fun at European pretensions of superpower status for many years. As one reminded readers in 2000, 'the Europeans couldn't fight their way out of a pastry shop (recall how the Bosnian Serbs tied Europe's hapless peacekeepers to telephone poles for kicks)'.[77]

At the height of Europe's embarrassment over its failure in Yugoslavia, rumours began circulating about secret negotiations taking place in Oslo, the Norwegian capital, between an Israeli delegation led by Uri Savir, the director-general of the foreign ministry, and Abu Alaa (Ahmed Qurei), a senior PLO figure and close associate of Arafat. Unexpectedly, it also looked as though these talks had resulted in a draft peace agreement.

Speculation was proved correct and on 13 September 1993, Israel's foreign minister Shimon Peres and the PLO's Mahmoud Abbas (Abu Mazen), Arafat's second in command, signed an agreement at a White House ceremony attended by leaders from across the world. Prime Minister Rabin and Chairman Arafat also attended the ceremony and they sealed the deal with a much-anticipated and highly symbolic handshake.[78]

The Oslo Accords set out a framework for providing for Palestinian self-rule in the entire West Bank and the Gaza Strip for a transitional period not to exceed five years, in anticipation of a permanent peace agreement. During this interim phase the Palestinian Territories would be administered by a Palestinian Authority (PA) to be freely and democratically elected after the withdrawal of Israeli military forces from Gaza and the populated areas of the West Bank.

As in the case of Sadat's visit to Jerusalem in November 1977, the US had not orchestrated the Oslo meetings. But, as occurred in the 1970s during the Camp David process, once Israel and the Arabs (in this case the PLO) decided to cooperate in the pursuit of peace, both parties looked to the US to act as host, mediator and guarantor.

Yet the Oslo signing ceremony in Washington represented a vision of peace much closer to that promoted by the Community following the Venice Declaration than to the US vision. Europe, as King Hussein of Jordan acknowledged, had been the 'forerunner'[79] in embracing the PLO, accepting long before either Israel or the US that Arafat's organisation was a key partner in the peace process.

During the Cold War the Middle East had been under the exclusive external influence of the Soviet Union and the US. On top of this, Europe's support for the PLO had led Israel to disqualify the Community as a legitimate external mediator to the conflict. Ongoing distrust of Euro-PLO cooperation resulted in numerous rumours, including the claim that the British Ambassador in Tunis had drafted Arafat's speeches from the late 1980s onwards.[80] Such suspicions did nothing to improve European credibility in Israeli eyes. In June 1982, in his characteristically blunt style, Shamir explained to West Germany's foreign minister Genscher that 'without [European] regard for Israel's positions and without co-operation there is no possibility for contributing to peace and stability'.[81] A decade later, little had changed. During his final visit to Israel in December 1992, Mitterrand's offer of French and European help to find Middle East peace was rebuffed by Rabin on the grounds that Israel was in 'no need of...mediation' from either France or Europe.[82]

The Israeli decision the following year to accept the PLO as the legitimate representative of the Palestinian people meant that it was no longer possible for Israel to use the Community's support for the PLO as a reason to exclude it from a substantive political role. In 1985, Peres had openly ruled out working with the Community because of its 'obsequious' attitude towards the PLO.[83] Less than a decade later, Peres himself was at the forefront of the attempt to legitimise the PLO as Israel's peace partner. As far as the Community was concerned, this changed everything.

On his trip to Paris following the signing of the Oslo Accords, Arafat was feted by President Mitterrand, Prime Minister Édouard Balladur and numerous senior officials precisely because they recognised that Oslo was both a vindication and validation of their long-time policy of support for the PLO.[84] These celebrations continued across the EU during Arafat's post-Oslo lap of honour in late 1993. During his two-day visit to Dublin in mid-December he held talks with President Mary Robinson as well as senior politicians from across the political spectrum. All poured praise on the PLO leader, reminding the media that Ireland had been the first member of the EEC to call for the PLO to represent the Palestinians in establishing their state, 13 years earlier. In turn, Arafat thanked his hosts for the fact that 'during our long march we have had real friends in Ireland who have given us unlimited support in difficult days when many others would not even listen to us...they have supported us on many occasions and on many levels'.[85] Arafat made comments that were similar in tone and content in visits to numerous other European capitals at that time.

The new post-Oslo reality offered a Community bruised and battered by its failure in the Balkans the opportunity to overcome its 'Bosnia Complex' by capitalising on its relationship with Arafat and the newly legitimised PLO to establish itself as a key external party in Middle East peacemaking. The exact form that this new role would take remained unclear, but it was certain that it would now be a central foreign policy priority of the European Union (EU) and its CSFP, both of which came into being in November 1993 just months after the signing of the Oslo Accords.

8

PAYER, NOT PLAYER

'Economic help... is not a substitute for the peace process, it is a supplement to it.'
Margaret Thatcher

In the years immediately preceding the Oslo Accords, the European Community chaired REDWG, the working group on regional economic development, the largest and most active of the five working groups established under the Madrid framework. However, it only played what the Commission termed a 'supportive complementary political role' to the US in the bilateral negotiations between Israel, the Palestinians and the Arab states.[1]

Following the signing of the Oslo Accords in September 1993, it was widely assumed that despite its close ties with the newly-legitimised PLO, the EU would continue to play its primary role in the multilateral track negotiations on regional development and economic issues. Patronage of the bilateral political talks between Israel and the PLO would remain a purely American preserve, as symbolised by the White House signing ceremony that launched the Oslo process. But an extraordinary European Council meeting on 29 October 1993 established that the Middle East would be one of five areas covered under the new CSFP and called on the EU to contribute to the peace process with the 'mobilisation of all political, economic, and financial resources';[2] it now appeared increasingly likely that any significant European economic commitment to the peace process would have political implications. The US wanted aid coordination for Oslo to be presided over by itself and

Russia, the joint sponsors of the Washington Conference to Support the Middle East Peace held in early October 1993. The EU put forward a counter-proposal for aid coordination to be under the control of the Palestine Economic Development Working Group (PEDWG), a sub-group of the EU-led REDWG. With neither side willing to back down, the US insisted that the World Bank took over the role of disbursing US aid to the Palestinians.[3]

Despite this setback, as Manual Marin, Vice President of the European Commission, would subsequently note, the EU 'reacted to this historic opportunity [Oslo] by making available the largest international pro-gramme of economic assistance to the peace process'.[4] On 12 September 1993, EU foreign ministers agreed to an initial US$600 million aid pack-age to the Palestinians. The following month, at the Washington Donors Conference, the EU signalled its desire to make a long-term commitment to financing the peace effort when it promised 38 per cent of the US$2.4 billion pledged at the meeting, by far the largest financial contribution to the nascent Oslo process (the US pledged 22 per cent; Japan nine per cent; the World Bank seven per cent and Saudi Arabia four per cent).

The vast majority of EU funds were intended to build and consolidate a strong Palestinian economy and society in the territories designated to the new Fatah-dominated Palestinian Authority (PA) under Arafat. This financial commitment represented a reaffirmation of Europe's long-time support for the PLO as the legitimate representative of the Palestinian people. The EU also took the lead in promoting four other related objec-tives: increasing Europe's purchase of Palestinian exports; increasing trade ties with Israel; finding and allocating international donors; and promot-ing regional economic development.

The first practical success to emerge from the Oslo Accords was the Israel-PLO Cairo Agreement of 4 May 1994, which established PLO rule in Gaza and Jericho. A peace agreement between Israel and Jordan followed in October 1994, and on 28 September 1995, the Israeli-Pales-tinian Interim Agreement (Oslo II) was signed. Oslo II extended Pales-tinian autonomy in the occupied territories and established a framework for Israeli military redeployment. This was intended to open the way for the much-anticipated but already postponed Palestinian presidential and legislative elections.

For the first half of the 1990s the EU accepted a more limited role in the politics of the Oslo process, because of its inability to establish itself as a serious force in the region during the Gulf Crisis of 1990–91 and its embarrassing failure in Yugoslavia, where 'aspirations exceeded... capabilities',[5] as the International Commission on the Balkans diplomatically put it. In late 1994 the French foreign minister, Alain Juppé, spoke for all of Europe when he informed a meeting of his country's ambassadors to the Middle East that regional priorities would be limited to participation in multilateral negotiations and 'a wide number of bilateral contacts' and transmission of messages.[6] As long as the Oslo process was making tangible progress the EU was content to let the US continue to dominate the bilateral political negotiations between Israel and the Palestinians and to focus its own primary effort on underpinning the 'economics of peace'.

On 4 November 1995, less than a week after the signing of Oslo II, Yitzhak Rabin was assassinated by an Israeli extremist opposed to the peace process. His death sent shock waves through the world, but the declarations of horror extended beyond sympathy for Israel and the Rabin family. They also underlined real international concern that the death of such a key player in the Oslo process might compromise the move towards a permanent settlement between Israel and the Palestinians. Rabin's murder occurred at a time of increased Palestinian terror attacks against Israeli targets. The violence worsened after Shimon Peres replaced Rabin as head of the Labour-led coalition government; in one eight-day period in February-March 1996, over 40 Israelis were killed and 200 injured in suicide attacks on Jerusalem and Tel Aviv.

The situation became so unstable by March 1996 that President Mubarak of Egypt and US President Bill Clinton felt compelled to convene an emergency meeting to provide momentum to the floundering peace process. The objective of this 'Summit of Peacemakers', held at Sharm El-Sheik in Egypt, was to 'demonstrate support for the peace process' by the international community. Unfortunately, it failed to stem terror attacks on Israel, which placed the interim Prime Minister Shimon Peres, a key architect of Oslo, in an increasingly untenable situation at home.

Israel began a major military operation in southern Lebanon codenamed Operation Grapes of Wrath shortly after the Sharm El-Sheik meeting, in response to the heavy shelling of Israeli towns by Hezbollah, the pro-Iranian Islamist group working to increase its political and military power in Lebanon. On 18 April, two weeks into the month-long operation, an Israeli missile hit the UN base at Qana, resulting in the death of over 100 Lebanese civilians who had been sheltering there under the protection of Fijian UN forces.

The EU's response to Qana was immediate. Within days of the tragedy the Italian foreign minister, Susanna Agnelli, led a high-level EU delegation to Beirut.[7] France capitalised on the international outcry by putting forward a unilateral peace proposal for the region. This called for an Israeli and Hezbollah agreement to stop targeting civilians and for Hezbollah to retain its right to resist the Israeli military occupation of the south of the country. It also called for a complete Israeli withdrawal from Lebanon and for the establishment of a committee to monitor any ceasefire, co-chaired by France and the US.[8]

This French proposal contradicted the US and Israeli demand that Hezbollah should give up its arms and agree to stop attacks on Israel, and Shimon Peres criticised it for causing 'confusion'.[9] Hervé de Charette, a long-standing political ally of Giscard d'Estaing and now France's foreign minister, was unmoved by such criticism. He shuttled between Jerusalem, Damascus and Beirut to promote his plan and was followed to the Lebanese capital by a disgruntled US Secretary of State, Warren Christopher. Things got worse for Christopher in Beirut when a jointly-convened and televised press conference was conducted in French and Christopher was left on the platform oblivious to proceedings until a French-speaking State Department official bounded onto the stage and started translating in his ear.

France's peace proposal failed to bring change, but its linguistic victory over the US at the Beirut press conference and the apparent willingness of the Lebanese government (and its Syrian patron) to accept the proposals conditionally meant that for a brief moment France had recaptured its place as the key Western power in Lebanon and as a leading external player in the Arab-Israeli conflict. There was some support inside the Community for the French move, with an Irish foreign ministry spokesman explaining that 'anything that the French can do to help improve the situation must be welcomed'.[10] But there was far more resentment over the fact that France had ignored official EU channels and had not informed its EU partners before putting forward its peace plan.

Such worries were part of a growing concern across the EU that the French President Jacques Chirac, who succeeded Mitterrand in May 1995, was implementing what one well-informed French commentator termed a 'modernised Gaullist formula'.[11] Upon taking office Chirac had been instrumental in pressuring the Clinton administration to take a hands-on role in the Balkans. He also ordered the resumption of nuclear testing, and refused to sign the Schengen agreement on European border controls without consulting his EU partners. This raised the 'curious paradox'[12] of France once again playing the dual role as the loudest advocate of a joint EU foreign policy and the EU's leading independent actor.

Likud's Benjamin Netanyahu became Israeli Prime Minister in May 1996. The EU's two main priorities at the time related to internal matters—consolidating Economic and Monetary Union (EMU) and preparing for the upcoming Intergovernmental Conference. Nevertheless, across the EU, Netanyahu's victory over Labour's Peres was viewed as a major setback to the Oslo peace process, not least because it threatened to marginalise the EU's influence on negotiations. Netanyahu, a former Israeli UN Ambassador, had been a vocal and scathing critic of Oslo while in opposition. On gaining power he backed down somewhat by acknowledging that the 'Oslo Accords and its consequences on the ground are a fait accompli'. He also promised to comply with Oslo commitments as long as there was 'reciprocity' from the Palestinians.[13]

Prior to the Likud election victory, and despite some setbacks such as the postponement of the Palestinian elections originally scheduled for July 1995, Oslo had resulted in two landmark agreements, Oslo I and Oslo II, that transformed the local political landscape. They also validated the EU's long-time policy of accepting the PLO as the legitimate representative of the Palestinian people. When the Palestinian elections finally took place in January 1996, under the watchful eye of 300 EU observers, Arafat won 88 per cent of the popular vote for president, with Fatah and pro-Fatah candidates securing 65 of the 88 seats on the legislative council. Fears that the anti-Oslo tendencies of Netanyahu's Likud-led government might derail progress and that Washington would do nothing to stop this explain the EU's growing dissatisfaction with what Eric Rouleau, the long-time Middle East correspondent of *Le Monde* and a special adviser to Mitterrand, termed the American 'insistence on monopolising the peace process'.[14]

In June 1996, immediately after Netanyahu's election victory, the European Council meeting at Florence took an unprecedented step by declaring the Oslo process a fundamental interest of the EU. This was restated at the Luxembourg General Affairs Council meeting of October 1996 and at the European Council meeting in Dublin in December 1996. The EU also issued a special 'Call for Peace' document following the Amsterdam European Council meeting in June 1997, while at the Luxembourg European Council meeting in December 1997, member states infuriated Israel by calling on it to make concessions in order to revive the peace process. On a practical level, at the beginning of the Irish EU presidency in June 1996 the EU established a mechanism to monitor Israeli settlement activity, which was later expanded to cover Jerusalem also. In September 1996, in the face of renewed Israeli-Palestinian clashes, following the Israeli decision to open a tunnel in the historic part of Jerusalem's Old City, that left 14 Israelis and 56 Arabs dead, the EU dispatched Ireland's foreign minister Dick Spring for intense shuttle diplomacy during which he met the Israeli foreign minister, David Levy, three times in one four-week period. Following a specially-convened meeting of the European Council in Dublin on 5 October, Spring once more travelled to the region to hold meetings with both Netanyahu and Arafat.[15] During these discussions Spring stressed the importance that the EU attached to a revitalisation of the Oslo process but, unlike some other senior European officials, he refused to blame Netanyahu publicly for the breakdown in the process.

Jacques Chirac visited Israel and the PA-controlled territories on a trip to the region in October 1996. While prime minister in 1987, Chirac had met a number of senior Israeli figures on a visit to the country that had passed without any major incidents. France's foreign minister at the time, Jean-Bernard Raimond, thought that in the late 1980s Chirac's approach to the Israel-Palestine conflict differed little from that of President Mitterrand.[16] On becoming president Chirac was determined to improve Franco-Arab ties, telling an audience at Cairo University in April 1996 that France's 'Arab policy must be an essential part of its foreign policy'.[17] He was also adamant that, with France in the lead, the EU would develop an independent political role in the Middle East peace process.[18]

At the same time, as Avi Pazner, Israel's Ambassador in Paris between 1995 and 1998, later recalled, relations between Chirac and Netanyahu were 'not good from the beginning'.[19] While in Israel, and in front of the world's media, Chirac very publicly rejected the protection of Israeli security personnel on a visit to East Jerusalem. He also refused to speak to members of the Knesset, though he did become the first Western head of state to visit Yasser Arafat in Ramallah, where he expressed the hope that Palestine would be a model of democracy for other states. This gesture resonated so deeply that during the 2002 French presidential elections Muslim audiences chanted 'Chirac to Ramallah, Chirac to Ramallah', recalling his landmark meeting with Arafat six years earlier.[20] During a speech in Israel, Chirac also called on the EU to play a role alongside the US and Russia as co-sponsors of the peace process, adding that a more active French and EU role would improve the chances for peace.[21] Senior Israeli officials dismissed Chirac's visit as a 'fiasco',[22] but it did mark the start of a new EU effort to increase its involvement in bilateral political negotiations between Israel and the PA, which up to this point had been the sole preserve of the US administration.

A few days after Chirac returned from his controversial trip to the region, the EU established the post of Envoy to the Middle East at a specially-convened European Council meeting in Dublin. Miguel Ángel Moratinos, previously Spain's Ambassador to Israel, was appointed to the new role with a mandate to report back to the EU on the opportunities for involvement in political aspects of the peace process, to assist Israel and the PA in their negotiations, and to monitor violations of existing agreements by both sides. France, Sweden, Ireland, Portugal, Italy, Greece and Spain supported this move. The Netherlands, Britain and Germany were far more sceptical, with the foreign ministers of the latter two, Malcolm Rifkind and Klaus Kinkel respectively, expressing concerns that the move could hinder US peace efforts. King Hussein of Jordan was equally cautious: 'Europe does not want a role contradictory to the US role, but complementary'.[23]

In response to Spring's earlier shuttle diplomacy in the region, Secretary of State Christopher had written to all 15 EU members warning them off any new attempt to intervene in Middle East peacemaking at such 'a delicate moment'.[24] Following Moratinos' appointment the US State Department issued another thinly veiled warning, on the grounds that the US was the 'only indispensable partner' to the local parties.[25] The establishment of the Middle East envoy post fell far short of French calls at the time for the EU to 'co-sponsor' peace talks,[26] but it still offered a potential challenge to the US monopolisation of the bilateral political negotiations between Israel and the PA. It was also part of the, albeit stilted, European attempt to move towards a more independent CSFP following the ratification of the Maastricht Treaty in November 1993.

The birth of the Euro-Mediterranean Partnership (EMP), better known as the Barcelona Process, was the latest of several attempts by the

EU to consolidate and strengthen its economic and political relationship with the Middle East and North Africa. Launched in the Spanish city in November 1995, it was immediately held up as evidence of the EU's importance as a party to peace negotiations between Israel and its Arab neighbours. As de Charette explained, the new framework could 'exert a positive influence on the peace process by endeavouring to develop concrete acts of cooperation, by planning its work over the long term by establishing a genuine partnership. The Barcelona process has today a decisive contribution to make in the restoration of trust in the region'.[27] Over subsequent years EU officials continued to make much of the fact the Barcelona process was the 'only forum where the Arabs and Israelis are continuously having discussions',[28] and they also drew on it repeatedly as evidence of the EU's key role in mediating regional conflict.

All these overlapping efforts suggested that Europe was finally succeeding in turning its economic power and significant financial investment in the peace process into political influence. The EU played a notable role in the negotiations that led to the Hebron Agreement on Israeli troop withdrawals at the end of January 1997. Following this, it sent a letter of assurance to the PA in which it vowed to 'use all its political and moral weight to ensure that all the provisions in the agreements already reached will be fully implemented'.[29]

During negotiations on the Hebron redeployment Israel, albeit grudgingly, acknowledged for the first time that the EU had a role to play in the bilateral political negotiations between itself and the Palestinians. EU leaders looked to capitalise on this. The British Foreign Secretary, Robin Cook, promised guests at the fiftieth anniversary dinner of the Anglo-Arab Association in London that from now on the EU would make a greater effort to 'complement' US efforts to mediate an Israeli-Palestinian peace.[30] At a meeting with Arafat in Paris soon afterwards, Chirac pushed his guest hard to lend support to a new proposal to restart peace negotiations with the EU as an equal partner of the US.[31]

This was not simply an emotional response to Europe's marginalisation in the region, which Paul-Marie de La Gorce, a well-known commentator who had served France under both de Gaulle and Pompidou, was now describing as 'abnormal'.[32] There was widespread agreement across the EU that it was time 'to rectify the imbalance between the EU's economic and political roles [in the peace process]', as Ireland's then minister for European affairs put it.[33] Romano Prodi, Italy's Prime Minister, was equally blunt: 'Europe must transform its simple economic presence into an economic and political presence'.[34] A greater role was also a practical necessity. As the European Commission acknowledged, the 'stalemate in the Palestinian track has had a progressive paralysing effect on the Multilateral track'.[35] At the end of March 1997, in response to the lack of progress in the ongoing peace talks, the Arab League foreign ministers officially suspended their involvement in the Oslo multilateral track discussions on matters such as regional security, development and arms control. This deprived the EU of its traditional, if imperfect, multilateral route for inserting itself in the peace process.[36]

By 1998 the European Commission felt that the EU had been 'instrumental' in ensuring 'the survival of the peace process' and expressed its 'determination to play a full political role in terms of promoting a comprehensive, just and lasting peace'.[37] In particular, it called for EU governments and the EU special envoy to the Middle East to participate 'alongside' US officials in order to assist in political negotiations, and to increase the EU role in coordinating donor funds as it was 'dwarfing the efforts of all other donors'.[38] Interestingly, this increasingly outspoken approach by the EU towards its role in the Middle East peace process coincided with its most assertive period of involvement in the Balkans. While the US flew 80 per cent of the air strikes, the EU provided 80 per cent of ground troops during the crisis in Kosovo in 1999. Unlike earlier in the decade, when the EU was plagued by division over how to deal with the war in Bosnia, it now managed to coordinate its response and maintain a common front, despite outspoken Greek opposition to military action against Serbia.

But tough talking aside, there remained a number of major obstacles that the EU had to overcome before it could play the role it desired in the Middle East peace process. The first was the attitude of the Netanyahu government. Likud had been elected on a platform that proclaimed that 'peace is based first of all on the security of Israel and its citizens'.[39] The government insisted that Oslo's success had to be judged in terms of the PLO's ability and willingness to take on Palestinian opponents of the peace process, notably Hamas and Islamic Jihad, in order to protect Israel from terrorism. This argument resonated not only among Netanyahu's core supporters inside the Likud party but among the vast majority of Israeli citizens and was, in the words of one veteran Israeli security analyst, 'an absolutely critical test of the Palestinians ability to "deliver" on peace'.[40]

The Netanyahu government was infuriated by the harsh attacks on Israeli security strategy by leading European figures such as France's foreign minister Hubert Védrine, who in September 1997 described Israeli policy as 'catastrophic'.[41] Speaking in early April 1997, before a visit to Europe, Netanyahu urged the EU to adopt a 'balanced, factual and responsible position' and argued that the Palestinians' belief that Europe would 'always line up behind all of their [the Palestinian] demands and violations and will overlook the facts' had led to the current impasse in the peace process.[42]

A government spokesman warned Europe that it would face staunch Israeli opposition to any attempt it made to 'impose a solution which endangers the State of Israel and runs counter to its interests'. In particular, Netanyahu's government was wary of any European attempt to force a settlement on Israel before the PA carried out its commitments under Oslo. This explained Israel's strong reaction to the EU's March 1999 Berlin Declaration, which called for the establishment of a Palestinian state in Gaza and West Bank as the 'best guarantee' for Israel's security.[43] In response, Netanyahu accused the EU of trying to 'force a dangerous solution upon Israel'.[44]

During a meeting with the Dutch Prime Minister Wim Kok in mid-1997, Netanyahu had argued that the EU's role in the peace process should be 'essentially economic'.[45] In European eyes, even this secondary role was made all but impossible by Israel's policy of closing off the West Bank and Gaza in response to terror attacks. The EU argued that this policy prevented Palestinians from entering Israel to work, and denounced the closure as a breach of Oslo that undermined the development of the Palestinian economy, 'invalidated' the donor effort and made a 'mockery of the economics of peace'.[46] Although it was not mentioned explicitly, the Israeli measures also undermined European influence profoundly by reducing the importance of the EU's role as the major donor to the PA under the Oslo framework.

Criticism escalated following the signing of the EU-Palestinian Interim Association agreement in July 1997. This had been intended to create a free-trade area between the EU and the West Bank and Gaza by 2001 and to establish a comprehensive framework for political, trade and financial cooperation. Though it entered into force in July 1997, its first meeting did not take place until May 2000 and the implementation of the agreement was, in the words of the European Commission, 'very low'.[47]

A second impediment to the EU achieving a greater role in the politics of the Israel-Palestine conflict was the ongoing US dominance of the process. In October 1996 an editorial in the Israeli daily *Ha'aretz* attacked Netanyahu for alienating the Clinton administration, which had sought to defend Israel from European attempts to insert itself into the peace process.[48] But in truth, for much of the Netanyahu era the Clinton administration was as critical as the EU of Likud government policies.[49] For example, the White House expressed 'disappointment' at the Israeli decision to build approximately 2,000 new houses in Har Homa, a disputed neighbourhood of Jerusalem, which the Palestinians claimed was occupied territory.[50] Israel refuted the accusation on the grounds that most of the land being built on was privately owned by Jews, and explained that the government intended to build 3,000 houses for Jerusalem's Arabs over the following three years.[51]

This did little to pacify Washington. Clinton had made no secret of his support for Shimon Peres in his unsuccessful election battle against Netanyahu in 1996. Subsequently, the US president was deeply frustrated by Netanyahu, telling one senior aide that the Israeli prime minister drove him crazy.[52] On his return from a visit to the US capital in October 1997 the Israeli President, Ezer Weizman, admitted that he was 'amazed at the degree of distrust felt by the administration towards Bibi [Netanyahu]'.[53]

Clinton's relationship with Arafat could not have been more different. Over the course of Clinton's two terms in office Arafat was a guest in the White House more times than any other international figure. Clinton's close relationship with Arafat and his much more strained ties with Netanyahu were very apparent in October 1998 when the US president hosted both of them at Wye River, Maryland, for peace talks. This meeting resulted in the Wye River Accords, under which the US agreed to undertake 23 roles and functions including the day-to-day on-the-ground monitoring of the peace. This intricate and extensive practical commitment by Washington led one US commentator to note that now 'Israel gives land; the Palestinians give promises; and America tries to fill the gaps'.[54]

The Clinton administration agreed to bear the cost of the land-for-security plan agreed at Wye, and in November it also pledged to 'substantially increase' the amount of assistance it would provide to the PA over the next five years.[55] This did not change the fact that since the Washington Conference of 1993 the EU had established itself as by far the largest donor to Palestinians. At the second international donors' conference, held in Paris in January 1996, the EU once more pledged the largest amount of funds to the PA. By 1998, the EU accounted for almost 55 per cent of all aid to the PA, compared with 11 per cent from the US. Again in November of that year, the EU once more pledged to act as the lead funder to the PA until 2003. But within a month of this announcement the EU financial role, totalling over €1.1 billion between 1994 and 1999, was all but forgotten as the Palestinian leadership clamoured to welcome Bill Clinton on an official visit to Gaza to attend a meeting of the PLO National Council. Describing this event as a 'landmark in Palestinian history', senior PA officials were ecstatic. Nabil Shaath, the Palestinian foreign minister who had headed the PLO's first delegation to the UN in 1974, exclaimed that 'the world will never be the same again', and compared Clinton's trip to Nixon's visit to China.[56]

This was a real blow to the EU's attempt to turn its financial commitment to Oslo into political influence, and highlighted how the local parties still ignored the EU's calls for it to be allowed to play a 'constructive role' in facilitating peace.[57] It was also a sharp reminder of the ongoing success of the Clinton administration in keeping the EU in its 'junior role',[58] as one State Department official put it in July 1996. Indeed, some even argued that Washington's decision to veto an EU-sponsored UN Security Council Resolution in March 1997 condemning Israel's plans for Har Homa, and its refusal to support an EU proposal for a joint initiative to restart peace talks the following month, were evidence of an active US policy to marginalise the EU's role in the peace process wherever possible.[59]

During the late 1970s, Sadat had set out the reason why both Egypt and Israel looked to the US to the exclusion of any other external partner during its peace negotiations. 'America is the only partner that has got cards in this game', he explained in a joint interview with Begin for French television. 'We need someone that can be trusted by both of us to come and help us create confidence'.[60] For much the same reasons, the Palestinians prized US political and diplomatic involvement above all else during the Oslo era. Like Sadat, they valued the US precisely because it was so close to Israel and, as such, was the only external party able to pressure the Jewish state to make concessions. In a 1990 interview William Waldegrave, then a junior minister in the British government, acknowledged this reality by saying 'Europe cannot seek to take over the American position', because 'we do not have that kind of relationship with Israel nor with the region as a whole'.[61]

Over the next decade little changed, and although a senior adviser to Arafat was happy to exclaim in 1997 that Europe 'completely supports Arafat',[62] the US still held the key. By the time of Clinton's visit to Gaza in late 1998 Shaath, for example, was emphatic on one point: it was the US special relationship with Israel, combined with the US special relationship with the Palestinians, that was 'best for the peace process'.[63]

No doubt Netanyahu's failure to establish the close relationship with Clinton that past Israeli prime ministers could claim with US presidents contributed in part to the fact that by 1999 he had lost the confidence of both the pro-Oslo and anti-Oslo constituencies in Israel and was defeated in elections by Labour's Ehud Barak. Initially Barak's victory was celebrated in Europe as an opportunity to restart the stalled peace process after three years of Likud obstructionism. Although Barak had been a gradual convert to the Oslo process, much comfort was taken in the apparent similarities between him and the late Yitzhak Rabin. Both men had been highly decorated army chiefs of staff prior to entering politics, and Rabin had brought Barak into the cabinet in September 1995 shortly before his death. Both were also more popular with the electorate than their party. As one European paper put it, after the aberration of Netanyahu, Barak was the 'natural heir to Rabin'.[64]

The similarities between these two military men turned Labour party leaders was emphasised following Barak's electoral pledge to reach framework agreements with all the Arab parties within 18 months of coming to power. The first week of May 1999 was the deadline that had been set out under the 1994 Gaza-Jericho Agreement for Israel and the Palestinians to reach a final agreement in permanent status talks. In anticipation of this, in February 1999, Arafat announced that he would declare a state unilaterally on 4 May 1999. This led the EU to issue a statement in March reaffirming the Palestinians' 'unqualified' right to self-determination 'including the option of a state' in the short term.[65] It also warmly welcomed Barak's decision to meet Arafat on his first day as prime minister, in contrast to Netanyahu who refused to meet the PA leader until two months after taking office.

Barak's election re-energised EU attempts to inject life into the moribund Oslo process. In June, after a meeting with the Egyptian foreign minister Amr Moussa in Cairo, the EU envoy Moratinos announced that the EU 'plans to shoulder [its] responsibilities' in order to push forward the peace process and informed his host that the EU was 'ready to remove any obstacles that impede the realisation of peace in the Middle East'.[66] A few days later, the EU Council 'reaffirm[ed]' its 'resolve fully to assume its role in the peace process'.[67] The following December, the EU 'invited' all parties back to the multilateral track discussions on the grounds that 'parallel progress on all tracks should be in the interests of all'.[68]

Few were surprised when this appeal found no takers among the local parties whose relations with each other were deteriorating rapidly. It was only in July 2000, in a move very reminiscent of Carter's efforts to mediate between Israel and Egypt in the late 1970s, that Clinton injected some momentum into the peace process by inviting Arafat and Barak to Camp David for talks. These discussions took place over an unprecedented 12 days between 12 and 24 July 2000; their goal was to find a permanent and lasting solution to the Israel-Palestine conflict acceptable to both sides. During the talks Barak agreed to a proposal by Clinton that offered the Palestinians a state comprising of all Gaza and 92 per cent of the West Bank, as well as Palestinian sovereignty over the Old City of Jerusalem's Muslim and Christian quarters and the city's Arab neighbourhoods. He also agreed to Palestinian 'custodial' sovereignty over the Temple Mount with Israel holding 'residual' sovereignty over the Muslim Holy Site. However, neither Clinton's major investment of time, credibility and political capital nor the Sadat-Begin precedent during the Carter presidency resulted in an agreement.[69]

Immediately after this failure, President Chirac invited Barak, Arafat and the US Secretary of State Madeleine Albright to Paris in the hope that disappointment over the failure to reach agreement at Camp David would result in all three parties signing a compromise deal under French auspices.[70] Some Israelis close to Barak subsequently claimed that Chirac had urged Arafat to reject the terms offered at Camp David so that he could play host to a settlement in Paris—a charge refuted outright by French officials. But Chirac's invitation was evidence of the deep frustration inside the EU over the refusal of the US, Israel and the Palestinians to embrace European attempts to move the peace process forward at times of deadlock. One French newspaper, *Le Canard Enchaîné*, even quoted a gloomy Chirac admitting that 'the Europeans don't count in these negotiations…we must not have any illusions. Clinton is running the whole thing'.[71]

True as this was, in late September 2000 'the whole thing' came crashing down with the outbreak of the Al Aqsa Intifada. In the months, and years, after the collapse of Oslo the Palestinian leadership, much of the Arab world and supporters of the Palestinian cause in Europe challenged the generosity of Barak's various peace proposals between July 2000 and January 2001. They explained the disintegration of the Oslo process and the outbreak of the Intifada in terms of general Palestinian frustration with ongoing statelessness and anger over the visit of then Israeli Defence Minister, Ariel Sharon, to the Temple Mount (location of the Al Aqsa Mosque, the holiest Muslim site in Jerusalem) in late September 2000.[72]

Others, perhaps most notably the senior US negotiator Dennis Ross and Nabil Amer, former PA Minister for Parliamentary Affairs,[73] argued that in the six-month period beginning with Camp David Israel did make significant concessions on the size of a prospective Palestinian state and the Palestinian claim to Jerusalem, as well as on the highly contentious issue of the 'right of return' of Palestinian refugees to their former homes in Israel (though agreeing to this in a way consistent with the continued status of Israel as the homeland for the Jewish people). What all agreed on was that with the outbreak of the Intifada the 'unprecedented tangible progress'[74] that the European Commission had applauded just a few years before evaporated overnight. For many in Europe charged with developing a Middle East policy it now seemed very possible that the EU's hard earned status as a credible political player in the politics of the Israel-Palestine conflict would disappear also.

9

THE CHORUS OF REFORM

'[The European Union is] in the chorus of reform...But they only scurry around sending emissaries to see Sharon and Arafat, they make ringing declarations in Brussels, they fund a few projects, and more or less leave it at that, so great is the shadow of the US over them.'

Edward Said

'The peace process must be saved, time is running out'[1] was a statement unexpected from an official declaration from EU leaders. But the Oslo peace process was hardly the average foreign policy concern for the EU, and by the time this statement was made in October 2000, the process was on the verge of total collapse. In the preceding months the EU had acknowledged that the process of mutual recognition between the PLO and Israel was 'slow and cumbersome'.[2] Yet few had expected the Oslo era to end so suddenly or to be replaced by a level of violence shocking even by the standards of the previous half-century of Arab-Israeli conflict. According to Israeli sources, from 29 September 2000 until early February 2003, there were 16,347 attacks against Israeli targets (7,230 in the West Bank, 8,455 in Gaza and 662 in Israel proper). These resulted in a total of 5,063 injured civilians and members of the security forces and 724 dead. Over the same time period the PA estimated losses in excess of 3,200 dead and 34,000 wounded.

For all the clashes between the EU and the Netanyahu government in the late 1990s, the success of Arafat and Fatah in the January 1996 elections appeared to have validated once and for all the EU's support for the

PLO over the previous two decades. The EU also made some progress in inserting itself into the political process, most notably in its mediatory role in negotiations leading to the Hebron Agreement of 1997. Despite Israel's border closure policy, there was also growing satisfaction in Brussels that the economic situation in the PA-ruled territories was improving and that the EU's major financial commitment of €1.1 billion between 1994 and 1999, over half the financial resources invested in the peace process, was starting to pay off. A number of international aid projects had also begun to show real results and the World Bank was reporting by early 1999 that the West Bank and Gaza had fully recovered from the economic decline of the previous years; the economic situation continued to improve well into the summer of 2000.

For all these reasons, even as failed peace process gave way to bloody Intifada, the EU continued to attach special importance to using aid and investment to preserve the PA as a partner for peace.[3] It pumped almost €250 million (US$280 million) into the PA between November 2000 and December 2002 in the form of budgetary support for institutions and infrastructure, as well as humanitarian, refugee and food aid. It also reprimanded Israel regularly for damage caused to EU-funded infrastructural projects including Gaza's international airport and seaport, the Palestinian Broadcasting Corporation (PBC), the Palestinian police headquarters, two schools, a research laboratory and a water treatment and pumping plant.

This continued emphasis on the economics of peace was also partly an attempt to consolidate the EU's gains in the political sphere over the previous few years. On 9 October 2000, within weeks of the effective collapse of Oslo, the EU Council of Ministers asked Javier Solana to travel to the region 'as a matter of urgency'.[4] Solana, the EU's High Representative for CSFP between 1999 and 2009, was well suited to the task. He had previously served as Spain's foreign minister, and he believed that his greatest achievement in that role was overseeing the Barcelona process because it had provided a forum for the EU, Israel and the Arab world to come together.[5]

The following January the EU's Middle East Envoy Moritanos was the only foreign representative present at the last-gasp attempt by Israeli and Palestinian negotiators to reach a deal at the Egyptian Red Sea resort of Taba. When this failed, the EU offered to assign a low profile security team, the EU Informal Group, to oversee and facilitate any ceasefire, and volunteered to play 'an active role' in any third-party monitoring mechanism that would contribute to a return to peace and stability between Israel and the PA.[6]

With no sign of an end to the violence in sight, Chris Patten, EU Commissioner for External Relations, summed up the mood in Europe in a speech to the European Parliament in December 2001, during which he argued that 'we must not allow ten years of political and financial investment to be wasted'.[7] In the same month the EU Council of Ministers once again instructed Solana to go to the region in order to 'contribute…to a speedy resumption of negotiations'. In explaining the decision, the Belgian foreign minister Louis Michel was clear: 'The situation in the Middle East is extremely serious, we cannot be inactive'.[8] Solana's shuttle diplomacy on behalf of the EU was complemented by back-to-back visits to the region by the British Foreign Secretary Jack Straw and his German counterpart Joschka Fischer, which fuelled speculation that the EU was now pushing ahead to promote its own peace proposal.

The Straw and Solana visits coincided with a proposal put forward by Saudi Crown Prince Abdullah, disseminated in the *New York Times*.[9] This 'land for normalisation initiative', as *Ha'aretz* termed it, called for full Israeli withdrawal from the West Bank, Gaza and part of Jerusalem, in return for Israeli sovereignty over Jerusalem's Jewish Quarter and Arab recognition of Israel. The EU immediately welcomed this Arab Peace Initiative (API) as it came to be known. On the eve of the Saudi announcement, Solana had told the European Parliament that 'today, we can't really talk about a peace process, because there is no process and there is no peace'.[10] So he then embraced Crown Prince Abdullah's proposal as 'an opportunity that has to be taken' and flew directly to Saudi Arabia to flesh out its details before heading to Cairo to brief President Mubarak. Solana was the first Western envoy to discuss the plan with Crown Prince Adbullah, and his diplomatic efforts made a significant impression on Saudi officials. One told journalists that 'we expect the EU to play a bigger role in the Middle East peace process in the light of today's talks'.[11]

President Chirac of France hailed the Saudi plan as 'strong and courageous'[12] and his foreign minister Védrine saw it as providing the EU with a real opportunity to increase its political role. 'The task ahead for the European Union is clear', Védrine exclaimed, before adding, 'we will work to remove obstacles to dialogue and we will work to strengthen a coalition for peace'.[13] In an attempt to build on the momentum generated by the Saudi initiative Védrine unveiled a French-sponsored 'non-paper', as he called it. It began with what was long considered an endpoint—the immediate establishment of a Palestinian state in the West Bank and Gaza that would be recognised by the international community. It would be followed by Palestinian elections and by negotiations on a final status agreement between Israel and a newly sovereign Palestinian government with an uncontestable mandate to make peace.

Védrine's proposal was both novel and controversial and revolved around 'bringing the endgame [of a Palestinian state] up front a little bit',[14] as one EU official described it. Consultation between Paris, London and Washington followed and by May the proposal had been watered down; Germany's Fischer now took over from Védrine as the lead voice on a less ambitious, EU-sponsored version of this proposal. Fischer's plan retreated from the French call for the immediate establishment of a Palestinian state and instead provided a detailed timetable to establish an emergency PA government, followed by elections and the declaration of a provisional Palestinian state in 2003, opening the way for final status negotiations on borders in 2004. Védrine had described his proposal as 'a political response to a consistent and insidious effort by Israel to sap the basis of the PA'.[15] In stark contrast, Fischer was far more diplomatic and far less critical of both US and Israeli policy than his French counterpart, preferring to describe his plan as a sincere attempt to 'build a bridge from the present to full independence for a fully responsible Palestinian state'.[16]

As the first year of the new millennium drew to a close the international community waited for the results of the US presidential elections for an indication of how a new administration, Democrat or Republican, would engage with the Israel-Palestine conflict, given Clinton's unprecedented and unsuccessful attempts to bring peace. Following the election of George W. Bush in November the consensus view was that he would likely 'cease the practice of Presidential summitry in the Middle East',[17] and would not look to 'micromanage the peace process'.[18] These predictions seemed to be correct in the earliest months of the Bush administration. In particular, the announcement that the new administration would not appoint a special envoy to move the peace process forward seemed to signal a significant US withdrawal from its long-time position as the external mediator and facilitator of Arab-Israeli peace efforts. So did the decision to end the CIA's close advisory relationship with the PA, a central component of US involvement since the Wye River Agreement of 1998.

In the immediate aftermath of the September 2001 al-Qaeda attacks on New York and Washington, America's three main European partners were unflinching in their support. Chancellor Gerhard Schröder of Germany described the attacks on the US as 'a declaration of war against the entire civilised world' and pledged Germany's 'unreserved solidarity'. President Chirac of France offered 'total solidarity', while the British Prime Minister Tony Blair promised that his country would be 'standing shoulder to shoulder' with the US.[19]

Eighty nations backed the US military action against al-Qaeda and the Taliban in Afghanistan, demonstrating the extent of international goodwill for the US across the globe. Even those countries that would later take the lead in opposing the US on Iraq supported and contributed to the war in Afghanistan. France deployed 5,000 military personnel in Central Asia and sent its only aircraft carrier, the *Charles de Gaulle*, to the region, while Germany, in what Chancellor Schröder termed a 'historic decision', agreed to deploy troops abroad in support of the US action in Afghanistan.[20]

The end of the military phase of the war against al-Qaeda and the Taliban in Afghanistan in early December 2001 provided the Bush administration with the opportunity to focus on preparing for a preemptive war against Iraq in the context of addressing the threat of 'rogue states' who were the 'most likely sources of chemical and biological weapons for terrorists'.[21] In January 2002, the President made the same argument in his 'Axis of Evil' State of the Union address. In June he argued that 'containment is not possible when unbalanced dictators with weapons of mass destruction can deliver those weapons on missiles or secretly provide them to terrorist allies'.[22] Tackling this paramount challenge was also at the heart of two major policy documents published in 2002 and 2003: the wide-ranging National Security Strategy of the United States of America, and the more focused National Strategy for Combating Terrorism.[23]

These documents promised to 'constantly strive to enlist the support of the international community'. But they also insisted that the US 'will not hesitate to act alone, or if necessary, to exercise our self defence by acting pre-emptively'. This resulted in an extensive, passionate and increasingly acrimonious debate in Europe over the nature of American power and the legitimacy and effectiveness of the Bush doctrine of pre-emption. Coming as it did after the US refusal to ratify the Kyoto Protocol on climate change and the Rome agreement setting up the International Criminal Court, it was too much to bear in some quarters. Chirac labelled it 'an extraordinarily dangerous doctrine'.[24] Patten condemned it as 'unilateralist overdrive' and Solana, his Brussels-based colleague, warned against US 'global unilateralism'.[25]

As the US determination to remove Saddam Hussein intensified in late 2002, so too did hostility over the issue of legitimacy of pre-emptive action. As early as November 2001, Schröder warned against targeting Iraq in the future, saying that such action could 'blow up in our faces'. During his subsequent re-election campaign in 2002, the German Chancellor ruled out German participation in any Iraq war, even one with UN approval,[26] while Solana, speaking as the EU's foreign policy chief, explained that 'we oppose a preventive war against Iraq'.[27] However, not all EU member states took this position. Britain, Italy, Spain, the Netherlands, Portugal, Denmark and, much to Chirac's disgust, the former Communist states of Central Europe formed a 'vague almost alliance'[28] sympathetic to Washington's Iraq strategy.[29]

There was much less disagreement inside the EU over the Israel-Palestine issue. Before 9/11 the EU viewed the Bush administration's absence from the politics of the Israeli-Palestinian conflict as an opportunity to increase its own political influence. But in its wake, the EU stressed that the peace process needed to be resumed with US participation and without any preconditions in order to address the region's wider anti-Western grievances. Preoccupied with the hunt for Bin Laden, the war in Afghanistan and preparations for the war in Iraq, Washington had little interest.

European anger at the Bush administration's neglect of Palestine was dismissed by some US commentators as 'anti-American grandstanding';[30] others urged Europe 'to stop fretting'[31] over perceived differences with Washington. But there existed some very substantive divisions that were clear to all by early 2002. While Javier Solana embarked on shuttle diplomacy across the region to promote the Saudi plan, the US response was far more cautious, with the White House press spokesman only describing it as a 'note of hope'.[32] The Bush administration was even less enthusiastic about the French-driven attempt to use the Saudi proposals as the basis for a European initiative. During a tense meeting in Washington in the first week of February 2002, Solana and Moratinos received no support for the idea of moving straight to Palestinian statehood under the French 'non-paper'.[33]

In response the EU commission president, Romano Prodi, noted that 'it is clear that American mediation efforts have failed, and we need new mediation'.[34] An enraged Védrine was more explicit: 'If we're not in agreement with US policy, we must say it', and he told French radio that 'Europeans today are unanimous in disagreeing with the White House's Middle East policy'.[35] By mid-2002 the 'profound gap',[36] as one leading US commentator put it, between the US and EU approaches to dealing with the Israel-Palestine conflict in the post-9/11 world was infuriating EU officials. Some now chose to brief the media anonymously that 'cooperation between the Americans and the Europeans has collapsed'.[37]

In an interview with an Israeli newspaper, Fischer was asked, 'What is Europe bringing to the table here that the United States isn't? What's its distinctive role?' In response, he argued that its 'unified position' made the EU 'a real asset to the process…economically, politically [and] has good relations with the Arabs…Palestinians'.[38] But prominent figures such as the new Syrian President, Basher al-Assad, and the renowned Palestinian-American academic Edward Said demanded that the EU do more than simply discuss solutions. Rashid Khalidi, Said's Columbia University colleague, called on Europe to adopt a genuinely united policy on the Palestine issue and then take a stand against Washington.[39]

In early 2000, Arafat had acknowledged that 'Europe has a considerable political role to play in this region…this awareness since Venice, has guided European involvement, and it is high time for Europe to act as a full partner in the shaping of our common future'.[40] Following the collapse of Oslo, the Palestinian leadership was not averse to the EU playing a greater role in mediating the conflict; Arafat told a delegation of senior EU officials that 'we are looking forward to your role',[41] and other senior PA figures welcomed the 'involvement of Europe in the process'.[42]

The EU looked to increase its mediating role in the conflict wherever possible. In May 2002 Italy, Spain, Greece, Portugal, Ireland and Belgium offered sanctuary to Palestinian militants who had been under Israeli siege in the Church of the Nativity in Bethlehem for 39 days, though there was no uniform basis for admitting the men (described by the Israeli authorities as the 'most wanted of men') into the various host countries; indeed, as a Spanish official noted the exceptional nature of the case meant that each state had to 'find a formula within humanitarian law' in order to accommodate them.[43] Despite such gestures, Palestinian leaders still saw the EU role as secondary to that of the US. Although the PA welcomed the 'French ideas' of early 2002, it still sounded a note of caution and emphasised, in the words of Nabil Shaath, that the 'role of the Europeans will be to obtain a commitment from the US and to put pressure on [Israeli Prime Minister] Sharon'.[44]

Although Fischer protested to the contrary, one reason for this Palestinian reluctance to embrace the EU as a full partner was that it was still unable to unite fully behind one position. In late December 2001 Britain, Germany, Denmark and the Netherlands abstained on a UN General Assembly draft resolution criticising Israeli behaviour, while the other 11 EU member states voted in favour.[45] The British government publicly blocked French efforts to get the EU to endorse the immediate establishment of a Palestinian state in April 2002. Moreover, despite a growing consensus that the Bush administration was nothing more than the 'callow instrument of neo-conservative ideologues'[46] acting in the interests of Israel, few EU nations followed the French in publicly expressing contempt for US policies. Fischer had taken over the lead role from Védrine in promoting a European initiative in part because the French foreign minister had been so openly hostile to the 'overriding predominance of the United States in all areas and the current lack of any counterweight'.[47] In particular, Védrine spoke of the 'error' of US Palestine policy as a specific example of the gulf between the US and EU in international affairs.[48]

Jack Straw spoke for the majority of EU governments when he argued in a newspaper article highly critical of Védrine's approach that 'any attempt to push for a solution without American support would be shortsighted and self-defeating'.[49] Following an unproductive April 2002 peace mission to Israel the Spanish foreign minister, Josep Pique, acknowledged that 'a solution is not possible without the United States. They cannot resolve the problem on their own, but we need them'.[50] Solana, who had accompanied Pique on his trip, was no less adamant later in the month that 'to solve the problem, the active presence of the United States with the European Union is fundamental'.[51] More junior EU officials also briefed the media that 'the ball' was 'still in Washington's court. The peace plans are there…We are waiting for the US to take a position'.[52]

The EU's refusal to follow the French lead and break ranks with the US at the height of the Intifada was heralded by some as the reason why it was unable to match economic clout and assistance with the commensurate political influence.[53] But this more cautious strategy appeared to be paying certain dividends. On a visit to Egypt in April 2002 the US Secretary of State Colin Powell told his hosts that the US was considering supporting a 'mechanism' whereby observers would be sent to monitor the implementation of any ceasefire, something the EU had called for since the start of the Oslo era.

The following month, the EU welcomed the announcement by Powell of American backing for an International Quartet made up of the US, the UN, Russia and the EU. Fischer said that it signalled—for the first time since the Bush administration took office—that 'the United States is back in the driver's seat'.[54] Denmark's foreign minister Per Stig Moeller, in his role as EU president, called on the US to work together with the EU to start a 'new, concrete and realistic peace process'.[55]

In 2003, the Bush administration went even further, in agreeing to coordinate its Palestine policy with the EU, as well as the UN and Russia, under the Road Map framework. The Road Map was first conceived during the Danish presidency of the EU in 2002. It was a performance-based plan that called for a three-phase move to ending the conflict—a return to the situation before the Intifada broke out in 2000; the establishment of a Palestinian state with provisional borders; and a final negotiated agreement. It was not only a European idea originally, the EU was also the major external donor to the Palestinians under the framework. In July 2003 it signed off on €100 million to the PA to finance the Road Map, with Patten explaining that the 'regeneration' of the Palestinian economy would 'help build confidence and [is a] commitment to the peace process'.[56] It was, as he rightly described it, 'A Road Map paid for in Euros',[57] and the EU was increasingly viewed as 'Shareholder No. 1 in the Palestinian Authority'.[58]

The Palestinians, as in the Oslo era, still looked primarily to the US to play the lead political role leaving the EU, as one former French ambassador in the Middle East put it, 'to play the passive part of banker'.[59] In September 2002, Denmark's Per Stig Moeller first raised with Arafat the idea of a phased agreement followed by elections and a state; the Palestinian leader had accepted the idea 'in principle' but expressed the need for the EU to get US backing for the proposal.[60] The following year Arafat appeared to have forgotten the European origins of the proposal altogether when he called for EU leaders to do more to promote the US-backed Road Map.[61]

In a June 2002 meeting with Alastair Crooke, security adviser to the Middle East Envoy Moratinos, the Hamas leader Sheikh Ahmed Yassin explained that 'we place great hope in Europe', but added that 'instead of being dragged behind the American policy, it must at the very least say "no" and refuse to accept that policy'. Crooke responded that Europe was 'trying to implement an independent policy, but whenever we want to work with the Palestinians on one matter or another—and I'm not trying to pass criticism on the Palestinian Authority here—we notice a Palestinian tendency to work with Washington'.[62]

This perception was all the more demoralising given the EU's great efforts to protect Yasser Arafat's position in the post-Oslo era. In December 2001, EU leaders stated in no uncertain terms that they did 'not accept attempts to weaken or discredit Arafat'.[63] They also issued harsh warnings against Israel adopting a policy of 'asphyxiating' or marginalising the PA president in any future negotiations.[64] Writing in a Danish magazine in mid-2002, Solana acknowledged that the EU has 'worked hard to ensure that President Arafat could recover his capacity to act'.[65] In the same month Straw explained that Britain was committed to a peace process including Arafat, on the grounds that 'we do not choose the leaders we deal with. We just have to deal with who we have got'.[66]

The EU took particular offence at a perceived Israeli attempt to block Arafat from meeting EU foreign ministers when the PA President was prevented from travelling to Europe in January 2002. The following April a high-level EU delegation, including Solana and Pique, was denied access to Arafat, who was now under Israeli siege in his Ramallah headquarters.[67] In response, Solana argued that Israel could not dictate who met Arafat, and that he was 'not an obstacle to peace'.[68]

By 2003 Israel was refusing to meet foreign representatives who visited Arafat on the same visit to the region. The Spanish foreign minister made two official visits in a five-day period to avoid the Israeli boycott, while the Italian Prime Minister Silvio Berlusconi refused to meet Arafat at all when he travelled to the region. It was not until June 2003 that the Irish foreign minister, Brian Cowen, became the first high-ranking international diplomat to choose to meet Arafat rather than Israeli officials.[69]

When Arafat misled President Bush in January 2002 over his knowledge of an arms shipment intercepted by Israel on its way from Iran to Gaza, Washington expressly challenged EU support for the PA President and Bush accused Arafat of 'enhancing terror' in his January 2002 State of the Union address.[70] Later in the year, in direct response to the EU's description of Arafat as an 'indispensable' partner, the White House announced that its decision just made (in June) to end all contact with the PA President was 'final'.[71] Arafat attempted to put a brave face on the Bush administration's attitude, describing it as a 'serious effort to push the peace process forward'.[72] The EU was less diplomatic. At the G8 Summit in June 2002, EU leaders clashed with the US President over his decision to 'cast [Arafat] into outer darkness' as the *Economist* put it.[73] One European official attending the G8 meeting said Europe agreed that 'there is need to reform the Palestinian Authority but that does not mean that Arafat has to go…we are not going to tell Arafat to go'.[74]

The following year President Bush promised to publish the Road Map once the Palestinians appointed a prime minister who held 'real authority' and was a 'credible and responsible partner'.[75] In June he set out his 'vision' of 'two states living side by side in peace and security' but made US support for this conditional on a 'different Palestinian leadership'.[76] The EU had no problem with the US demand that Arafat cede power to a 'credible' alternative willing to bring transparent and democratic government to the Palestinians.[77] In 2002 Fischer had called for the appointment of a 'strong independent prime minister' to oversee the reform of the PA,[78] and Solana was no less categorical in his demand that the PA needed 'more transparency, more accountability, greater efficiency'.[79]

Mahmoud Abbas (Abu Mazen) was appointed as the PA's first ever prime minister in March 2003. The EU supported this move but it refused to condemn Arafat for opposing the disarming of militant groups, the first precondition of the Road Map, or for accusing Abu Mazen of not extracting greater concessions from Israel in return for a ceasefire even though the Road Map called for an immediate and unconditional ceasefire. Instead, the vast majority of EU leaders focused their criticism on President Bush's demand that Arafat give up political power and his refusal to meet the Palestinian leader during the last three years of his life.

Martin Indyk was one of many in Washington frustrated over all this. He argued that the Quartet was 'not a particularly useful mechanism' because with four mediators 'it is impossible to get anywhere'. Indyk held the EU primarily responsible for this impotence because it 'always out bid us on the Palestinian side. And the Palestinians will always have an opportunity to do an end run around us in the negotiations'.[80]

Following Abu Mazen's resignation from the post of prime minister in September 2003, citing Arafat's refusal to cooperate, the EU governments joined much of the international community in rejecting the Israeli cabinet's decision (in principle) to expel Arafat from Palestinian-controlled territories as a 'terrible mistake', a 'grave error' and 'not the best way to stabilise the situation'.[81]

By mid-February 2004 reports from the PA were noting the rising anger over the 'political bankruptcy' of the Arafat regime and the growing discontent even within Arafat's Fatah organisation.[82] Over a hundred Palestinian policemen, in a desperate attempt to draw attention to the failings of the PA leadership that it served, briefly occupied a security base run by members of Force 17, Arafat's personal bodyguard, in late May 2004. Before surrendering, they warned that unless something was done about corruption, thousands of their fellow officers would be forced to mutiny.[83]

The following month President Mubarak of Egypt, King Abdullah of Jordan and a number of prominent Palestinian officials and personalities gave Arafat an ultimatum to implement reforms. Khalil Shikaki, head of the Ramallah-based Centre for Policy and Survey Research, blamed the crisis of governance on the refusal of the Arafat-controlled Palestinian National Security Council to take measures 'to maintain public order'.[84] The Palestinian Legislative Council (the Palestinian parliament) also issued a report noting that the failure of Arafat and the PA to live up to the responsibilities of leadership was a significant contributing factor to the growing anarchy and disillusionment among the Palestinian people.[85] Even the UN, which had championed Palestinian rights since the 1970s, began to adopt a firmer approach to Arafat when it acknowledged that any security reforms that the PA had reluctantly agreed to implement had been 'slow and mostly cosmetic'.[86]

But the EU still refused to take Arafat to task for his part in Abu Mazen's failure to establish effective government, or to admonish the PA leader for ignoring, and in many cases causing, the chronic corruption and instability that plagued the PA. The IMF had estimated that in its first five years in existence between 1995 and 2000, the PA was unable to account for US$900 million. Even in 2003, despite the best efforts of Salam Fayyad, the former IMF official who had been appointed PA Finance Minister the previous year to implement new conditions for EU budgetary support, Arafat's office was unable to account for US$34 million of the US$74 million it spent.[87]

In August 2004, Arafat bowed to growing external and domestic pressure and grudgingly admitted that he had made 'unacceptable mistakes'. Soon afterwards, it became public knowledge that he was terminally ill and had only months to live. 'Mr Palestine', as he was known for his long-time embodiment of the Palestinian struggle, died in a French hospital in mid-November. In a highly symbolic display of solidarity, his coffin, draped with the Palestinian flag, was moved to the Villacoublay air force base and loaded onto a waiting military cargo plane by French soldiers while a military band played Chopin's Funeral March and the French and Palestinian national anthems. Arafat's body was then flown to Cairo accompanied by another plane, with France's foreign minister Michel Barnier on board.[88] Speaking on behalf of the EU Presidency, the Dutch foreign minister Bernard Bot paid tribute to Arafat as a 'historic leader' of the Palestinian cause. National leaders across the EU paid similar tributes while embassies, municipal offices and government buildings opened books of condolence for the European public to express their own feelings of loss on Arafat's death.

For Israelis from across the political spectrum it was difficult to understand the EU's tendency to uphold Arafat as a great statesman rather than reject him as an arch-terrorist. In their attempts to explain this some pointed to Europe's long-time indifference to the suffering of Israelis, which in turn was attributed to a visceral anti-Israeli feeling within Europe due to guilt over the Holocaust and a belief that Israel was the last bastion of colonialism in the Middle East. Some went even further and blamed it on anti-Semitism. Others explained it as the inevitable function of Europe's post-1945 world-view, which placed a premium on negotiation and non-confrontation as well as a commitment to finding economic solutions to political problems. In 2002, Harry Kney-Tal, Israel's Ambassador in Brussels, explained that as the largest financial donor to the PA since its establishment, the EU 'simply cannot accept' that Arafat or the Palestinian leadership was either inherently opposed to peace or incapable of reform as this would 'entail rejection of the creature they've created'. Kney-Tel also argued that the EU had refused 'to play any part in a process that might lead to the collapse of the Palestinian side'.[89] Certainly, many Israelis, including those on the Left who wholeheartedly endorsed Oslo, were angered at what they interpreted as the EU's determination to apportion blame equally for a crisis that most of them believed was initiated, and perpetuated, by the Palestinian leadership either directly or through incitement.

Israeli officials, with much public support, were very wary lest Europe should attempt to embark on an independent policy and push the process forward on its own.[90] In these terms the mid-February 2002 publication by *Ha'aretz*[91] of Moratinos' account of what happened at the Taba talks the previous year, and its subsequent dismissal as 'utter nonsense' by Israelis who attended the meeting, was of note.[92] So was the statement by Victor Harel, the head of the Israeli foreign ministry's Western Europe department, that Israel 'expect[s] more from the EU...a much more balanced and unbiased approach'.[93]

Ariel Sharon, a politician who had long been discounted as a realistic candidate for prime minister, defeated Ehud Barak in national elections in February 2001. On taking office he was consistently suspicious of European intentions. Speaking at a press conference in 2003, he made it clear that the EU could only play a future role in peace negotiations if its 'attitude towards Israel and the Arabs and the Palestinians [is] ... balanced'.[94] In taking this position, Sharon had the backing of much of the Israeli electorate, as demonstrated by a mid-2003 poll finding that 74 per cent of Israelis believed the EU unfairly favoured the Palestinian side. Israel's foreign minister Silvan Shalom admitted, 'I find myself challenged to convince the Israeli people that the EU is a partner we can trust'.[95]

Relations worsened following the publication of a number of lengthy reports by both the Israeli government and pro-Israeli organisations in the US and Europe[96] claiming that EU funds had been misappropriated by the PA for propaganda and terror purposes. In response to the call by over 170 MEPs for answers to these accusations, the EU anti-Fraud Office (OLAF) opened an investigation 'in relation to allegations of misuse of funds donated by the European Union in the context of EU budgetary support to the Palestinian Authority'.[97]

OLAF's findings were inconclusive, but the charges were rejected by top EU officials, with Patten dismissing the claim that the Palestinians received EU money with 'no strings attached' as 'complete balls' and a 'total fabrication'.[98] By mid-2003 Israel claimed to be in possession of documents confiscated during raids on PA offices in the West Bank proving that EU aid was being used to fund terror attacks against Israeli civilians. As a consequence the Sharon government announced that there would be 'no Europeans' in any monitoring process implemented under the Road Map framework.[99]

In October 2003, Yossi Beilin, an architect of Oslo, and the former Labour party leader Amram Mitzna, joined forces with two former PA ministers, Yasser Abed Rabbo and Nabil Kassis, to launch a peace plan.[100] This Geneva initiative, as it was known, was an unofficial proposal promoted in a private capacity, but it gained the public backing of the EU, including an offer of US$7 million from France and Belgium towards the cost of promoting it inside Israel.[101] This was denounced as EU interference in domestic politics by the Israeli government and further complicated relations.

In late 2004, an internal Israeli government report was leaked to the media predicting that relations with Europe would deteriorate further and the EU would look to harness its growing power to isolate Israel.[102] Such concerns were a response to Israel's increasing unpopularity across Europe. In November 2003, an EU commissioned survey found that 59 per cent of Europeans believed that Israel posed a threat to world peace; this was a higher percentage than those who saw Pakistan, North Korea or Iran posing a similar problem.[103]

Israeli attitudes were also fuelled by the growing support for an academic, cultural and economic boycott of Israel across the EU. In 2004, the Irish branch of the International Palestine Solidarity Campaign (PSC) submitted a petition—signed by 275 European parliamentarians, 210 European NGOs, and 12,000 Irish citizens—calling for sanctions against Israel. The PSC also sponsored the Boycott Israeli Goods campaigns across Europe, an effort that targets Israeli products like sage, rosemary, basil, coriander, thyme, oranges, and potatoes. For its part, a British group called Architects and Planners for Justice in Palestine called for an economic boycott of Israel's construction industry.

Then came the April 2005 decision of Britain's 48,000-strong Association of University Teachers (AUT) to boycott two Israeli universities, followed nine months later by the General Synod of the Church of England's announcement that it would back a campaign urging disinvestment in companies 'profiting' from Israel's occupation of the West Bank. And while the AUT's boycott was quickly rescinded owing to heavy international pressure by Jewish academics and organisations, a year later a larger teaching union, the National Association of Teachers in Further and Higher Education (NATFHE), voted to boycott Israeli academics and institutions of learning that did not disassociate themselves from the government's 'apartheid' policy in the occupied territories.

Britain's Prime Minister Tony Blair worked hard during this period to convince Israel that the EU had no intention of isolating or boycotting it and would not let the endemic hostility towards Israel across Europe's growing Muslim population negatively influence bilateral ties. Throughout the turbulent years of the al-Aqsa Intifada, Blair also avoided the inflammatory and even derogatory language employed by other EU leaders. This did not prevent some public statements and comments emanating from both Downing Street and the Foreign Office that fuelled Anglo-Israeli tensions.

Both the Foreign Secretary Jack Straw and Cherie Blair, the wife of the Prime Minister, made the headlines for appearing to express sympathy with the motives, if not the actions, of Palestinian suicide bombers. But in April 2002, when much of Europe was wrongly accusing Israel of genocide during its military operations in the Palestinian town of Jenin, it was the Blair government that opposed the decision to condemn Israel at the UN Human Rights Commission. France, Spain, Sweden, Portugal and Belgium backed the resolution. Again, it was the Blair government that took the lead inside the EU in demanding a crackdown on the Islamist group Hamas, urging the introduction of strict limits on charities raising funds for the organisation in Europe.

Blair quickly came to be viewed as one of the best friends Israel ever had in Downing Street. Zvi Shtauber, Israel's Ambassador in London between 2001 and 2004, argued that, Germany aside, Blair's Britain was the 'most pro-Israeli country in Europe'.[104] In an interview in the British media on the eve of a 2004 visit to London, even Sharon was full of praise for Blair, a 'friend of Israel' whose efforts made the Israeli prime minister think that 'Europe and Britain should be involved more here in the political process'.[105]

Blair's relatively sympathetic approach to Israel was not, as one senior French diplomat wrongly claimed, due to his obsession with keeping Washington happy.[106] Far from Britain playing a 'blind, apparently subservient role' vis-à-vis the US,[107] as the former US President Jimmy Carter charged, the Palestine issue was actually a major thorn in Anglo-American relations. As one senior Foreign Office official later acknowledged, it was the 'most difficult, protracted issue between us and the Americans over the whole ten-year period of Blair's premiership'.[108] In early October 2002, for example, Bush rebuffed Blair's call for 'a 'massive mobilisation of energy to get the peace process moving again'.[109] Three years later, in 2005, Bush and Blair disagreed publicly over the EU's plan to recognise a Palestinian state immediately. Bush explained during a

White House meeting with Abbas in May 2005 that this was the wrong way forward because democratisation had to precede, rather than follow, such a move.[110]

Blair certainly had no need to win over Israel for domestic reasons. As noted above, British teaching unions led Europe in calling for a boycott of Israeli academic institutions. Much of the British media, including the BBC and national newspapers like the *Independent* and *Guardian*, were among the most hostile critics of Israel in Europe during the Intifada. Between 2001 and 2004, for example, the BBC aired 20 major documentaries on Israel and its conflict with the Palestinians, one every two to three months, and 88 per cent of these documentaries 'paint either a negative impression of Israel or (in two cases) a positive image of the Palestinians'.[111] In 2002, a Guardian/ICM opinion poll showed that British voters who claimed to have more sympathy for Palestinians outnumbered two to one those who said they supported Israel.[112] A January 2005 British poll asking respondents to rate two dozen countries on the basis of twelve separate criteria voted Israel the country least worthy of international respect and one of the world's 'least democratic countries'; Israel came bottom in four of the twelve categories and in the bottom five in all the remaining categories.[113] By 2007, 65 per cent of respondents to a BBC poll believed that Israel had a 'mainly negative' influence.[114]

While Blair believed that the British position in the Middle East was 'somewhat unique',[115] his more conciliatory approach to Israel compared with his EU partners was not a way of asserting an independent British policy. As far back as 1998, during his government's first presidency of the EU, Blair underlined his commitment to coordinate Palestine policy with his EU partners. For the most part he honoured that commitment. In early 2001, the Blair government supported the EU's public condemnation of Israel's destruction of EU-funded infrastructural projects in the occupied territories, a move orchestrated by Chris Patten, Blair's nominee for the post of EU External Affairs Commissioner. The Labour government also joined its EU partners in opposing Israel's policy of targeted assassination of known Palestinian militant leaders and, unmoved by Israeli foreign minister Silvan Shalom's explanation that it was 'a security fence, not a political fence',[116] it also expressed opposition to the construction of Israel's security barrier/separation fence that was erected through parts of Palestinian territory during the Intifada.

However, having found himself in the middle of an acrimonious breakdown in the transatlantic alliance after 9/11, Blair's primary goal was to minimise the increase in tension between the US and the EU due to the Israel-Palestine conflict. As he explained in a 2002 interview, 'I regard it as one of my tasks to say to people the whole time, don't pull apart Europe and America...the only people who rejoice in those circumstances are the bad guys'. This explains his pledge to make the resolution of the conflict his own 'personal priority' as well as a 'central priority' of British foreign policy, and hence his description of this tragic feud as the 'single most pressing political challenge in our world'.[117]

In March 2002, while Javier Solana and the governments of France, Sweden, Ireland, Belgium and Greece were explicit in their condemnations of Israel's increased isolation of Arafat in Ramallah, Britain (in the company of Germany) chose only to call for restraint and a return to negotiations on both sides.[118] The following June, unlike most other EU leaders who condemned President Bush's statement calling on Arafat to give up political power, Blair expressed understanding for this approach. In early July 2003, following a visit to Arafat by a junior Foreign Office minister, Downing Street issued a statement expressing support for the visit but added that 'it is no secret that we believe that Yasser Arafat is somebody who has let down the Palestinian people. We do not believe that the PA...and Arafat have done all they could do to bear down on terrorism'.[119]

But at the same time his government steadfastly refused to abandon the Palestinian leader. At a London meeting with Blair in mid 2003, Ariel Sharon argued that continued British support for Arafat was an obstacle to the peace process. In response Blair was adamant that Britain would continue to deal with Arafat because he was the legally elected head of the Palestinians, and because there was no way to influence him in a positive way except by contact.[120]

Overall, Blair's outlook benefited Israeli interests on occasion, but he did not hesitate to adopt a stance detrimental to Israel when he felt that this was the best way to bring the EU closer to Washington. From the time of the invasion of Iraq in March 2003, and following Arafat's death in November 2004, Blair spent much of the political capital he had earned since 9/11 trying to influence President Bush to make concessions on the Palestine issue that Israel opposed but which he felt would help reduce resentment in Europe over the Iraq war. Both Blair and Straw antagonised Israel by publicly linking the Iraq crisis to the Israel-Palestine conflict on more than one occasion, with Straw going somewhat further than his prime minister in remarking that the West was guilty of a certain amount of hypocrisy in its response to Israel's lack of compliance with UN resolutions compared with the West's own response to Iraq's non-compliance.[121]

Blair, who arrived in Washington for a meeting with Bush on the day of Arafat's death, considered the passing of the long-time Palestinian leader as a real opportunity for building bridges. He urged Bush to support the convening of an international conference on the peace process, something that Israel had opposed for decades. Again, in the immediate aftermath of Arafat's death, believing that Abbas' accession to the top post provided the opportunity for a reinvigorated peace process, the EU once more looked to take the initiative. Solana put forward a proposal to re-launch the Road Map in a 'less incremental manner'.[122] This diplomatic language was widely interpreted as nothing more than a restatement of France's 2002 proposal for immediate recognition of a Palestinian state. Blair had opposed it then because he believed that it would damage US-EU ties; he supported it in 2005 because he believed that it would bring the US and EU closer together.

Blair also took a lead role in the EU response to Israel's decision to withdraw unilaterally from Gaza in August 2005. This unprecedented decision led to the dismantling of all 21 Jewish settlements in Gaza (as well as four in the northern West Bank).[123] Across the EU the move was viewed as the first stage of a complete Israeli withdrawal from territories captured during the 1967 war, as well as the first real opportunity since the 1994 Cairo Agreement established Palestinian self-rule in Gaza and Jericho for the Palestinians to govern themselves, free from Israeli military intervention or settlements.

The five criteria that the EU insisted Israel must meet before it would support any unilateral disengagement made clear its overriding interest. Firstly, it had to take place in the context of the Road Map, which in its original form called for a permanent status agreement on the boundaries of a Palestinian state between Israel and the PA no later than the end of 2005. The EU also insisted that the disengagement process had to be a step towards a two-state solution; it could not involve a transfer of settlement activity to the West Bank, and must involve an organised and negotiated handover of responsibility to the PA. In addition, it demanded that Israel should facilitate the rehabilitation and reconstruction of Gaza.[124]

Satisfied that Israel was serious about meeting all these requirements, the EU acknowledged the huge political and personal risks that Sharon had taken by going through with his disengagement plan in the face of staunch domestic opposition. Praise was forthcoming even before the implementation of disengagement. In June 2005 President Chirac, who had cancelled a planned visit by the Israeli leader a year earlier, invited Sharon to Paris. Calling the Gaza disengagement 'determined and courageous', the French President commented, 'more than ever, France with its European partners wants to be by your side so that the withdrawal sets off a positive dynamic'.[125] Even the former foreign minister Védrine, an outspoken critic of Israel since the collapse of Oslo, credited Sharon with having 'removed the stumbling block' by leaving Gaza.[126] Following the successful completion of the disengagement plan in August, Blair summed up the general attitude among EU leaders when he wrote to Sharon:

I greatly admire the courage with which you have developed and implemented this policy. I believe you are right to see disengagement as an opportunity to pursue a better future for Israelis and Palestinians. I look forward to working with you to help achieve this, and to continue working together towards a just and lasting peace, free from the scourge of terrorism.[127]

The EU's foreign policy chief, Javier Solana, was the first high-level international visitor to the region after the disengagement. Solana praised the work of the IDF, and the political leadership that oversaw disengagement:

Sharon kept his word, and did so in an intelligent and professional manner. The IDF acted professionally, by the book, and reduced the potential damage. There was a government decision here, approved by the parliament, and that is how a democratic country behaves. The law was implemented and that should be emphasised, considering the difficulty involved in the operation.[128]

Solana was followed to Israel by the French foreign minister, Philippe Douste-Blazy, and his Spanish counterpart, Miguel Ángel Moratinos, who commended Israel in the wake of disengagement: 'Sharon had the courage to make the decision, which was implemented in a highly professional manner'.[129]

Following its practice at every stage since the beginning of the Oslo process in the early 1990s, the EU pledged significant sums of money to help the Palestinians develop Gaza's infrastructure and economy following the Israeli withdrawal. At the March 2005 London Meeting on Supporting the Palestinian Authority, Blair announced that the EU would be providing US$330 million for this purpose. In July, France,

Britain, Italy and Germany were part of the G8 group of leading industrial nations that promised a further US$3 billion for Gaza. In September, just weeks after the Gaza withdrawal, the EU announced that it would increase its 2005 funding to the Palestinians to over US$340 million, around 17 per cent more than originally planned. In the same year the PA also expected to receive an additional US$270 million in donations from individual EU member states.[130] At the end of 2005 the European Commission announced that the EU intended to double its annual aid to the PA between 2006 and 2008 in order to fund the reform of the Palestinian civil service, finance election observer missions, rebuild air and sea ports in Gaza, and help the Palestinians find investments and markets for their goods.[131]

In addition to providing funds to the PA, in November the EU agreed to 'undertake the third party role proposed in the agreement' and to launch, 'as a matter of urgency', an EU Border Assistance Mission (BAM) to monitor the operation of crossing points at Rafah on the Egyptian-Gaza border.[132] This was part of the EU's revamped European Security and Defence Policy (ESDP), the successor to the CSFP. Although officials acknowledged that the EU would play a supporting role on the border and admitted that 'there is not much we can do until the two parties agree on the role of the third party',[133] this was a notable development as it entailed Israeli acceptance of the EU's third party role in security matters.

EU leaders also began to urge Abbas and the governing Fatah party to try harder to re-establish control over Gaza, in the face of growing Hamas influence, before the legislative elections scheduled for January 2006. Blair told Abbas that 'more clearly needs to be done for the Palestinian Authority to make a success of governing Gaza... Your personal leadership will be crucial'.[134] Solana was insistent that 'both for the sake of disengagement, but also to promote a return to political negotiations afterward, the PA must move against those individuals and groups who continue to use violence'.[135] In late September 2005, the International Quartet threw its weight behind this argument, urging the PA 'to maintain law and order and dismantle terrorist capabilities and infrastructure'.[136] With the success of the unilateral withdrawal from Gaza providing a real opportunity for improved relations with Israel and a practical involvement on the ground through the Rafah border mission, the EU seemed poised to finally establish itself in the role it believed it deserved. Little did its leaders know that very soon an upheaval in internal Palestinian politics would challenge this newfound status directly.

10

THE BEST LAID PLANS

'The Middle Eastern conflict has a vitality of its own.'
Zbigniew Brzezinski

In January 2006, the Islamic Resistance Movement, better known by its Arabic acronym Hamas, found little resistance among voters as it stormed to victory in the Palestinian legislative elections. Three months earlier, in a speech before an audience of American Jewish leaders, Ariel Sharon had described such a future development as 'unbearable'.[1] Now his government faced the dilemma of either engaging with Hamas politicians who openly called for Israel's destruction or refusing to deal with the legitimately-elected representatives of the Palestinian people. Hamas gained 74 out of the 132 parliamentary seats, and this victory posed an even more formidable problem for Mahmoud Abbas, whose Fatah party had been badly beaten at the polls.[2]

Hamas was the offspring of the Palestinian branch of the Muslim Brotherhood established in Gaza in the wake of the June 1967 war. It rose to prominence as a serious player in internal Palestinian politics during the first Intifada with its outspoken opposition to the Israeli occupation, its challenge to Fatah's attempt to 'dominate control of the uprising'[3] and its provision of shelter for orphans, widows, the elderly and families displaced during the crisis.

By 1990–91 Hamas, with the growing support of Iran, was publicly calling for an alternative to PLO leadership in the occupied territories. Its propaganda war also turned violent, with clashes between pro-Hamas and pro-Fatah groups in Gaza and those West Bank towns like Nablus where Hamas had its strongest following. At the same time Hamas consolidated its position by developing an extensive social services network that included clinics, kindergartens, primary and secondary schools, orphanages, colleges, summer camps, sports clubs and even matchmaking agencies. Most of these services were free or charged nominal fees. Hamas-run clinics in the West Bank and Gaza treated patients for less than one-fifth of the cost of going to a private clinic and prescriptions were almost always free for needy families. By the time Israel and the PLO signed the Oslo Accords in 1993, one in three Palestinians in Gaza received some kind of financial support from Hamas. In the West Bank it was one in five.[4] This significant role in Palestinian society meant that by the time that Arafat and the PLO leadership arrived in the Palestinian territories from their former base in Tunis in July 1994, they faced significant 'competition for the hearts and minds of Palestinians'.[5]

This was especially true in Gaza where much of the population were either grateful beneficiaries of Hamas' social welfare handouts or suspicious of the newly-arrived PLO elite, which apart from Arafat had little grassroots support. As early as 1994 Gaza's chief pollster told *Ha'aretz* that he refused to ask respondents if they supported Arafat, on the grounds that such a question would be too embarrassing.[6] In the same year other informed commentators were noting that Hamas 'dominates the streets of Gaza' and that 'true democratic elections in Gaza will only bring the Islamic fundamentalists to power'.[7]

On their signing in September 1993, Hamas immediately rejected the Oslo Accords and refused to participate in any of the PA institutions established within the Oslo framework. It also boycotted the Palestinian legislative and presidential elections in the West Bank and Gaza in 1996 on the grounds that participation in the ballot would legitimise the Oslo process that it opposed. Instead, it focused its energies on organising anti-Oslo demonstrations and boycotts and on leading the Palestinian terror assault on Israel between 1993 and 2000. It also engaged Fatah militarily and in late 1994, shortly after the Fatah-run PA took control of Gaza, 16 died and over 200 were injured in Hamas-Fatah clashes at Gaza's Palestine Mosque.[8]

Despite numerous attempts to calm the internal divisions, culminating in a meeting between PA and Hamas officials in Cairo in 1995, little progress was made on the political front. Instead, following a spate of

Hamas suicide bombings in March 1996, the PA was pressured by Israel and the US to jail hundreds of known Hamas activists. For the remainder of the Oslo era, a PA security crackdown and Hamas' tactical decision to limit its military campaign against Israel resulted in a lull in the group's activities.

The collapse of Oslo highlighted the extent of the divide inside Hamas between those who favoured engaging in the political process and those who preferred to continue the twin strategy of social welfare payments and violent struggle. Because of Palestinian frustration over the failure of Oslo to bring peace, public support for suicide attacks had doubled from 20 to 40 per cent over the course of the 1990s.[9] But at the same time polls were also providing an increasingly persuasive argument in support of those looking to take the political route. In August 2001, a Palestinian poll gave Hamas 27 per cent of the vote in Gaza compared to 26 per cent for Fatah.[10] By 2005 there was majority support for the view, expressed by Hamas' West Bank spokesman Hassan Yousef, that 'we can no longer leave the decision-making to one political stream [Fatah]'.[11] In the third round of the Palestinian municipal elections in May 2005, Hamas won 27 local councils compared to Fatah's 33, gaining more than twice as many votes as Fatah—450,000 compared to 190,000.[12] This result led Abbas to postpone the parliamentary elections to the PNC, first from July to November and then to January 2006. This served only to further alienate a Palestinian electorate keen to demonstrate dissatisfaction with Fatah rule at the ballot box.[13]

By the time Israel unilaterally disengaged from Gaza in August 2005, Hamas ruled the Gaza streets. Boasting on its official website that it had killed more Israelis in Gaza than any other militant group, it skilfully convinced a large section of the Palestinian population that its strategy of violence, rather than the PA's diplomacy, had forced Israel out of the area. Abbas, the leader of a faction-ridden Fatah, now found himself in the unenviable position of facing a power struggle against a highly moti-vated and disciplined Hamas to fill the vacuum following the Israeli departure

In late 2005, when EU leaders like Javier Solana and Tony Blair, as well as the International Quartet, pleaded with Abbas 'to maintain law and order and dismantle terrorist capabilities and infrastructure',[14] they were primarily thinking of Abbas' previous inability to disarm or dismantle Hamas while PA Prime Minister in 2003 and following his accession to the PA presidency after Arafat's death in late 2004.[15] But the EU's Hamas policy was no more coherent or consistent than that of Abbas and Fatah. From 2001, when the EU first adopted the US precedent of annually publishing its terrorist blacklist, there began a major debate over whether Hamas should be added to that list. In December 2001, the EU agreed to proscribe Izzedin al-Kassam, Hamas' military wing, but the majority view remained that Hamas' political wing had a role to play in the political process and should not be isolated.

This differed from the evolving US position in the wake of 9/11. In his infamous 'Axis of Evil' State of the Union address in January 2002, President Bush classified Hamas as one of four non-state Islamist groups (along with Hezbollah, Islamic Jihad and Jaish-e-Mohammed) that were enemies of the US. Over the coming year the US Department of Justice stepped up its investigations into Hamas finances and the State Department became increasingly outspoken in its calls for the EU to add Hamas to its terror list.[16]

There was no consensus on the issue inside the EU. In December 2002, the Middle East Envoy Miguel Moratinos told the European Parliament's Foreign Affairs Committee that Hamas still faced 'a clear choice between the Turkish model of democratic Islam, and the Al-Qaeda model'.[17] Spain, Ireland, Belgium, Greece and France all shared a similar reluctance to write off Hamas' political potential, with the Élysée Palace explaining that only 'if a conclusion will be reached that Hamas [and Islamic Jihad] are terror organisations that do not want peace, then it may be necessary to change the European position'.[18] Britain, the Netherlands, Portugal and Italy rejected this 'wait and see' approach on the grounds that, as Jack Straw argued, the military and political wings of Hamas were 'extensively intertwined [in] literally trying to blow [up] this peace process'.[19]

In June 2003, after meeting the EU Commission President Romano Prodi and the Greek foreign minister Costas Simitis in Washington, President Bush was categorical: 'In order for there to be peace Hamas must be dismantled…I urge the leaders of Europe to take swift, decisive action'.[20] The Hamas decision to agree to a three-month ceasefire in July 2003 somewhat relieved US pressure on the EU to take a decision, but the renewal of suicide attacks against Israel in August, in response to the targeted assassination of a top Hamas official, marked a decisive shift in European attitudes.[21] In September, EU foreign ministers agreed to des-

ignate the political wing of Hamas a terrorist organisation. This prohib-
ited contact between the EU and the Islamist group, and member states
were required to place financial restrictions on Hamas and provide each
other with the widest possible assistance through police and judicial coordination in order to counter the group's operations.[22]

In late 2004, in the course of a BBC interview, Solana divulged that
he had held secret meetings with Hamas officials in the period of uncertainty and opportunity following Yasser Arafat's death.[23] Although he
subsequently retracted this statement,[24] the incident underlined the EU's
ongoing failure to develop and apply a consistent approach to Hamas.

Those inside the EU who supported the blacklisting of Hamas, including the serving governments of the member states, pointed out that
between 2000 and 2004 the group was estimated to have carried out 425
terrorist attacks that killed 377 Israelis (including 53 suicide bombings
that claimed 289 victims). They also pointed to Hamas' rejection of all
talk of truce following Arafat's death and the very public statements by
senior Hamas officials calling for the destruction of Israel and explaining
the decision to accept a truce brokered by Abbas and Sharon at Sharm
el-Sheik in February 2005 in purely tactical terms. This was certainly a
powerful argument. Speaking at the Conference of the International
Campaign Against American and Zionist Occupation in Cairo in 2005,
Muhammad Nasal, a senior Hamas figure, told 1,000 delegates that his
group's ceasefire was 'a fighter's rest to rebuild the Palestinian house' as
'resistance is the only way we can liberate our lands'.[25] Khaled Mashal,
the Damascus-based head of Hamas' political wing, spoke in similar
terms. He refused to accept 'the 1967 borders alone and see it as a permanent solution', and following Israel's Gaza disengagement he predicted
that 'today it is Gaza, tomorrow it will be the West Bank, and later it will
be all of the Land—it is the beginning of the end of Israel'.[26]

There also existed an increasingly outspoken group of European politicians, civil servants, political advisers, and security officials who believed
that it had been a major miscalculation to place Hamas on the EU's terror
list, and that the West must create a framework for discussions with
Hamas and other Islamist groups.[27] Alistair Crooke, a former British
intelligence officer and former adviser to the European Commission who
acted as the EU's liaison with Islamist groups in the West Bank and Gaza
from 1997 to 2003, promoted this argument most effectively. From 2002
onwards Crooke held a series of secret talks with Hamas and other Isla-

mist groups, and when these became public he became the most vocal champion of European engagement with Hamas.[28]

The Hamas success in the May 2005 municipal elections gave credibility to those in Europe calling for dialogue with the group. They argued that Hamas' electoral victory was no real cause for concern and that the group's growing legitimacy at the ballot box would cause it to morph from a militant organisation into an ordinary political party that eschewed violence and terrorism—as had other revolutionary movements in the Third World. *The Times* encapsulated this increasingly popular view: 'The very fact that Hamas is participating in elections is a bonus for Mr. Abbas's strategy to wean the gunmen off violence by co-opting them into the political process'.[29]

The Hamas municipal election victory even appeared to be winning over policy-makers in the Netherlands and Britain, the original sponsors of the Hamas ban. The Dutch foreign ministry urged the EU to consider revising its Hamas policy; while contrary to the statements of Foreign Secretary Straw, Foreign Office officials acknowledged that they were engaged in 'limited, low-profile, working-level contacts in the occupied territories with Hamas politicians not implicated in violence'.[30] By mid-June 2005 the EU was informing Washington that European diplomats below ambassadorial level were maintaining contacts with Hamas members seeking election to the Palestinian parliament.[31] Hamas officials confirmed this. Mushir al-Masri, a spokesman for the group in Gaza, admitted that EU diplomats had discussed both municipal and wider political issues with Hamas mayors. His colleague, Mohammed Ghazal, was even more specific: 'Every ten days to two weeks we have at least one meeting with a European diplomat'.[32]

Despite these increasing contacts, the Hamas election victory in the 2006 legislative elections caught European policy-makers by surprise. Patten noted the 'astonishment of the West's diplomatic and intelligence services'[33] following the election. Even Tony Blair, who was more involved in the intricacies of the conflict than most of his EU counterparts, was taken aback. One official who worked closely with him on Middle East issues acknowledged that 'no one had expected the result….the election had been intended as a way of neutralising Hamas and for it to suddenly turn round and bite us in that way was astonishing'.[34]

The Israelis' unilateral withdrawal from Gaza had resulted in a significant improvement in EU-Israeli diplomatic ties, and the EU's attempt to insert itself into the politics of the Israel-Palestine conflict in the final months of 2005 had been successful. This was most apparent in Israel's approval of the EU monitoring role on the highly sensitive Rafah border. It had been hoped that Fatah would repeat its previous emphatic victory in the 1996 elections and that this would further consolidate the EU's involvement in the final status negotiations when they inevitably arrived. The Hamas victory shattered these hopes as Fatah was weakened, perhaps fatally. Israel was demanding that the EU embrace fully its own policy of isolating Hamas and even the EU border mission became increasingly untenable.

In the immediate aftermath of the election result, the Austrian presidency of the EU, speaking on behalf of what was now a 25-nation bloc, acknowledged that the Palestinian people had 'voted democratically and peacefully' for Hamas. But it issued a statement calling for 'all factions to disarm, renounce violence and recognise Israel's right to exist'. It also made clear that the EU believed that there was 'no place in a political process for groups or individuals who advocate violence'.[35] Thus it called for Hamas to recognise Israel, abandon terror, and abide by previously signed international agreements before the EU would engage with it. This echoed the statement by President Bush following the elections that 'a party that articulates the destruction of Israel is a party with which we will not deal'.[36]

Israel had welcomed the original EU decision to blacklist Hamas in September 2003, but by mid-2005 it had become increasingly disillusioned with the EU's developing ties with the group and warned Brussels that 'anything that demonstrates acceptance of Hamas as a legitimate player is a problem'.[37] Hence Israeli officials responded to the EU's categorical rejection of engagement with an unreformed Hamas following its election victory with a mixture of relief and uncertainty, intensified after seemingly contradictory statements by Solana in February. During a trip to Cairo he was clear that in order for Hamas to be eligible to play a role in the political process it had to say yes to 'peace, …two states, and the recognition of the other [Israel]'.[38] On his return to Europe Solana was less emphatic, telling a gathering of MEPs that 'at the moment, we can't regard Hamas as an appropriate partner' but that the EU 'doesn't and shouldn't want the Hamas government to fail'.[39]

The EU's response to the decision of Russia, its partner in the International Quartet, to invite senior members of Hamas to Moscow in the same month was no less ambiguous. Solana explained that the EU had 'no problem' with the Russian invitation;[40] France's Prime Minister Dominique de Villepin described it as an 'important historic event', though one his own country disagreed with.[41] Not for the first or last time de Villepin's rhetorical style baffled observers, and a report published the same month by the Congressional Research Service of the US Library of Congress stated that the Russian move was made 'with French support'.[42]

Within months of the Hamas-dominated Palestinian parliament's swearing-in on 18 February, Sweden granted a visa to a Hamas government minister. Shortly afterwards Italy's foreign minister, Massimo d'Alema, asserted that Hamas, unlike al-Qaeda, had a 'political side', and compared the group to the Irish Republican Army (IRA) and the Basque Fatherland and Liberty Organisation (ETA). Subsequently his Prime Minister, Romano Prodi, was reported to have called for the EU to deal with the 'democratic and cooperative Hamas, rather than [support] its marginalisation'.[43] Finland's foreign minister, Erkki Tuomioja, also suggested that the EU should work with Hamas, claiming that 'it is not the same party it was before the elections'.[44] The former EU External Relations Commissioner, Chris Patten now a member of the British House of Lords, was even more to the point: Europe's policy of boycotting the Hamas government was pointless and it was 'high time to get real'.[45]

Solana also appeared to be backtracking. Following a meeting with the Israeli foreign minister, Tzipi Livni, in Tel Aviv in late 2006 he told reporters that it was 'not impossible' for Hamas to change and added, 'I don't think the essence of Hamas is the destruction of Israel. The essence of Hamas is the liberation of the Palestinians'.[46] By the end of the year the EU had endorsed a peace plan put forward by France, Spain and Italy comprising five points, none of which explicitly demanded that Hamas recognise Israel's right to exist.[47]

It was such mixed messages that engendered the belief among senior Hamas officials that they could have '[both] weapons and the legislative council' and that there would be no need to 'sell our policies for money' in order to develop a formal relationship with the EU.[48] Hamas' belief that the EU would inevitably begin dealing with it on normal terms and that this would, in turn, gradually lead to more widespread international legitimacy was also based upon its assessment of the approach used with great success by Yasser Arafat and the PLO from the early 1970s onwards. Despite tough European talk about how the PLO needed to abandon its violent struggle and accept Israel's right to exist, the group managed to normalise its position in Europe via backdoor channels. As noted previously, although the PLO was not an official party to the EAD established in 1974, its representatives could travel to Europe for ostensibly non-political reasons as members of EAD delegations. This led to the PLO's gradual political acceptance in key European capitals like Paris and Bonn. The willingness of EEC governments, as well as Spain, Austria and Portugal, to host PLO officials and the Community's endorsement of the PLO's increasingly formal status at the UN also provided the group with further recognition on the international stage.

In a 2005 interview in the Italian media, Franco Frattine, the European Commissioner for Justice, Freedom and Security, described initial attempts by Hamas to make contact with the EU as 'a stone thrown in a pool' to evaluate how the EU would respond to its overtures, adding that the group's international priority was 'gaining legitimacy within the EU'.[49] In an April 2006 interview in *The Times*, Mahmoud Zahar, foreign minister in the Hamas-led government, acknowledged this tactic and promised that he was 'ready to go to Europe to the countries that are ready to accept us'.[50] The following month the Hamas minister Atef Edwane visited Germany in an unofficial capacity after gaining a visa from Sweden to enter Europe. Edwane met three German parliamentarians for what was described as 'a private, unofficial exchange of ideas'. Hamas hoped that this 'unofficial exchange of ideas', which a displeased German Chancellor Angela Merkel described as 'vexing',[51] would follow the PLO precedent during the 1970s and prepare the way for Hamas officials to meet senior politicians in Europe and beyond on a more formal basis. Soon after Edwane's visit, it was reported that a group of senior US Democrats met Hamas representatives in an undisclosed European country. A Hamas source quoted on the matter claimed that it had been previous meetings with European representatives that 'broke the ice' and facilitated the group's discussions with this influential US delegation.[52]

Just when it looked as though Europe would prove the Hamas strategy correct and succumb to its efforts to gain legitimacy by bringing it in from the cold, the group's mid-2007 overthrow of Fatah in Gaza ended any chance of this happening. In only four days, Hamas overran Fatah strongholds and seized control of all of Gaza in what the PA President Abbas described as a 'criminal war' and an 'armed rebellion' by Hamas 'outlaws'.[53] Hamas' overthrow of Fatah rule in Gaza directly threatened a fundamental assumption underpinning the EU's Middle East policy since the late 1970s—that when the inevitable Palestinian state was established it would be led by a Fatah-dominated secular Palestinian government with close ties to Europe. Consequently, the EU immediately condemned the Hamas move and joined the US in backing Abbas. 'The presidency of the European Union', a German foreign ministry spokesman said on behalf of the EU, 'condemns in the strongest terms the violent seizure of power by the Hamas militia in the Gaza Strip'.[54]

The EU supported Abbas' dissolution of the national unity government established the previous March and led by a Hamas Prime Minister— Ismail Haniyeh, the former dean of Gaza's Islamic University—on the dubious grounds that this move was 'in accordance with the Palestinian constitution'. The EU also backed immediately Abbas' decision to form an emergency government led by the former Finance Minister Salam Fayyad, based in Ramallah. As Solana explained, 'this [new Fatah-led PA] government is a legitimate government and is the only legitimate government that we should support, and whatever they decide to do, and to move forward, we do not have to interfere'.[55]

From 1994 to the end of 2005, the EU committed approximately €2.3 billion in assistance to the Palestinians (excluding bilateral assistance from individual EU member states). Following the Hamas election victory in 2006, the EU's Ambassador to Israel, Ramiro Cibrian-Uzal, explained that the EU would continue to 'honour [its] financial commitment to the PA to the extent that Hamas will honour the political commitments to the EU'.[56] However, Hamas' refusal to meet the EU preconditions for engagement—recognition of Israel, a renunciation of violence and acceptance of previously signed agreements—resulted in the EU decision to boycott any direct funding of the Hamas-run government.

Hamas condemned this move on the grounds that it had been democratically elected, and because the 'Palestinian people are [being] punished for their [electoral] choice'.[57] In a show of solidarity with Hamas, Iran and Qatar offered to provide US$100 million to the new government to make up for the shortfall in EU funding.[58] Despite EU restrictions on funding, it still provided €680 million to the PA in 2006.[59] Of this €188 million went through the Temporary International Mechanism (TIM), an initiative designed to minimise the impact of the aid boycott on civilians while bypassing Hamas and enabling the EU and other donors to target financial assistance directly at citizens. It provided social allowances to almost one million Palestinians including almost 90 per cent of non-security public sector employees, as well as the poorest members of society. It also funded emergency assistance and food aid to 73,000 low-income households.[60]

Following the Hamas election victory, Prime Minister Sharon called on the EU to undermine popular Palestinian support for Hamas by taking over its role as provider of medical, educational and other social services in Gaza.[61] Senior European officials doubted that substituting the European social welfare model for the Islamist one would in itself bring stability. Speaking in late 2006 the British Foreign Secretary, Margaret Beckett, explained that 'we as the EU…are substantial funders of aid and support to the Palestinian people, but in the end aid from outside is not the answer, the answer is to move to a more peaceful settlement in the Middle East so natural and normal economic development can take place'.[62]

By mid-2007, TIM was proving itself incapable of providing sufficient humanitarian assistance, especially fuel and welfare payments, to the people of Gaza without engaging directly with Hamas. In an effort to address this the EU's External Relations Commissioner, Benita Ferrero-Waldner, announced that she would review the EU ban on direct aid to the Hamas-led Palestinian government. This generated renewed speculation that EU engagement with Hamas was inevitable in the near future.[63] But the Hamas overthrow of Fatah in Gaza halted any move in this direction. Instead the EU decided to freeze all direct funding to Hamas, which by now was solely responsible for the civilian administration of Gaza including everything from schools and hospitals to the administration of justice.[64] Only after Abbas dismissed the national unity government and appointed a Hamas-free administration did the EU resume direct aid channelled through the PA's Finance Ministry and supervised by an accounting firm. As the British Foreign Office explained, this was intended to 'boost the economy, and demonstrates our clear support for the new [Abbas] government'.[65]

The dissolution of the Palestinian unity government had facilitated new talks between Israel and Abbas at a US-sponsored summit at Sharm el Sheik, also attended by Egypt and Jordan. The EU welcomed this move and endorsed President Bush's decision to convene an international peace conference at Annapolis in late 2007. The goal of this meeting was to consolidate international support for Abbas and to provide momentum for a new round of peace talks between a Fatah-led Palestinian government and Israel. Leaders from over 50 nations including a dozen Arab states and all the interested EU parties attended an elaborate and stage-managed meeting intended primarily to isolate Hamas in the region and beyond.

The Paris Donors Conference held the month after Annapolis pledged a record US$7.7 billion in aid to the PA. In May 2008 Britain's former Prime Minister Tony Blair, in his role as the International Quartet's Middle East envoy, organised an investment conference in Bethlehem that raised another US$1.4 billion.[66] In early 2008, after almost two years, the EU replaced TIM with a new mechanism, PEGASE. Its function was to provide a channel for close EU cooperation with the PA through the provision of development assistance and aid, but with the caveat that no development assistance would be provided to Gaza as long as Hamas was in power.[67] As the challenges faced by TIM confirmed, this was by no means an easy task given that Hamas controlled one of two cabinets, Gaza and the Legislative Council and Fatah controlled the West Bank, the presidency and the other cabinet.[68]

Europe's refusal to engage with Hamas, combined with the Israeli blockade of Gaza imposed following the 2006 elections and the US boycott of the Islamist group, increasingly took its toll on the Hamas government. In September 2008, it called for a return to a national unity government with Fatah.[69] By November, Hamas' situation deteriorated further when the Egyptian-brokered six-month ceasefire with Israel, agreed the previous June, almost collapsed. Following clashes between Hamas fighters and Israeli troops in the course of an Israeli raid on a tunnel suspected of being dug to house kidnapped soldiers, Hamas increased its rocket attacks on Israel, which had continued even during the ceasefire, and declared that it would not return to the ceasefire unless Israel ended its siege of Gaza.

Following the expiry of the ceasefire on 19 December, and in the context of continuing rocket attacks by Hamas and an Israeli general election scheduled for 10 February 2009, Israel responded. Israel was determined to avoid the mistakes of the war with Hezbollah in Lebanon in mid-2006, and this campaign saw the IDF enter Gaza in force while at the same time attacking major Hamas strategic locations by air in a military action codenamed Operation Cast Lead.[70]

Since Israel withdrew from Gaza in 2005, Hamas had improved the range of its missile capability greatly, from 12 to 40 kilometres. The Israeli government explained that its goal on returning to Gaza was to neutralise the missile threat to Sderot, Ashkelon, and other southern Israeli towns and cities. It also looked to destroy the infrastructure that was being used to develop even more sophisticated rockets that could soon target Israel's key industrial and population centres and transport hubs further north. Some senior Israeli leaders, notably the foreign minister Tzipi Livni, who was the ruling Kadima party's candidate for prime minister in the upcoming elections, and her main rival, the Likud leader Benjamin Netanyahu, expressed the hope that the military action would also deal a 'palpable, conspicuous and concretely visible'[71] blow to Hamas.

On 18 January 2009, Israel unilaterally declared a ceasefire and hostilities ceased. Although its military operation had inflicted significant damage on Hamas' capacity to wage war, it did not succeed in weakening fundamentally Hamas' political legitimacy or capacity to govern.[72] Instead, in the wake of the war, as Palestinian society came to terms with the civilian losses and the extensive damage to much of Gaza's non-military infrastructure, both Abbas and Fatah faced even greater challenges to their own legitimacy. Polls showed that 46.7 per cent of Palestinians in Gaza and the West Bank combined believed that Hamas had emerged from the war victorious (53 per cent of respondents in the West Bank and 35.2 per cent in Gaza).[73] This did little to reduce the EU's support for Fatah or its criticism of Hamas. In a much publicised statement made during a visit to Gaza in late January, Louis Michel, the EU Commissioner for Development and Humanitarian Aid, chastised Hamas. Placing 'overwhelming responsibility' for the Gaza crisis on the Islamist group, he dismissed it as a 'terrorist movement' that 'has to be denounced as such'.[74] For her part, Ferrero-Waldner acknowledged that 'we have been at the side of the Palestinian population always and we will be at their side, but at the same time it's also for the Palestinian population on both sides to say "we want this peace"'.[75] Although Hamas was not mentioned in her statement it was clear that she was linking future coordination with Hamas in supplying humanitarian aid to Gaza with the group's willingness to abandon violence.

In a statement highlighting the fact that Eastern European countries' entry into the EU in 2004 had not fundamentally changed Europe's political approach towards the Israel-Palestine question any more than previous enlargements, the Czech Republic's foreign minister, Karel Schwarzenberg, restated the EU's long-held position that 'Palestinian reconciliation behind president Mahmoud Abbas is fundamental to prog-ress'.[76] Mahmoud Abbas, though less outspoken in his support for the Israeli attack on Hamas than other anti-Hamas Palestinian leaders like Mohammad Dahlan, refused to criticise the Israeli military action, and when he did comment on it he described Hamas as being responsible for 'the massacre'.[77]

In the immediate aftermath of the Gaza war senior figures from Germany, France, Britain, Italy and the EU presidency visited the region to express their continued support for Abbas' government and to promote their plan to host high-level talks between Israel, the PA, Egypt, Jordan and Turkey.[78] At the same time, in a symbolic act intended to underscore continued EU backing for the beleaguered Palestinian president, Abbas was invited to speak before the European Parliament. During his visit he combined public calls for Europe to assist the Palestinian people in achieving their state[79] with more discreet requests that the EU maintain its boycott of Hamas. Following the collapse of Egyptian-sponsored Hamas-Fatah talks in Cairo in March, the Palestinian foreign minister Riyad al-Malki was more public in making his own appeal to Europe not to ease restrictions on Hamas, as any such move could give the impression that the 'international community, and especially the EU, is ready to change its position'.[80]

Such warnings by senior allies of Abbas emphasised how much the Fatah leadership was still concerned that the EU could provide Hamas with a diplomatic lifeline that would help it to garner further international legitimacy. Hamas also continued to hold out hope that the EU's united front would soon crack and that European foreign ministries would begin dealing with it on normal terms. But despite ongoing pressure from supporters of engagement with Hamas, most notably ex-President Jimmy Carter who described the EU's Hamas policy as 'supine' and its support for a Fatah-only government as 'subterfuge',[81] the group's overthrow of Fatah in Gaza in mid-2007 made this increasingly unlikely.

The reality was that although the EU acknowledged Hamas as a key Palestinian actor, now it also viewed the group's aspiration to become the dominant Palestinian party as hugely detrimental to its primary objective—working for the establishment of a Fatah-led Palestinian state, which had long been viewed in European policy-making circles as the key prerequisite for peace, stability and prosperity in Europe as well as the Middle East. As the EU Parliament's President, Josep Borrell Fontelles, explained during a visit to Israel in 2005, 'The conflict in the Middle East is dangerous for us. We are not just here, as the good guy who says, please do not fight between you. We need this conflict to be finished because of its impact on life in Europe'.[82]

On top of this, in the post-9/11 world the Islamist ideology of Hamas and its growing links to Iran failed to hold the same appeal as Fatah's freedom fighter slogans and anti-colonial language, which stirred so many Europeans in previous decades. Hamas also failed to take into account the fact that any EU decision to legitimise it while it refused to abandon its call for the destruction of Israel would have a very negative impact on ongoing EU efforts to improve ties with Israel following the low point in relations between 2002 and 2004. Israel had welcomed the EU's mid-2004 announcement of its European Neighbourhood Policy (ENP, also known as the new neighbourhood or wider Europe policy). First proposed in March 2003, the ENP was intended to offer the EU's neighbours in the Middle East and North Africa, and in the European areas of the former Soviet Union, new opportunities to develop trade and investment ties with the EU and to achieve greater social and working rights for citizens living inside the European single market. It also allowed the EU to impose conflict resolution, human rights, and governance conditions upon partner states through bilateral Action Plans.

While the EU-Palestinian Authority Action Plan negotiated under the ENP called for the 'effective implementation of political, economic, social and institutional reforms',[83] the EU-Israel Action Plan avoided imposing conditionality on its relationship with Israel. Instead, it encouraged Israel to 'strengthen political dialogue and identify areas for further cooperation' and focused its energies on ways to 'enhance political dialogue and cooperation'. Under the heading 'Situation in the Middle East', the Action Plan also set out the objective of cooperation with Israel in the political sphere on a 'bilateral basis'.[84]

On its adoption in mid-2005, the EU presented this agreement as an 'additional instrument for involvement in the Middle East peace process'.[85] In particular, as the EU's Ambassador in Israel, Giancarlo Chevallard, explained, it was a 'major step forward' because Israel agreed in writing to European involvement in the political dialogue of the peace process.[86] Ferrero-Waldner drew attention to much the same point, arguing that through the Action Plan 'Israel clearly acknowledges the role of the EU in the Quartet...Israel has never been willing to make such commitments in writing to any other partner'.[87]

Apart from the EU desire to improve political relations, the absence of any conditionality clauses in the EU-Israel Action Plan was due to the fact that Israel was by far the most advanced economy included in the initiative and had established itself as a key player, and a leading collaborator with the EU, in the global hi-tech and scientific sectors. During the latter half of the 1990s, the desire of EU member states to cooperate with Israel in the R&D and hi-tech spheres meant that even EU member states politically committed to the Palestinian cause and highly critical of Israeli policies had been keen to develop links with Israel. By the time of the collapse of Oslo in late 2000, Israel was experiencing unprecedented economic ties with EU member states from the Netherlands and Denmark to Ireland and France, and could claim the most progressive trade and co-operation agreements with the EU of any non-member Mediterranean state. It was also the only country in the world that had simultaneous free trade agreements with the EU, the US and the European Free Trade Association (EFTA).

Despite the subsequent downturn in the global hi-tech sector, after 2000 Israel maintained its position as a global technology leader, and by the beginning of 2005 hi-tech industries accounted for almost 15 per cent of Israel's Gross Domestic Product (GDP). It had the highest rate of Research and Development (R&D) investment per GDP in the world and spent a record five per cent of GDP on R&D. Seventy Israeli companies were quoted on the NASDAQ stock market, more than any other country outside North America. Israel could also boast more US-registered patents than China, India and Russia combined.

In proportion to its population, Israel had the largest number of start-up companies in the world, and in absolute terms it had more start-up companies than any other country in the world apart from the US (3,500 companies, mostly in hi-tech). Israel was also ranked second in the world (again behind the US) for venture capital funds, and on a per capita basis had the largest number of biotech start-ups. According to Dow Jones VentureSource, the top four economies, after the US, in attracting venture capital for start-ups in the first quarter of 2008 were: Europe US$1.53 billion, China US$719 million, Israel US$572 million and India US$99 million. Israel, with 7 million people, attracted almost as much venture capital for start-ups as China with its population of 1.3 billion. In parallel to this, in 2007 Israeli companies occupied the first, second and third spots in the Deloitte Touche 'Fast 500' list of the fastest

growing firms in the technology, media and telecommunications industries in the Europe, Middle East and Asia region.[88]

These were remarkable achievements for a country the size of the state
of Vermont, with a population not much larger than that of Dallas. In
political terms it meant that despite EU-Israeli relations reaching an all-
time low between 2000 and 2004, bilateral cooperation in the R&D and
hi-tech sphere (in the words of the European Commission) 'increased
significantly' over the same period.[89]

During the Netanyahu era in the late 1990s, despite political disagree-
ments with Israel and mounting pressure from the Arab world, the EU
sought to benefit from Israel's position (in the words of *Newsweek* magazine) as the only serious rival to California's Silicon Valley in the hi-tech
sphere.[90] In 1996 Israel became the only non-EU member state invited
to participate in the EU's Fourth Framework Technology Programme for
Research and Technical Development. In 1999, Israel and the EU signed
a bilateral agreement on scientific co-operation, by which Israel joined
the Fourth and Fifth Community R&D Framework Programmes. In
March 2000, Israel gained 'Co-operating State' status in the COST
(Research) programme, and from June 2000 Israel was a member of the
Eureka (Research) Network.[91] In December 2002, just months after Israel
clashed publicly with a number of EU member states over the (false)
allegation that the IDF had committed a massacre of civilians in the Palestinian town of Jenin, the EU and Israel signed a landmark agreement
that enabled Israel to participate in the EU's flagship Sixth Framework
Programme on Scientific and Technical Cooperation.

By this time Israel had succeeded in separating politics from its economic and hi-tech relationship with the EU, something that was most
apparent in the case of France. In the understated words of the French
foreign ministry, the Franco-Israeli political relationship has been 'often
heated since 1967'.[92] Following the collapse of Oslo, as French leaders
established themselves as among the most outspoken critics of Israel in
the EU, relations entered 'a glacial era...of attacks, rifts and misunderstanding'.[93] But over the same period Franco-Israeli trade almost doubled,
and by early 2005 Israel was France's sixth largest market for its exports
and France was Israel's third biggest partner in joint projects in the areas
of scientific and technological research. In 1984 the then French Prime
Minister, Laurent Fabius, had highlighted the importance of Israel to
France in the high-technology sphere, which was Paris' 'priority'.[94] Exactly

two decades later, despite profound political differences, a new Paris-based joint initiative, the French-Israeli High Scientific Authority, was established to consolidate the great strides in bilateral research that had developed in the decade since the Oslo process began.[95]

These developments explain why, in June 2008, the EU eagerly agreed to begin negotiations with Israel to discuss upgrading bilateral ties despite a plea by the PA Prime Minister Salam Fayyad for it to postpone such a move until there was progress on the political front.[96] The talks included discussions on the institutionalisation of diplomatic dialogue by senior EU and Israeli officials through regular annual senior level meetings; Israeli membership of European agencies, programmes and working groups, with a special focus on hi-tech; and a joint working group to examine the areas in which Israel was capable of integrating into the European single market.[97] Israel even succeeded in convincing the EU that any reference to the peace process should be included in a separate declaration, despite reservations from Britain, Belgium, Ireland, Cyprus and Malta.[98]

Israel hoped that these developments would 'usher in a new era of Israeli-European relations'.[99] But in reality the 'double game of economic passion and political hostility'[100] that had come to define the EU-Israeli relationship continued in the wake of the Gaza war. For while Israel had succeeded in separating politics from its thriving trade and hi-tech relationship with the EU, it was unable to use these ties to pressure the EU member states to moderate their political support for the Palestinian cause. In the early 1960s Yigal Allon had hoped that the EEC could provide an example of a framework that was needed for peace in the Middle East, and had even called on the EEC to invite Israel and the Arab states to join the Common Market simultaneously as a way of achieving this.[101] By 1975 Allon, now Israel's foreign minister, was far less optimistic over the positive role that the Community could play in the peace process and he cautioned against any assumption that rising trade relations with the EEC would improve Europe's political attitude towards Israel.[102]

The prescience of this observation was very apparent in the post-Oslo era. And so, despite the excellent state of EU-Israeli trade and technology cooperation, something David Ben-Gurion had envisaged during a meeting with the European Commission President Walter Hallstein in 1961,[103] no Israeli prime minister visited Brussels between 2000 and 2009. The Czech presidency of the EU in the first half of 2009 had planned to hold an EU-Israel summit, but this idea was abandoned in the wake of Operation Cast Lead and the subsequent Israeli elections.

Moreover, disagreement and distrust continued to define the political relationship. In April 2009, the EU External Affairs Commissioner Ferrero-Waldner made a number of pubic attacks on the new Netanyahu government's willingness to make concessions for peace. The Israeli foreign ministry's response was reminiscent, in both tone and content, of any number of statements emanating from Jerusalem since the 1970s: 'We want the EU to be a partner [in the diplomatic process but]…Israel is asking Europe to lower the tone and conduct a discreet dialogue [otherwise] Europe will not be able to be part of the diplomatic process, and both sides will lose'.[104] By the summer of 2009 EU concerns that the new Israeli government would place obstacles in the way of peace led to the postponement of a final agreement on the proposed upgrade in bilateral ties.[105]

At the same time, by 2009 the EU found itself faced with another familiar challenge: dealing with the peace proposals put forward by a new US president. The Gaza war broke out three weeks before Barack Obama's presidential inauguration, but long before the first Israeli tank entered Gaza, many of the 300 professors, pundits and foreign policy experts who had been working for the Obama campaign since his nomination had called on him to make solving the Israel-Palestine conflict a priority of his presidency.

In the early months, he appeared to have significant levels of goodwill in a region where US popularity was at an all-time low.[106] Yet his 'transformational image', as Colin Powell put it, and his status as the 'anti-Bush' could only go so far in what is a decidedly unsentimental part of the world. The fact that Obama had a Muslim father, spent part of his childhood in Indonesia, the world's largest Muslim state, and has the middle name Hussein did not count for much. Indeed, within hours of Obama's victory, the much-vaunted 'Arab street' was already showing signs of scepticism over whether he would make any difference. A group of Egyptians polled by Al-Jazeera in the wake of the election was almost unanimous in the view that 'it makes no difference who wins. The US will always pursue the same policies in the region'. Similar sentiments were expressed on the streets of Rabat, Baghdad, Beirut and Damascus.[107]

In an attempt to disprove these suspicions President Obama presented himself across the Arab media as a 'kind of empathiser-in-chief'[108] and promised that the US would now seek to engage with both America's allies and its adversaries in the region on the basis of 'mutual respect and mutual interest'.[109] In June 2009, in an address in Cairo entitled 'A New Beginning' Obama expanded on his vision for relations between the US and Arab and Muslim nations. He also addressed the 'situation between Israelis, Palestinians and the Arab world'. He reminded his global audience that America's bond with Israel 'is unbreakable'. But he also made it clear that he was sensitive to the 'the daily humiliations—large and small—that come with occupation. So let there be no doubt: The situation for the Palestinian people is intolerable. And America will not turn our backs on the legitimate Palestinian aspiration for dignity, opportunity, and a state of their own'.[110]

The Cairo speech was praised for marking a clear break with the Bush administration and for establishing the foundations of a new US foreign policy paradigm based on a 'friendly', non-belligerent approach that differed from the traditional US diplomatic and military involvement in the region. It also raised expectations that the new administration would succeed where its predecessors had failed in finding a solution to the Israeli-Palestinian conflict.

Since that time US-Israeli relations have been sorely tested in the course of a number of very public disputes between the Obama administration and the Netanyahu government. For their part Abbas and Fatah continue their tenuous hold on power while Hamas continues to wait and see if either the EU or the Obama administration (or possibly both) will succumb to pressure at home and realities on the ground and finally engage with it.

Whether this happens or not one factor will remain constant. Europe, as one Israeli diplomat recently commented, will continue to play 'second fiddle'[111] to an American administration intent on making an Israeli-Palestinian peace deal a central goal of its time in the White House.

NOTES

INTRODUCTION: A CAUSE LOOKING FOR AN OPPORTUNITY

1. *Washington Post*, 25 Feb. 2002.
2. Shada Islam, 'Craxi Tried Hard', *Middle East International* (hereafter, *MEI*), 254, 12 July 1985, p. 9.
3. *The Times*, 21 May 2002.
4. Jewish Telegraphic Agency (JTA), 17 Nov. 2006, www.jta.org
5. Noel Malcolm, 'The Case Against "Europe"', *Foreign Affairs*, 74, 2, March–April 1995, pp. 52–68, p. 68.
6. Marc Otte, 'Europe has a central role to play in the Middle East', *Europe's World*, 13 April 2009, www.europesworld.org/New-English/Home/Article/tabid/191/ArticleType/articleview/ArticleID/21436/Default.aspx.af
7. Leon Brittan, *A Diet of Brussels: The Changing Face of Europe*, London: Little, Brown and Company, 2000, p. 150.
8. Henri Simonet, 'Energy and the Future of Europe', *Foreign Affairs*, Vol. 53 No. 3 (April 1975), pp. 450–63, p. 461.
9. See Efraim Inbar, *Rabin and Israel's National Security*, Washington, DC: Wilson Centre and Johns Hopkins University Press, 1999.
10. See Bill Clinton, *My Life*, New York: Knopf, 2004.
11. See joint interview with President Sadat and Prime Minister Begin on French Television, 7 Sept. 1979, *Israel's Foreign Relations: Selected Documents*, Vol. 6, Meron Medzoni (ed.), Jerusalem: Ministry of Foreign Affairs, 1976, pp. 116–23 (hereafter, *Israel Documents*, followed by date of document and volume).
12. *Guardian*, 26 May 2008.

1. THE FRENCH (DIS)CONNECTION

1. F.R. Allemann, 'The End of the Adenauer Era', *Encounter*, XX, 2, Feb. 1963, pp. 59–63, p. 59.

2. In February 1958 Syria and Egypt joined together to form the United Arab Republic under the leadership of the Egyptian President, Gamal Abd al Nasser. Despite the dissolution of the union during the 1960s Nasser demanded that Egypt be known by this name until his death in 1970.

3. See UN General Assembly Resolution 1000 (ES-1), passed on 4 Nov. 1956. See *UN General Assembly Official Records*, First Emergency Special Session, 1–10 November 1956, Plenary Meetings and Annexes, New York: United Nations, p. 89.

4. See statement to the UN General Assembly by Foreign Minister Golda Meir, *Israel Documents*, 1 March 1957, Vol. 1, pp. 604-7 (hereafter, *Israel Documents*, followed by date of document and volume).

5. Tom Segev, *1967: Israel, the War and the Year That Transformed the Middle East*, New York: Little, Brown, 2007, p. 207.

6. Walter Laqueur, 'Israel, the Arabs, and World Opinion', *Commentary Magazine*, Aug.1967, pp. 49–59, p. 53.

7. See Declaration by President Charles de Gaulle at the Council of Ministers of France on 2 June 1967 and M. Couve dc Murville before the National Assembly on 7 June 1967, reprinted in Samuel Seguev, *Israël, les Arabes et les Grandes Puissances, 1963–1968*, Paris: Calmann-Levy, 1968.

8. For the full content of this and other draft resolutions put forward on the 4 July see meetings 1547 and 1548 of the UN General Assembly Special Session, 4 July 1967, *Official Records of the General Assembly*, 5th Emergency Special Session, New York: United Nations, pp. 1–18.

9. Neither the Yugoslav nor the Latin American draft resolutions succeeded in gaining the necessary two-thirds majority required for adoption. Fifty-seven UN member states voted in favour of the Latin American draft, whereas 63 states either voted against (43) or abstained (20). The Non-Aligned draft received 53 votes in favour to 46 against, with 20 abstentions. Of the 46 countries that opposed the Non-Aligned draft, 45 voted in favour of the Latin American draft (the exception being Israel). These 45 were joined by nine states that had abstained in the vote on the Non-Aligned draft; in addition, three member states voted in favour of both the Latin American and Non-Aligned drafts. For the voting of UN member states during the Special Session of July 1967 see Arthur Lall, *The UN and the Middle East Crisis*, *1967*, New York: Columbia University Press, 1968.

10. See *Justice Will Triumph*, New York: The Palestine Arab Delegation, 5 June 1968, p. 4.

11. See meeting 1382 of UN Security Council, 22 November 1967, UN Security Council Official Records, 22nd Year, pp. 1–8.

12. Raymond Aron, 'The Age of Suspicion', reprinted in *De Gaulle, Israel and the Jews*, trans from French by John Sturrock, London: Andre Deutsch, 1969, p. 21.

13. Gilles Kepel, 'Self and Other: The Heart of the Franco-Arab Paradox', in L. Carl Brown and Mathew S. Gordon (eds), *Franco-Arab Encounters: Studies in Memory of David C. Gordon*, Syracuse, NY: Syracuse University Press, 1997, pp. 306–26, p. 315.

14. Laqueur, 'Israel, the Arabs, and World Opinion', p. 53.

15. Segev, *1967*, p. 561.

16. Laqueur, 'Israel, the Arabs, and World Opinion', p. 55.

17. See Zach Levey, *Israel and the Western Powers, 1952–1960*, Chapel Hill & London: University of North Carolina Press, 1997.

18. The most important studies of the Israeli-French collaboration that led to the acquisition of the Dimona reactor by Israel are Binyamin Pinkus, 'Atomic Power to Israel's Rescue: French-Israeli Nuclear Cooperation, 1949–1957', *Israel Studies*, 7, 1, 2002, pp. 104–13 and Pierre Péan, *Les Deux bombes*, Paris: Fayard, 1981.

19. Sylvia K. Crosbie, *A Tacit Alliance: France and Israel from Suez to the Six Day War*, Princeton, NJ: Princeton University Press, 1974, p. 122.

20. Ibid., p. 139.

21. *The Times*, 11 May 1967.

22. See confidential report from Irish ambassador in Paris to Department of Foreign Affairs, Dublin, 2 June 1967, National Archives of Ireland (hereafter, NAI) 2001/43/98.

23. See, for example, the view of Jacques Chaban-Delmas, *Mémoires Pour Demain*, Paris: Flammarion, 1997, p. 263. Chaban-Delmas was the French minister of defence at the peak of the Franco-Israeli relationship in 1957–58. He was later French prime minister under President Georges Pompidou.

24. Richard Lowenthal, 'A World Adrift', *Encounter*, XXXVIII, 2, Feb. 1972, pp. 22–9, p. 24.

25. Interview with Maurice Couve de Murville, *Revue d'Etudes Palestiniennes*, 39, Spring 1991, p. 33

26. Aron, *De Gaulle, Israel and the Jews*, p. 33.

27. See confidential report from Irish Ambassador in Paris to Department of Foreign Affairs, Dublin, 2 June 1967, NAI 2001/43/98.

28. *Yediot Aharonot*, 6 Dec. 1967.

29. Raymond Aron, 'Why?', *Le Figaro*, 7 July 1967.

30. *The Times*, 1 July 1967.

31. 'The Khartoum Resolution', 29 Aug.-1 Sept. 1967, reprinted in Yeduda Lukacs (ed.), *The Israeli-Palestinian Conflict: a Documentary Record, 1967–1990*, Cambridge, New York: Cambridge University Press, 1992, pp. 78–9.

32. See Déclaration de President Nasser, 23 Nov. 1967, quoted in André Nouschi, *La France et le monde arabe depuis 1962*, Paris: Librairie Vuibert, 1994, p. 104.

33. *Al-Nahar*, 21 June 1967.
34. *Le Monde*, 7 Feb. 1968.
35. *The Times*, 6 Dec. 1967.
36. G.H. Jansen, *Zionism, Israel and Asian Nationalism*, Beirut: The Institute for Palestine Studies, 1971, pp. 274–5, Table 1.
37. See statement by Prime Minister Levi Eshkol in the Knesset Concerning Diplomatic Relations with the German Federal Republic, 16 March 1965, in Henry M. Christman (ed.), *The State Papers of Levi Eshkol*, New York: Funk & Wagnalls, 1969, pp. 52–3.
38. Nureddin Abdulhaddi, 'Willy Brandt's Crossfire Dilemma', *Middle East International (MEI)*, 1, April 1971, p. 47.
39. On the factors considered by the Community before agreeing to an association agreement with the Mediterranean states see J. Redmond, 'The European Community's Approach to Association: Applicability to the Case of Israel', in Ephraim Ahiram and Alfred Tovias (eds), *Whither EU-Israeli Relations? Common and Divergent Interests*, Frankfurt: Peter Lang, 1995, pp. 129–46.
40. Irish Embassy, The Hague, to Secretary, Department of Foreign Affairs, 8 June 1967, NAI, 98/3/337.
41. European News Agency, 8 June 1967 and *Financial Times*, 12 June 1967.
42. Kepel, 'Self and Other: The heart of the Franco-Arab Paradox', p. 310.
43. *The Times*, 19 July 1967.
44. *The Times*, 6 Dec. 1967.
45. *Le Monde*, 1 June 1967.
46. *Le Figaro*, 28 June 1967.
47. Europe Agency Reports, 22 June 1967.
48. Europe Agency Reports, 24 Nov. 1967.
49. Robert S. Wistrich, 'Left-Wing Anti-Zionism in Western Societies', in Robert S. Wistrich (ed.), *Anti-Zionism and Antisemitism in the Contemporary World*, New York: New York University Press, 1990, pp. 46–52, p. 50.
50. *Irish Times*, 10 Feb. 1970.
51. Moshe Shemesh, 'The Founding of the PLO 1964', *Middle Eastern Studies*, 20, 4, Oct. 1984, pp. 105–41, p. 108.
52. Eric Rouleau, 'The Palestinian Quest', *Foreign Affairs*, 53, 2, Jan. 1975, pp. 264–83, p. 273.
53. See telegram from Department of State to US Embassy in Israel, 14 Dec. 1966, document 366, *Foreign Relations of the United States, 1964–1968, XVIII*, Arab-Israeli Dispute 1964–1967, Washington, DC: US Government Printing Office, 2000, p. 715.
54. *New York Times*, 22 Feb. 1980.
55. Edward Said, 'The Theory and Practice of Banning Books and Ideas', *Al-*

Hayat, 4 Sept. 1996, reprinted in Edward W. Said, *The End of the Peace Process*, 2nd edition, London: Granta, 2002, p. 70.

56. *The Economist*, 8 Feb. 1969, p. 25.

57. On the rise of Fatah and Arafat to the leadership of the PLO's see Hisham Shirabi, *Palestine Guerrillas: Their Credibility and Effectiveness*, Beirut: Institute for Palestine Studies, 1970.

58. Turki Fawaz, *Exile's Return: The Making of a Palestinian-American*, New York: The Free Press, 1994, p. 189.

59. Bruce Hoffman, *Inside Terrorism*, New York: Columbia University Press, 2006, p. 64.

60. Stephen Sloan, 'Foreword: Responding to the Threat' in Robert J. Bunker (ed.), *Networks, Terrorism and Global Insurgency*, London, New York: Routledge, 2005, pp. xx-xxvi, p. xxiii.

61. Don Peretz, 'Arab Palestine: Phoenix or Phantom?', *Foreign Affairs*, 48, 2, Jan. 1970, pp. 322–33, pp. 326–7.

62. *The Economist*, 19 July 1969, p. 18.

63. *The Times*, 10 April 1969.

64. *The Times*, 7 Feb. 1969.

65. *Le Monde*, 10 Feb. 1969.

66. Michael Stewart, 'Britain, Europe and the Alliance', *Foreign Affairs*, 48, 4, July 1970, pp. 468–659, p. 655.

67. See Michael Brecher, *The Foreign Policy System of Israel: Setting, Images, Process*, London, Toronto: Oxford University Press, 1972, p. 348.

68. Walter Eytan, *The First Ten Years: A Diplomatic History of Israel*, New York: Simon & Schuster, 1958, p. 212.

69. See, for example, Europe Agency Reports, 8 Feb. 1964, 19 Feb. 1964 and 16 April 1964.

70. European News Agency, 27 Jan. 1967.

71. European News Agency, 12 Dec. 1967.

72. Irish Mission to the EEC, Brussels, to Department of Foreign Affairs, 24 Oct. 1969, NAI 99/3/136.

73. Philippe Rondot, 'France and Palestine: From Charles de Gaulle to François Mitterrand', *Journal of Palestine Studies*, XVI, 3, Spring 1987, pp. 87–100, p. 89.

74. *The Times*, 27 Nov. 1969.

75. See Phillippe de Schoutheete, *La Coopération politique européenne*, Paris and Brussels: Fernand Nathan, 1980, p. 45.

76. See *UN General Assembly Official Records*, 25th Year, Verbatim Records, 15 September-17 December, 1970, Vol. 2, p. 12.

77. *The Times*, 4 March 1969.

78. See statement to the Knesset by Prime Minister Golda Meir, 15 Dec. 1969, *Israel Documents*, Vol. 2, p. 890.

79. George Lavy, *Germany and Israel: Moral Debt and National Interest*, London: Frank Cass, 1996, p. 172.
80. *Herald Tribune*, 14 May 1971.
81. Ilan Greilsammer and Joseph Weiler, *Europe's Middle East Dilemma: The Quest for a Unified Stance*, Boulder, CO and London: Westview Press, 1987, p. 26.
82. Alain Dieckhoff, 'Europe and the Arab World: The Difficult Dialogue', in Ilan Greilsammer and Joseph Weiler (eds), *Europe and Israel, Troubled Neighbours*, Berlin and New York: Walter De Gruyter, 1988, pp. 255–82, p. 278. Alain Gresh, 'The European Union and the Refugee Question', in Naseer Aruri (ed.), *Palestinian Refugees, The Right of Return*, London: Pluto Press, 2001, pp. 82–6, p. 83.
83. See *Jerusalem Post*, 19 May 1971; *Die Welt*, 11 July 1971 and *Der Spiegel*, 21 July 1971.
84. Jacob Abadi, 'Constraints and Adjustments in Italy's Policy toward Israel', *Middle Eastern Studies*, 38, 4, Oct. 2002, pp. 63–94, p. 81; Omer De Raeymaeker, 'Belgium' in David Allen and Alfred Pijpers (eds), *European Foreign Policy Making and the Arab Israeli Conflict*, The Hague, Boston and Lancaster: Martinus Nijhoff Publishers, 1984, pp. 60–79, p. 66.
85. *Le Monde*, 9 November 1972.
86. See UNRWA Memorandum, 1 May 1975, in British National Archives (hereafter, BNA), Foreign & Commonwealth Office (hereafter, FCO) 30/3027.
87. See memorandum on proposed contributions to International Aid Agencies, 5 December 1970, NAI DFA 2002/19/243.
88. See UNRWA Memorandum, 28 April 1975, BNA/FCO 30/3027.
89. Peter Geyl, 'Waiting for Britain', *Encounter*, XXIV, 5 May 1965, pp. 59–61, p. 66.
90. See address by President Charles de Gaulle Outlining the Principles of French Foreign Policy, 31 May 1960, in *Major Addresses, Statements and Press Conferences of General Charles de Gaulle, May 19, 1958-January 31, 1964*, New York and Paris: French Foreign Ministry, Press & Information Division, 1964, p. 75.
91. Eric Roussel, *Jean Monnet, 1888–1979*, Paris: Fayard, 1996, pp. 736–7. For a more expansive discussion on Monnet's view of a supranational Europe and the Atlantic alliance see Klaus Schwabe, 'Jean Monnet, les Etats-Unis et le rôle de l'Europe au sein de la Communauté atlantique', in Gerard Bossuat and Andreas Wilkens (eds), *Jean Monnet, L'Europe et Les Chemins de la Paix*, Paris: Sorbonne, 1999, pp. 273–93.
92. Donald Tyerman, 'Going into Europe—Again', *Encounter*, XXXVII, 1, July 1971, p. 19.

93. Quoted in Paul Balta and Claudine Rulleau, *La Politique arabe de la France: de Gaulle a Pompidou*, Paris: Sindbad, 1974, p. 60.

94. See Jobert's foreword to Mustapha Benchenane, *Pour un dialogue euro-arabe*, Paris: Berger-Levrault, 1983, p. 11.

95. See Georges Pompidou, *Entretiens et Discours, 1968–1974*, Vol. II, Paris: Flammarion, 1984, pp. 83–5. Also see the view of Michel Debré, *Gouverner autrement: Mémoires*, Vol. IV, 1962–1970, Paris: Albin Michel, 1993, p. 285. Debré served as minister for both defence and foreign affairs under Pompidou. He remained a guardian of the Gaullist tradition until his death in the mid-1990s.

96. Philippe Rondot, 'France and Palestine', pp. 90–1.

97. See Ambassador Tekoah's statement to the UN General Assembly, 10 December 1969, *Israel Documents*, Vol. 1, p. 456.

98. Interview with Ghassan Tueni, *MEI*, 9, Dec. 1971, p. 12.

99. Quoted in Elizabeth Stephens, *US Policy towards Israel: The Role of Political Culture in Defining the "Special Relationship"*, Brighton, Portland: Sussex University Press, 2006, p. 134.

100. Lord Gladwyn, 'Atlantic Dreams and Realities, *Encounter*, XXI, 6, Dec. 1963, pp. 57–63, p. 57.

101. Joe Haines, *The Politics of Power*, London: Jonathan Cape, 1977, p. 79.

102. Michael Stewart, *Life and Labour: An Autobiography*, London: Sidgwick & Jackson, 1980, p. 259.

103. Anthony Hartley, 'Europe Between the Superpowers', *Foreign Affairs*, 49, 2, Jan. 1971, pp. 271–82, p. 272.

104. Luigi Barzani, *The Impossible Europeans*, London: Weidenfeld & Nicolson, 1983, p. 61.

105. Quoted in Theo Sommer, 'The Community is Working', *Foreign Affairs*, 51, 4, July 1973, pp. 747–60, p. 751.

106. Ibid., p. 747.

107. *The Times*, 2 Nov. 1973.

108. Rt Hon. Sir Christopher Soames, *Three Views of Europe*, London: Conservative Political Centre, 1973, p. 20.

109. Second Report of the Foreign Ministers to the heads of Government of the European Community (Copenhagen Report), 23 July 1973, reprinted in Greilsammer and Weiler, *Europe's Middle East Dilemma*, pp. 118–35.

110. Aron, 'Why?', *Le Figaro*, 7 July 1967.

111. 'The Year of Europe: Address by Henry Kissinger, 23 April 1973', *The Department of State Bulletin*, LXVIII, 14 May 1973, pp. 593–8.

2. 'INGLORIOUS DISARRAY'

1. Michael Howard, 'The World of Henry Kissinger', *Encounter*, LIX, 5, Nov. 1982, pp. 52–5, p. 53.
2. Edward Heath, *The Course of My Life: My Autobiography*, London: Hodder & Stoughton, 1998, p. 493.
3. Michel Jobert, *Les Américains*, Paris: Albin Michel, 1987, p. 159.
4. See Georges Pompidou, *Entretiens et Discours, 1968–1974*, Vol. II, p. 286. Some years later Kissinger did admit that the 'Year of Europe' was perhaps 'too grandiloquent', but he stuck to the analysis that lay behind it. See Henry Kissinger, *Years of Renewal*, New York: Simon & Schuster, 1999, p. 600.
5. Michel Jobert, *Mémoires d'avenir*, Paris: Grasset, 1974, p. 126.
6. *Corriere della Sera*, 7 Oct. 1973.
7. Geneviève Bibes, *L'Italie a-t-elle une politique étrangère*, Paris: Centre d'Etudes des Relations Internationales, 1974.
8. Walter Laqueur, *Confrontation: The Middle East War and World Politics*, London: Abacus, 1974, pp. 142–3.
9. Daniel Colord, 'La Politique méditerranéenne et proche-orientale de G. Pompidou', *Politique Etrangère*, 43, 3, 1978, pp. 283–96.
10. *Daily Telegraph*, 26 Oct. 1973.
11. Phillipe Simonnot, La 'fin du pétrole à bon marché', *Le Monde*, 25 Oct. 1993.
12. In 1973, OPEC also had four non-Arab members—Iran, Venezuela, Indonesia and Nigeria.
13. *Irish Press*, 4 March 1963.
14. *The Times*, 29 May 1967.
15. British Embassy, Beirut, to Foreign Office, 16 & 17 Sept. 1947, BNA/FCO 371/61529, cited in Efraim Karsh, *Palestine Betrayed*, London, New Haven: Yale University Press, 2010, p. 87.
16. *The Times*, 1 July 1967.
17. Nadav Safran, 'The War and the Future of the Arab-Israeli Conflict', *Foreign Affairs*, 52, 2, Jan. 1974, pp. 215–36, p. 221.
18. Cecil Hourani, 'The Moment of Truth: Towards a Middle East Dialogue', *Encounter*, XXIX, 5, Nov. 1967, pp. 3–14, p. 9.
19. *Süddeutsche Zeitung*, 6 Feb. 1971.
20. Walter J. Levy, 'Oil Power', *Foreign Affairs*, 49, 4, July 1971, pp. 652–68, p. 658.
21. The Hon Parker Thompson Hart, 'US Middle East Policy in 1971', *MEI*, 1, April 1971, p. 6.
22. By mid-1973, at least 300 billion of the world's proven 500 million barrels of oil were estimated to be in the Arab world. In the same year oil made up

60 per cent of the Community's energy needs, of which 43 per cent came from the Arab world: *International Economic Report of the President*, Washington, DC: US Government Printing Office, March 1975, p. 7.

23. James E. Atkins, 'The Oil Crisis: This Time the Wolf is Here', *Foreign Affairs*, 51, 3, April 1973, pp. 462–90, p. 467.

24. Address by Vice President Henri Simonet, 27 March 1973, reprinted in *Europe: Documents*, 729, 3 April 1973, pp. 1–4.

25. Jobert, *Mémoires d'avenir*, p. 125.

26. *Economist*, 15 Dec. 1973, p. 41.

27. Romano Prodi and Alberto Clo, 'Europe', in 'The Oil Crisis in Perspective', DAEDALUS, 14, 4, Fall 1975, pp. 91–112, pp. 101–2.

28. Memorandum on the Fourth Arab-Israel War, 7 Jan. 1974, BNA/FCO 93/561.

29. *L'Express*, 5 Nov. 1973.

30. *Le Monde*, 30 June 1967.

31. Greilsammer and Weiler, *Europe's Middle East Dilemma*, p. 29.

32. *Jewish Chronicle*, 2 Nov. 1973.

33. Laqueur, *Confrontation*, p. 153.

34. Tom Little, 'News Desk Notes', *MEI*, 3, Dec. 1973, p. 26.

35. Laqueur, *Confrontation*, p. 214.

36. Heath, *The Course of My Life*, pp. 501–2.

37. Jobert, *Mémoires d'avenir*, p. 125.

38. Karl Kaiser, 'Europe and America: A Critical Phase', *Foreign Affairs*, 52, 4, July 1974, pp. 725–41, p. 725 and Louis Turner, 'The Politics of the Energy Crisis', *International Affairs*, 50, 3, July 1974, pp. 404–15, p. 404.

39. Statement by European Community Foreign Ministers, 6 November 1973, reprinted in Lukacs (ed.), *The Israeli-Palestinian Conflict: a Documentary Record, 1967–1990*, p. 14.

40. UN Security Council Resolution 338 called for an immediate cease-fire, the 'implementation' of UNSC Resolution 242 'in all its parts' and for 'negotiations' to begin between the warring parties.

41. Statement by European Community Foreign Ministers, 6 November 1973.

42. P.E.L. Fellowes, 'The Oil Weapon in Action', *MEI*, 3, Dec. 1973, p. 8.

43. 'Memorandum on European Political Cooperation: Middle East Guarantees', 12 May 1975, BNA/FCO 30/3027.

44. Quoted in Haifaa A. Jawad, *Euro-Arab Relations: A Study in Collective Diplomacy*, Reading: Ithaca Press, 1992, p. 61.

45. Lavy, *Germany and Israel*, p. 164.

46. See Jan Deboutte and Alfred Van Staden, 'High Politics in the Low Countries', in William Wallace and W.E. Patterson (eds), *Foreign Policy Making*

in *Western Europe: A Comparative Approach*, Farnborough: Saxon House, 1978, p. 71.

47. *Ha'aretz*, 9 Nov. 1973.

48. *Yediot Aharonot*, 26 July 1974.

49. See statement by Foreign Minister Eban in response to the EEC Declaration of 6 November, *Israel Documents*, Vol. 2, pp. 1066–7.

50. *The Times*, 12 May 1975.

51. *Daily Telegraph*, 17 Nov. 1973.

52. Heath, *The Course of My Life*, p. 501.

53. Kenneth Lewan, 'West Germany Waits for the US', *MEI*, 58, April 1976, pp. 10–1.

54. André Fontaine, 'Une dernière chance pour les Neuf? Le révélateur pétrolier', *Le Monde*, 7 Nov. 1973.

55. Declaration of the Arab Summit Conference at Algiers, 28 Nov. 1973, *Israel Documents*, Vol. 2, pp. 1074–6.

56. *Guardian*, 29 Nov. 1973.

57. *Al-Nahar*, 4 Dec. 1973.

58. M. Abdel-Kader Hatem, *Information and the Arab Cause*, London: Longman, 1974, p. 291.

59. *Economist*, 23 Sept. 1972, p. 41.

60. Mohamed Hassanein Heikal, 'Egyptian Foreign Policy', *Foreign Affairs*, 56, 4, July 1978, pp. 714–27, p. 724.

61. Memorandum on the Fourth Arab-Israel War, 7 Jan. 1974, BNA/FCO 93/561.

62. Tom Little, 'News Desk Notes', *MEI*, 31, Jan. 1974, p. 25.

63. Fitzgerald, *All in a Life*, p. 128.

64. Daniel Yergin, *The Prize: The Epic Quest for Oil, Money and Power*, London, New York: Simon & Schuster, 1991, p. 627.

65. *International Economic Report of the President*, p. 7.

66. *New York Times*, 9 Nov. 1973.

67. *Le Monde*, 25 Dec. 1973.

68. Gideon Rafael, *Destination Peace: Three Decades of Israeli Foreign Policy, A Personal Memoir*, New York: Stein and Day, 1981, p. 359.

69. See 'An Open Letter from Europe to President Nixon', *Eurabia*, Paris, 14 May 1973.

70. Editorial, *MEI*, 30, Dec. 1973, p. 3.

71. Nadav Safran, 'Engagement in the Middle East', *Foreign Affairs*, 53, 1, Oct. 1974, pp. 45–63, p. 45. See also *New York Times*, 3 Nov. 1973.

72. Quoted in Elizabeth Stephens, *US Policy towards Israel*, p. 152.

73. *International Herald Tribune*, 29 Oct. 1973.

74. *Corriere della Sera*, 24 Dec. 1973; *Economist*, 3 Nov. 1973, p. 12.

75. *Die Welt*, 7 Nov. 1973.
76. 'Z', 'The Year of Europe?' *Foreign Affairs*, 52, 1, Jan. 1974, pp. 237–48, p. 240.
77. Henry A. Kissinger, *The Troubled Partnership: A Re-Appraisal of the Atlantic Alliance*, New York: McGraw-Hill, 1965, p. 40.
78. Jobert, *Les Américains*, p. 164.
79. Jobert, *Mémoires d'avenir*, p. 126.
80. Kissinger, *Years of Renewal*, p. 603.
81. Rayner Heppenstall, 'Going into Europe—Again', *Encounter*, XXXVII, 1, July 1971, p. 29.
82. Memorandum on the Fourth Arab-Israel War, 7 Jan. 1974, BNA/FCO 93/561.
83. Lord Home, *The Way the Wind Blows: An Autobiography*, London: Collins, 1976, p. 260.
84. *MEI*, 19, Jan. 1973, p. 10.
85. Heath, *The Course of My Life*, p. 492.
86. Memorandum on the Fourth Arab-Israel War, 7 Jan. 1974, BNA/FCO 93/561.
87. *International Herald Tribune*, 14 Nov. 1973.
88. *The Times*, 2 Nov. 1973; *Bulletin of the European Communities*, 6 Nov. 1973.
89. Laqueur, *Confrontation*, p. 183.
90. *The Times*, 19 Nov. 1973.
91. Lavy, *Germany and Israel*, p. 185.
92. *The Times*, 6 July 1974.
93. See *Le Monde*, 10 Dec. 1973 and Jobert, *Mémoires d'avenir*, p. 126. See also Laqueur, *Confrontation*, p. 183.
94. Speech by Sir Alec Douglas-Home to the Foreign Press Association, 26 Nov. 1973, reprinted in *MEI*, 31, Jan. 1974, p. 31.
95. Heath, *The Course of My Life*, p. 502.
96. Hatem, *Information and the Arab Cause*, p. 290.
97. Jobert, *Mémoires d'avenir*, p. 126.
98. James O. Goldsborough, 'France, the European Crisis and the Alliance', *Foreign Affairs*, 52, 3, April 1974, pp. 538–56, p. 541.

3. DIALOGUE OF THE DEAF

1. "Z", 'The Year of Europe?', p. 243.
2. Christopher Serpell, 'Europe and the Middle East: A Time for Re-appraisal', *MEI*, 31, Jan. 1974, pp. 6–7.
3. Pompidou, *Entretiens et Discours, 1968–1974*, Vol. II, p. 285.
4. Safran, 'The War and the Future of the Arab-Israeli Conflict', p. 224.

5. Communiqué of European Summit Meeting at Copenhagen, 14–15 Dec. 1973, Washington, DC: European Community Information Service, 20 Dec. 1973.

6. *Economist*, 26 Jan. 1974, pp. 36–7.

7. Jobert, *Mémoires d'avenir*, p. 287.

8. Goldsborough, 'France, the European Crisis and the Alliance', p. 539.

9. Barzani, *The Impossible Europeans*, p. 101.

10. Ibid., p. 539.

11. Kissinger, *Years of Renewal*, p. 605.

12. *Le Monde*, 14 Feb. 1974.

13. See Press Conference given by Michel Jobert, Washington, 13 Feb. 1974, reprinted in *La Politique étrangère de la France: 1e semestre 1974–Nov. 1974*, pp. 90–3.

14. Final communiqué of the Washington Conference, 13 Feb. 1974, reprinted in *Bulletin of the European Communities*, 2, Feb. 1974, pp. 19–22.

15. See interview with Christopher Mayhew, MP, *MEI*, 35, May 1974, pp. 19–20.

16. Prodi and Clo, 'Europe', p. 106.

17. European Parliament resolution on Community energy policy, 20 Feb. 1975, reprinted in *Official Journal of the European Communities*, 60, 13 March 1975, p. 36.

18. Euro-Arab Dialogue Minutes, 17 and 22 Dec. 1975, BNA/FCO 30/3045.

19. Document de travail de la présidence dialogue euro-arabe, 18 Feb. 1975, BNA/FCO 30/3023.

20. Joint Communiqué: Euro-Arab Dialogue, Cairo, 14 June 1975, BNA/FCO 30/3031.

21. Jim Callaghan, *Challenges and Opportunities for British Foreign Policy*, London: Fabian Bureau, 1975, p. 13.

22. Interview with Christopher Mayhew, p. 20.

23. Lakhdar Brahimi, 'Who is Speaking to Whom in the Euro-Arab Dialogue', *Euro-Arab Dialogue Lectures II*, The Hague: The Luftia Rabbani Foundation, 1986, p. 15.

24. Rory Miller and Ashraf Mishrif, 'The Barcelona Process and Euro-Arab Economic Relations: 1995–2005', *Middle East Review of International Affairs*, 9, 2, June 2005, http://meria.idc.ac.il/journal/2005/issue2/jv9no2a6.html

25. British Embassy, Algiers, to Foreign Office, 20 Jan. 1975, BNA/FCO 30/2022.

26. Memorandum on Danish Foreign Minister's Visit to the Gulf States, 4–11 May 1975, 14 May 1975, BNA/FCO 30/3027.

27. Ahmad Yousef Ahmad, 'The Dialectics of Domestic Environment and Role Performance: The Foreign Policy of Iraq', in Bahgat Korany and Ali E. Hil-

lal Dessouki (eds), *The Foreign Policies of Arab States*, Boulder, CO and London: Westview Press, 1984, pp. 147–67, p. 163. See also British Embassy, Baghdad, to Foreign Office, 31 May 1975, BNA/FCO 30/3030.

28. *The Times*, 12 June 1975.
29. *Financial Times*, 25 Nov. 1975.
30. *The Times*, 20 Sept. 1976.
31. Minutes and Report of Euro-Arab Dialogue Meeting of Experts, Cairo, 11 June 1975, BNA/FCO 30/3030.
32. *Al Thawra*, 23 May 1975.
33. EAD: Meeting of Coordinating Group, Dublin, 22 Jan. 1975, 3 Feb. 1975, BNA/FCO 30/3022.
34. Ibid.
35. *Al Thawra*, 23 May 1975.
36. Robert Swann, 'Europe and the Arabs: the Dialogue Takes Shape', *MEI*, 39, Sept. 1974, p. 8.
37. Minister of State Memorandum on Euro-Arab Dialogue, 10 Jan. 1975, BNA/FCO 30/3022.
38. Ibid.
39. Jobert, *Mémoires d'avenir*, p. 124.
40. Swann, 'Europe and the Arabs: the Dialogue Takes Shape', p. 8.
41. Philip Ziegler, *Wilson, The Authorised Life of Lord Wilson of Rievaulx*, London: Weidenfeld & Nicolson, 1993, p. 388.
42. Quoted in Ziegler, *Wilson*, p. 463.
43. Marcia Falkender, *Downing Street in Perspective*, London: Weidenfeld & Nicolson, 1983, p. 178.
44. Ziegler, *Wilson*, pp. 463–4.
45. Memorandum on Middle East: General Situation, 27 Aug. 1975, BNA/FCO 30/3027.
46. Robert Stephens, 'Europe in Search of a Policy', *MEI*, 35, May 1974, p. 17.
47. British Embassy, Paris, to Foreign Office, 6 Jan. 1975, BNA/FCO 30/3022.
48. EAD: Meeting of Coordinating Group, Dublin, 22 Jan. 1975, 3 Feb. 1975, BNA/FCO 30/3022.
49. Foreign Office to British Embassy, Brussels, 17 Jan. 1975, BNA/FCO 30/3022.
50. EAD: Meeting of the Co-ordinating Group, Paris, 17 Dec. 1974, BNA/FCO 30/3022.
51. Harold Wilson, *The Chariot of Israel: Britain, America and the State of Israel*, London: Weidenfeld & Nicolson and Michael Joseph, 1981, p. 377.
52. *Filastin al-Thawra*, 15 Aug. 1973.
53. *The Times*, 29 Sept. 1970.

54. Interview with Mahmoud Darwish, *Sh'un Filastiniya*, 27 Sept. 1973.

55. *Le Monde*, 29 Nov. 1973.

56. *The Times*, 16 May 1981.

57. See Arab League Summit Conference communiqué, Rabat, 29 October 1974, reprinted in Yeduda Lukacs (ed.), *The Israeli–Palestinian Conflict: a Documentary Record, 1967–1990*, p. 464. The Rabat summit also introduced the PLO's new phased strategy (first put forward in June 1974), whereby the Palestinians agreed to take whatever territory Israel offered to them as a springboard for further territorial gains until the 'complete liberation of Palestine' could be achieved. See 'PLO Phased Political Programme, Resolutions of the 12th Palestine National Council, 1–9 June 1974', reprinted in Aryeh Y. Yodfat and Yval Arnon-Ohanna (eds), *PLO Strategy and Tactics*, New York: St. Martins Press, 1981, pp. 173–5.

58. *The Times*, 23 Dec. 1969.

59. Richard H. Ullman, 'After Rabat: Middle East Risks and America Roles', *Foreign Affairs*, 53, 2, Jan. 1975, pp. 284–96, p. 284.

60. *Le Monde*, 2 November 1974.

61. Ziegler, *Wilson*, p. 389.

62. Balta and Rulleau, *La Politique arabe de la France*, p. 198.

63. Barzani, *The Impossible Europeans*, p. 147.

64. Israeli Foreign Ministry statement on UN General Assembly Resolution 3210, 15 Oct. 1974, *Israel Documents*, Vol. 3, p. 104.

65. Avi Beker, *The United Nations and Israel: From Recognition to Reprehension*, Lexington Mass., and Toronto: Lexington Books, 1988, p. 82.

66. Valéry Giscard d'Estaing (with Agathe Fourgnaud), *Mémoire vivante*, Paris: Flammarion, 2001, p. 164.

67. British Embassy, Paris, to Foreign Office, 2 Jan. 1975, BNA/FCO 30/3022.

68. Interview with Jean Lacouture, *Al-Nahar*, 26 Oct. 1974.

69. *Frankfurter Allgemeine Zeitung*, 3 Dec. 1974.

70. Bernard Lewis, 'The Anti-Zionist Resolution', *Foreign Affairs*, 55, 1, Oct. 1976, pp. 54–64, p. 57.

71. This UN General Assembly Resolution 3379 (XXX) was passed on 10 Nov. 1975. 72 member states voted in favour of this resolution, 35 voted against and 35 abstained (3 were absent).

72. Helena Cobban, *The Palestinian Liberation Organization—People, Power and Politics*, Cambridge: Cambridge University Press, 1984, p. 234.

73. EAD: Meeting of Coordinating Group, Dublin, 22 Jan. 1975, 3 Feb. 1975, BNA/FCO 30/3022.

74. Minutes of Euro-Arab Dialogue, 17 Dec. 1975, BNA/FCO 30/3045.

75. Memorandum on Euro Arab Dialogue, 10 Jan. 1975, BNA/FCO 30/3022.

76. EAD: Meeting of Coordinating Group, Paris, 17 Dec. 1974, BNA/FCO 30/3022.

77. Euro-Arab Dialogue, Ministers Meeting, Dublin, 13 Feb. 1975, BNA/FCO 30/3023.

78. EAD: Meeting of Coordinating Group, Paris, 17 Dec. 1974, BNA/FCO 30/3022.

79. Safran, 'Engagement in the Middle East', p. 45.

80. See, for example, the Israeli Prime Minister Yitzhak Rabin's emphatic rejection of a role for the PLO or Palestinians in negotiations in *Ma'ariv*, 5 Dec. 1975.

81. Memorandum on the Political Director's Committee, 22–24 Jan. 1975, BNA/FCO 30/3022.

82. *New York Times*, 6 March 1974.

83. *The Times*, 16 March 1974.

84. *The Times*, 20 March 1974.

85. *Le Monde*, 4 April 1974.

86. Atkins, 'The Oil Crisis: This Time the Wolf is Here', p. 487.

87. Stephens, 'Europe in Search of a Policy', p. 17.

88. Community Briefing on Prime Minister Wilson and Foreign Minister Callaghan's Meeting with President Ford and Dr Kissinger, 31 Jan. 1974, BNA/FCO 30/3023.

89. West German briefing to ambassadors on Kissinger visit to Bonn, 19 Feb. 1975, BNA/FCO 30/3023.

90. Kissinger, *Years of Renewal*, p. 1055.

91. Memorandum on Euro-Arab Dialogue, 10 Feb. 1975, BNA/FCO 30/3023.

92. Henri Simonet, 'Energy and the Future of Europe', *Foreign Affairs*, 53, 3, April 1975, pp. 450–63, p. 461.

93. Memorandum on President Ford and North Atlantic Council: Middle East, 24 June 1975, BNA/FCO 30/3031.

94. British Embassy, Washington, to Foreign Office, 1 July 1975, BNA/FCO 30/3032

95. Foreign Office to British Embassy, Brussels, 17 Jan. 1975, BNA/FCO 30/3022.

96. *The Times*, 18 May 1976.

97. Euro Arab Dialogue: Palestinian Participation, 3 Jan. 1975, BNA/FCO 30/3022.

98. Minister of State Memorandum on Euro-Arab Dialogue, 10 Jan. 1975, BNA/FCO 30/3022.

99. Euro-Arab Dialogue: Ministers Meeting, Dublin, 13 Feb. 1975, BNA/FCO 30/3023.

100. Ibid.

101. Memorandum on Euro Arab Dialogue, 10 Jan. 1975, BNA/FCO 30/3022.

102. British Embassy, Paris, to Foreign Office, 12 Feb. 1975, BNA/FCO 30/3023.

103. Community Briefing on Prime Minister Wilson and Foreign Minister Callaghan's Meeting with President Ford and Dr Kissinger, 31 Jan. 1974, BNA/FCO 30/3023.

104. British Embassy, Cairo, to Foreign Office, 10 Feb. 1975, BNA/FCO 30/3023.

105. 'Joint Communiqué: Euro-Arab Dialogue, Cairo, 14 June 1975', BNA/FCO 30/3031

106. Alan R. Taylor, 'How to Bridge the Gap', *MEI*, 67, Feb. 1977, pp. 11–2.

107. See Agreement between the European Economic Community and the State of Israel, 11 May 1975, *Israel Documents*, Vol. 2, p. 211.

108. Address to Knesset by Prime Minister Rabin on the presentation of his government, 3 June 1974, *Israel Documents*, Vol. 3, p. 7.

109. Statement by Foreign Minister Allon to Knesset on EEC-Israel Trade Agreement, 26 May 1975, *Israel Documents*, Vol. 2, pp. 218–21.

110. Minutes on Euro-Arab Dialogue, 11 June 1975, BNA/FCO 30/3030.

111. See *El-Moudjahid*, 13 May 1975 and *Al-Ahram*, 13 May 1975.

112. Address by the Chairman of the Arab Delegation, Meeting of the Euro-Arab Dialogue, 10–14 June 1975, BNA/FCO 30/3031.

113. Palestine News Agency, 16 July 1975.

114. Memorandum, European Political Cooperation: Political Committee Meeting, Dublin, 12–13 May 1975, 14 May 1975, BNA/FCO 30/3027.

115. Fitzgerald, *All in a Life*, pp. 159–61.

116. See 'Dr Fitzgerald visits Middle East' and 'EEC Ministers in Dublin' in *Bulletin of the Department of Foreign Affairs*, 866, 9 June 1975, pp. 7–8.

117. Minister of State Report on Euro-Arab Dialogue at Dublin Meeting, 28 May 1975, BNA/FCO 30/3028.

118. Fitzgerald, *All in a Life*, p. 61.

119. Memorandum on Euro-Arab Dialogue, 27 May 1975, BNA/FCO 30/3028.

120. Bat Ye'or, *The Euro-Arab Axis*, Madison, Teaneck: Fairleigh Dickinson University Press, 2005, pp. 10, 57.

121. Minutes of Meeting of the EAD Coordinating Group, Dublin, 20 June 1975, BNA/FCO 30/3032.

4. GET CARTER

1. West German briefing to ambassadors on Kissinger visit to Bonn, 19 Feb. 1975, BNA/FCO 30/3023.
2. Moshe Dayan, *Story of My Life*, New York: Morrow, 1976, p. 572.
3. EAD-Committee of Permanent Representatives, 19 June 1975, BNA/FCO 30/3031.
4. Michel Jobert, 'Les Véritables dialogues', *La Pensée Nationale*, 25–26 Feb. 1980, p. 23.
5. Goldsborough, 'France, the European Crisis and the Alliance', p. 543.
6. Rafael Israeli, *The Public Diary of President Sadat. Vol. 3, The Road of Pragmatism: June 1975-October 1976*, Leiden: E.J. Brill, 1979, p. 925.
7. *The Times*, 28 Jan. 1975. See also Valéry Giscard d'Estaing, *Le Pouvoir et la vie*, Vol. 1, *La Rencontre*, Paris: Cie 12, 1988, p. 191.
8. See interview with Dr George Habash, *Al-Hadaf*, 3 Aug. 1974.
9. Kissinger, *Years of Renewal*, p. 383.
10. Israel-US Memorandum of Understanding, 1 Sept. 1975, *Israel Documents*, Vol. 3, p. 290.
11. *MEI*, 61, July 1976, p. 18.
12. *The Times*, 1 June 1976.
13. Ibid., 22 May 1976.
14. *MEI*, 63, Sept. 1976, p. 3.
15. Text of Final Communiqué of the General Committee of the EAD, Tunis, 10–12 February 1977, BNA/FCO 93/1253.
16. *Le Monde*, 12 Feb. 1977.
17. Alan R. Taylor, 'Europe and the Arabs: A Disappointing Dialogue', *MEI*, 78, Dec. 1977, p. 14.
18. Ibid.
19. William B. Quandt, *Peace Process: American Diplomacy and the Arab-Israeli Conflict Since 1967*, Los Angeles: Brookings Institute Press and University of California Press, 3rd edition, 2005, p. 128.
20. John Bosworth, 'The British in Europe: A Balance Sheet', *Encounter*, XLVI, 2, Feb. 1976, pp. 20–6.
21. Memorandum on Euro-Arab Dialogue General Committee: Political Matters, 17 Nov. 1977, BNA/FCO 93/1253.
22. Ibid.
23. Ahmad Sidqi Al-Dajani, 'The PLO and the Euro-Arab Dialogue', *Journal of Palestine Studies*, IX, 3, Spring 1980, pp. 81–98, pp. 90, 93.
24. See British Embassy, Bonn, to Foreign Office, 13 Aug. 1976, BNA/FCO 93/909.
25. British Embassy, Brussels, to Foreign Office, 29 Oct. 1977, BNA/FCO 93/1253.

26. Palestine National Council, Political Declaration, 22 March 1977, reprinted in Yeduda Lukacs (ed.), *The Israeli-Palestinian Conflict: a Documentary Record*, pp. 333–5.

27. Extract from Note of a Meeting between the Foreign and Commonwealth Secretary and Israeli Foreign Minister, Mr Yigal Allon', 1 March 1975, 3 March 1975, BNA/FCO 30/3024.

28. *The Times*, 9 Feb. 1977.

29. Statement on the Middle East by members of the EEC, 29 June 1977, *Israel Documents*, Vol. 4, pp. 19–20.

30. Giscard d'Estaing, *Le Pouvoir et la vie, Vol. 1, La Rencontre*, p. 195.

31. Memorandum on Euro-Arab Dialogue General Committee: Political Matters, 17 Nov. 1977, BNA/FCO 93/1253.

32. Ibid.

33. EAD: General Committee, Brussels, 3rd Day, 29 Oct. 1977, BNA/FCO 93/1253.

34. *Toward Peace in the Middle East, Report of a Study Group*, Los Angeles: Brookings Institute, 1975.

35. Quandt, *Peace Process*, p. 180.

36. *New York Times*, 10 May 1977.

37. *Economist*, 28 May 1977, p. 13.

38. See Lawrence Freedman, *A Choice of Enemies: America Confronts the Middle East*, London: Orion Books, 2008, pp. 43–4.

39. *Economist*, 19 Nov. 1977, p. 15.

40. Abba Eban, 'Camp David-The Unfinished Business', *Foreign Affairs*, 57, 2, Winter, 1978–1979, pp. 343–54, p. 344.

41. William B. Quandt, 'The Middle East Crises', *Foreign Affairs*, 58, 3, 1979, pp. 540–62, p. 547.

42. Kissinger, *Years of Renewal*, p. 361.

43. Raymond Barre, *Au tournant du siècle*, Paris: Plon, 1988, p. 53.

44. 'Statement by Foreign Ministers of the EEC, Brussels, 22 Nov.1977', reprinted in *European Political Cooperation*, 3rd edition, Bonn: Press and Information Office, 1978, p. 34.

45. Lily Gardner-Feldman, *The Special Relationship between West Germany and Israel*, Boston: Allen & Unwin, 1984.

46. Record of Conversation between the Minister of State, the Rt Hon Roy Hattersley and Dr Martin Bangemann, Secretary General of the FDP, 1 July 1975, BNA/FCO 30/3034.

47. Prime Minister James Callaghan, *Parliamentary Debates* (Hansard) Fifth Series, Vol. 940, House of Commons Official Report, Session 1977–78, 7 Dec. 1977, col. 872, p. 1401.

48. *The Times*, 21 Dec. 1977.

49. Statement on the Middle East by the Heads of Government of the EEC, London, 29 June 1978, *Israel Documents*, Vol. 5, p. 442.

50. *Frankfurter Allgemeine Zeitung*, 21 Sept. 1978.

51. *Le Monde*, 19 Sept. 1978.

52. *Economist*, 11 February 1978, p. 25.

53. Kissinger, *Years of Renewal*, p. 367.

54. *Financial Times*, 27 March 1979.

55. Jawad, *Euro-Arab Relations*, p. 146.

56. *Financial Times*, 26 March 1979.

57. Sam Younger, 'US Turns a Blind Eye to PLO', *MEI*, 104, 20 July 1979, p. 3.

58. *Le Monde*, 21 Sept. 1978; *The Times*, 5 Nov. 1981.

59. *Le Monde*, 13 March 1979.

60. See Report of the Security Council Commission on Palestine, 25 Nov. 1980, Document S/14268, UNSC Official Records, 35th Year, Supplement for October, November and December 1980, p. 61.

61. *MEI*, 97, 13 April 1979, pp. 2–3.

62. *Le Monde*, 31 March 1980.

63. Communiqué du Conseil des ministres du 29 mars 1979, reprinted in *France-Pays Arabes*, April-May 1979, p. 10.

64. See Fiorella Seiler, '"King of the Armed Ghetto": Israel in the West German National Press during Menachem Begin's First Government (1977–1981)', Unpublished PhD Thesis, University of London, 2001, pp. 100–80.

65. Text of speech by James Callaghan in House of Commons debate, 25 March 1975, Vol. 889, col. 286, http://hansard.millbanksystems.com/commons/1975/mar/25/foreign-affairs

66. Record of Conversation between the Minister of State, the Rt Hon Roy Hattersley and Dr Martin Bangemann, Secretary General of the FDP, 1 July 1975, BNA/FCO 30/3034.

67. Kenneth O. Morgan, *Callaghan: A Life*, Oxford University Press, 1997, p. 608; James Callaghan, *Time and Chance*, London: Collins, 1987, p. 292.

68. See, for example, Louis Heren, 'Israel's founding father reaps the rewards of terrorism', *The Times*, 19 May 1977. See also an editorial entitled 'A killer calls', *Sunday Express*, 9 Jan. 1972.

69. *The Times*, 23 May 1977.

70. Text of speech by David Owen in House Commons debate, 15 June 1977, Vol. 933, col. 368, http://hansard.millbanksystems.com/commons/1977/jun/15/israel

71. *The Times*, 3 Dec. 1977.

72. Statement to Knesset by Prime Minister Begin presenting Israel's Peace Plan, 28 December 1977, *Israel Documents*, Vol. 6, p. 274.

73. *The Prime Minister talks to the* Observer: interview by Kenneth Harris, London: Observer Publications, 1979.

74. Statement by EEC on its Middle East Policy, 26 March 1979, reprinted in *MEI*, 96, 30 March 1979, p. 15.

75. Statement by the Council of Foreign Ministers of the EEC, 18 June 1979, *Israel Documents*, Vol. 6, p. 69.

76. *Al-Ahram*, 9 and 16 November 1978, quoted in David Hirst and Irene Beeson, *Sadat*, New York and London: Faber and Faber, 1981, p. 312.

77. *The Times*, 27 May 1979.

78. *Al Ahram*, 24 March 1979 and 2 April 1979, quoted in Hirst and Beeson, *Sadat*, p. 263.

79. Quandt, *Peace Process*, p. 217.

80. *The Times*, 6 Sept. 1975.

81. Damascus Domestic Radio, 17 Nov. 1977.

82. Quoted in Hirst and Beeson, *Sadat*, p. 340.

83. See Transcript of President Sadat's Press Conference with Israeli editors, 15 Sept. 1979, *Israel Documents*, Vol. 7, pp. 112–3.

84. *MEI*, 111, 26 Oct. 1979, p. 3.

85. Foreign Minister Dayan to Foreign Ministers of the EEC, 20 June 1979, *Israel Documents*, Vol. 6, p. 70; Address to UN General Assembly by Foreign Minister Dayan, 27 Sept. 1979, *Israel Documents*, Vol. 6, p. 136.

86. See Address to the Council of Europe by Foreign Minister Dayan, 10 Oct. 1979, *Israel Documents*, Vol. 6, pp. 139–43.

87. *New York Times*, 28 March 1979.

88. *Le Monde*, 15 July 1979.

89. Text of speech by Lord Carrington at the Arab Community dinner in London, 21 Jan. 1981, reprinted in *MEI*, 143, 13 Feb 1981, p. 15.

90. *The Times*, 15 Nov. 1979.

91. Abba Eban, 'Camp David-The Unfinished Business', p. 345; *The Times*, 13 June 1980.

92. Sir Harold Beeley, 'Extending the Euro-Arab Dialogue', *MEI*, 72, June 1977, p. 11.

93. Sam Younger, 'US Turns a Blind Eye to PLO', p. 3.

94. *International Herald Tribune*, 2 July 1979.

95. Livia Rokach, 'Is the Euro-Arab Dialogue On or Off?', *MEI*, 110, 12 Oct. 1979, p. 3.

96. Walter J. Levy, 'Oil and the Decline of the West', *Foreign Affairs*, 58, 5, Summer 1980, pp. 999–1015, p. 1004.

97. John Reddaway, 'Western Opinion and the Palestinians', *MEI*, 115, 21 Dec. 1979, p. 4.

98. *New York Times*, 26 Sept. 1979.

99. See speech by Mr Michael O'Kennedy, UN General Assembly, 34th Session, 25 Sept. 1979, *Official Records of the UNGA*, p. 121.

100. See Fred Khouri, *The Arab-Israeli Dilemma*, New York: Syracuse University Press, 1985, p. 415.

101. *MEI*, 109, 28 Sept.1979, p. 2.

102. See Address to the Council of Europe by Foreign Minister Dayan, 10 October 1979, *Israel Documents*, Vol. 6, p. 141 and Interview with Foreign Minister Dayan on Israel Television, 19 Oct. 1979, *Israel Documents*, Vol. 6, p. 144.

103. Foreign Minister Dayan to Foreign Ministers of the EEC, 20 June 1979, *Israel Documents*, Vol. 6, p. 70; Address to UN General Assembly by Foreign Minister Dayan, 27 Sept. 1979, *Israel Documents*, Vol. 6, p. 136.

104. *Le Monde*, 27 July 1979.

105. Ibid., 27 October 1979.

106. *New York Times*, 30 Oct. 1979.

107. Uri Bar-Joseph, *The Watchman Fell Asleep: the Surprise of Yom Kippur and Its Sources*, Albany, New York: State University Press of New York, 2005, p. 95.

108. *The Times*, 5 Sept. 1978.

109. Aaron David Miller, 'The PLO', in Robert O. Freedman (ed.), *The Middle East Since Camp David*, Boulder and London: Westview Press, 1984, pp. 193–228, p. 205.

110. Christopher Hitchens, 'Interview with Chancellor Kreisky', *MEI*, 126, 6 June 1980, p. 7.

111. *Le Monde*, 11 July 1979.

112. See Statements in the Knesset by Prime Minister Begin and Labour Party Chairman Peres on the Visit of Yasser Arafat to Austria, 5 July 1979, *Israel Documents*, Vol. 6, pp. 79–86.

113. *Le Monde*, 11 July 1979.

114. See Interview with Chancellor Bruno Kreisky, *al-Safir*, 16 June 1980.

115. Stephen J. Artner, 'The Middle East: A Chance for Europe?', *International Affairs*, 56, 3, Summer 1980, pp. 420–42, p. 438.

5. BET IN VENICE

1. Theo Sommer, 'Europe and the American Connection', *Foreign Affairs*, 58, 3, 1979, pp. 622–36, p. 623.

2. Emanuele Gazzo, 'Sadat must be given backing', *Europe*, 12 Feb. 1981.

3. Hisham Sharabi, 'Can Europe Help?', *MEI*, 106, 17 Aug. 1979, p. 10.

4. *MEI*, 97, 13 April 1979, pp. 2–3.

5. Quandt, 'The Middle East Crises', p. 548.

6. *Guardian*, 19 Sept. 1979.
7. *MEI*, 111, 26 Oct. 1979, p. 5.
8. 'Memorandum on Euro-Arab Dialogue prepared by European Integration Department, 17 Dec. 1975', BNA/FCO 30/3045.
9. Jawad, *Euro-Arab Relations*, p. 159.
10. *MEI*, 119, 29 Feb. 1980, p. 4.
11. Livia Rokach, 'No Progress in Euro-Arab Dialogue', *MEI*, 120, 14 March 1980, p. 5.
12. Ibid.
13. See Communiqué on the Palestinian right to self-determination, published following the visit of President Giscard d'Estaing's visit to Kuwait, 1–3 March 1980, reprinted in *MEI*, 120, 14 March 1980, p. 15.
14. *Le Monde*, 4 March 1980.
15. Paul-Marie de La Gorce, 'Europe and the Arab-Israeli Conflict: A Survey', *Journal of Palestine Studies*, XXVI, 3, Spring 1997, p. 11.
16. Alexander M. Haig Jr., *Caveat: Realism, Reagan, and Foreign Policy*, New York: Macmillan, 1984, p. 327.
17. Text of speech by Lord Carrington, House of Lords debate, 17 March 1980, Vol. 407, col. 5, http://hansard.millbanksystems.com/lords/1980/mar/17/the-palestine-liberation-organisation
18. Speech by Douglas Hurd, MP, Minister of State at the Foreign Office, to the Middle East Association, 30 Jan. 1980, reprinted in *MEI*, 118, 15 Feb. 1980, p. 1.
19. See text of interview with Mr Douglas Hurd, Minister of State at the Foreign and Commonwealth Office, BBC Arabic Service, 5 March 1980, reprinted in Artner, 'The Middle East: A Chance for Europe?', p. 435
20. Interview with Yasser Arafat, *Le Monde*, 10 March 1980.
21. *The Times*, 13 June 1980.
22. Text of speech by James Callaghan in House of Commons debate, 16 June 1980, Vol. 986, col. 1132, http://hansard.millbanksystems.com/commons/1980/jun/16/european-council-venice-meeting
23. Rondot, 'France and Palestine, p. 94.
24. Belgian-Iraqi Joint communiqué, 13 July 1979, reprinted in *MEI*, 106, 17 Aug. 1979.
25. *Le Monde*, 27 Oct. 1979.
26. See speech by Mr Michael O'Kennedy, UN General Assembly 34th Session, 25 Sept. 1979, *Official Records of the UNGA*, p. 121.
27. Irish Government Communique, 10 Feb. 1980, Dublin: Irish Government Information Service. See also *Irish Times*, 20 Feb. 1980.
28. See 'Bahrain Declaration: Ireland's Definitive Official Commitment to an Independent Palestine', Dublin: Eurabia Irish Office, 1980.

29. *Ma'ariv*, 12 Feb. 1980.

30. *The Times*, 14 March 1980; *New York Times*, 21 April 1980.

31. Prime Minister Begin's statement in the Knesset on Israel's foreign policy, 2 June 1980, *Israel Documents*, Vol. 6, pp. 268–9. See also *Yediot Achronot*, 25 April 1980.

32. See *The Times*, 28 April 1980.

33. *Tishrin*, 25 March 1980.

34. *Al-Tali'a*, 13 March 1980.

35. *Al-Safir*, 13 March 1980.

36. *Filastin al-Thawra*, 17 March 1980.

37. *Al Hadaf*, 15 March 1980.

38. *Al-Hurriya*, 10 March 1980.

39. Council of Europe, Parliamentary Assembly, 32nd Ordinary Session, Resolution 728 on the situation in the Middle East, Strasbourg, 24 April 1980, http://assembly.coe.int/Mainf.asp?link=/Documents/AdoptedText/ta80/ERES728.htm

40. Foreign Ministry statement on Council of Europe Resolution, 24 April 1980, *Israel Documents*, Vol. 6, p. 241.

41. *Yediot Achronot*, 25 April 1980; *The Times*, 20 Feb. 1980.

42. Interview of Prime Minister Begin with French speaking journalists, 21 March 1980, *Israel Documents*, Vol. 6, pp. 208–13.

43. *Ma'ariv*, 19 April 1979. See also similar arguments made earlier by Dayan in interviews with *Ma'ariv*, 19 Aug. 1977 and *Yedioth Aharonoth*, 19 Sept. 1977.

44. See Interview with Foreign Minister Shamir on Israel Radio, 20 March 1980, *Israel Documents*, Vol. 6, 205–7

45. *MEI*, 122, 11 April 1980, p. 1.

46. *New York Times*, 19 April 1980.

47. John Palmer, 'The EEC Goes its Own Way', *MEI*, 125, 23 May 1980, p. 2.

48. Letter to Prime Minister Begin from a group of Members of the House of Commons, 21 May 1980, *Israel Documents*, Vol. 6, pp. 272–3.

49. Text of Open letter to presdient Carter signed by joint presidents of Parliamentary Association for Euro-Arab Cooperation, reprinted in *MEI*, 126, 6 June 1980, p. 3.

50. Kissinger, *Years of Renewal*, p. 394.

51. *New York Times*, 31 May 1980.

52. Saleh A. Al-Mani, *The Euro-Arab Dialogue: A Study in Associative Diplomacy*, London: Palgrave Macmillan, 1983, p. 127.

53. Greilsammer and Weiler, *Europe's Middle East Dilemma*, p. 45.

54. *MEI*, 104, 20 July 1979, p. 4.

55. Robert Swann, 'New Success for Palestinians in Europe', *MEI*, 124, 9 May 1980, pp. 3–4.

56. Artner, 'The Middle East: A Chance for Europe?', p. 433.
57. John Cooley, 'The West's Ever Widening Rift over Palestine', *MEI*, 126, 6 June 1980, p. 3.
58. *New York Times*, 31 May 1980.
59. Statement in Knesset by Prime Minister Begin on Israel Foreign Policy, 2 June 1980, *Israel Documents*, Vol. 2, pp. 266–72.
60. John Palmer, 'The EEC goes its own way', *MEI*, 125, 23 May 1980, p. 2.
61. *New York Times*, 14 June 1980.
62. *Al-Far*, 9 March 1980.
63. See Resolutions of the fourth congress of Al-Fatah, 1 June 1980, reprinted in *UN Security Council Official Records*, 35th Year, Supplement April, May, June 1980, p. 87.
64. André Fontaine, 'Transatlantic Doubts and Dreams', *Foreign Affairs*, 59, 3, 1980, pp. 578–93, p. 589.
65. See the 'Resolution of the Heads of Government and Ministers of Foreign Affairs of the European Council (the Venice Declaration) 13 June 1980', reprinted in Yeduda Lukacs (ed.), *The Israeli–Palestinian Conflict: a Documentary Record*, pp. 17–19.
66. *New York Times*, 13 June 1980.
67. Interview with Prime Minister Margaret Thatcher, *Al-Ahram*, 12 Sept. 1985.
68. *New York Times*, 13 June 1980.
69. Peter Carrington, *Reflect on Things Past: The Memoirs of Lord Carrington*, London: Collins, 1988, p. 341.
70. *New York Times*, 14 June 1980.
71. *New York Times*, 15 June 1980.
72. *The Times*, 16 June 1980.
73. *Daily Telegraph*, 16 June 1980.
74. *New York Times*, 15 June 1980.
75. *Le Monde*, 7 August 1980.
76. Al-Mani, *The Euro-Arab Dialogue*, p. 117.
77. Yezid Sayigh, *Armed Struggle and the Search for State: The Palestinian National Movement, 1949–1993*, Washington, DC and Oxford: Oxford University Press, 1997, p. 502.
78. Cooley, 'The West's Ever Widening Rift over Palestine', p. 3.
79. *Le Figaro*, 14 June 1980.
80. *Ha'aretz*, 15 June 1980.
81. Israeli cabinet statement in response to the Venice Declaration, 15 June 1980, *Israel Documents*, Vol. 6, pp. 276–7.
82. Statement in Knesset by Foreign Minister Shamir, 19 June 1980, *Israel Documents*, Vol. 6, pp. 281–3.

83. Ibid.

84. *The Times*, 17 June 1980; See also Press Conference with Foreign Minister Peres, 28 January 1987, *Israel Documents*, Vol. 10, p. 586.

85. *The Times*, 18 March 1981

86. Ibid., 14 Jan. 1981.

87. *New York Times*, 21 June 1967.

88. *The Times*, 16 Oct. 1980.

89. *Le Figaro*, 14 June 1980.

90. Address by Foreign Minister Shamir at the Herut Central Committee, 24 Aug. 1980, *Israel Documents*, Vol. 6, pp. 333–9.

91. Sergio Minerbi, 'Israel et l'Europe', *Politique Etrangère*, 46, 2, 1981, p. 440.

92. *Europe*, 12 Feb. 1981.

93. John Palmer, 'Thorn Reports to the Community', *MEI*, 134, 12 Sept. 1980, p. 3.

94. *The Times*, 3 Sept. 1980.

95. *New York Times*, 21 May 1981.

96. Livia Rokach, 'Is the Euro-Arab Dialogue On or Off?', *MEI*, 110, 12 Oct. 1979, p. 3.

97. Steve Coll, *The Bin Ladens: The Story of a Family and its Fortune*, New York, London: Allen Lane, 2008, p. 157.

98. *New York Times*, 17 Feb. 1976.

99. Ibid., 7 Oct. 1979.

100. Text of speech by Lord Carrington in House of Lords debate, 9 July 1980, Vol. 411, col. 1192, http://hansard.millbanksystems.com/lords/1980/jul/09/africa-and-the-middle-east#column_1192.

101. Carrington, *Reflect on Things Past*, p. 340.

102. Text of speech by Lord Carrington, House of Lords debate, 9 July 1980, Vol. 411, col. 1187, http://hansard.millbanksystems.com/lords/1980/jul/09/africa-and-the-middle-east#column_1192.

103. Lord Carrington, 'European Political Co-Operation: America Should Welcome it', *International Affairs*, 58, 1, Winter 1981–82, pp. 1–6, p. 4.

104. Carrington, *Reflect on Things Past*, p. 340.

105. Al-Mani, *The Euro-Arab Dialogue*, p. 110.

106. Philip Robins, 'Always the Bridesmaid: Europe and the Middle East Peace Process', *Cambridge Review of International Affairs*, 10, 2, Winter-Spring, 1997, pp. 69–83, p. 74.

107. *Los Angeles Times*, 14 June 1980. See also Valéry Giscard d'Estaing, *Le Pouvoir et la vie, Vol. II, L'Affrontement*, Paris: Cie, 1991, p. 448.

108. *MEI*, 129, 19 July 1980, p. 5.

6. DUE SOUTH

1. Interview with Prime Minister Begin on Israel Radio, 7 May 1981, *Israel Documents*, Vol. 7, p. 28; *New York Times*, 30 April 1981.

2. Elfi Pallis, 'Holocaust Politics', *MEI*, 150, 22 May 1981, pp. 9–10.

3. Interview with Prime Minister Begin on French Television, 25 Nov. 1981, *Israel Documents*, Vol. 7, p. 195.

4. *The Times*, 3 Nov. 1981.

5. *Ma'ariv*, 15 May 1981.

6. *MEI*, 149, p. 1, 8 May 1981; *Economist*, 9 May 1981, p. 81.

7. Margaret Thatcher, press conference following Venice Council meeting, 13 June 1980, in Margaret Thatcher, 'Complete Public Statements, 1945–1990'. Database and Compilation (CD-Rom) (hereafter, Thatcher, Complete Public Statements, 1945–1990), Oxford University Press, 1999.

8. Margaret Thatcher, interviews with BBC television and radio, 13 June 1980, in Margaret Thatcher, Complete Public Statements, 1945–1990.

9. Margaret Thatcher, Press Conference for American Correspondents in London, 25 June 1980, in Margaret Thatcher, Complete Public Statements, 1945–1990.

10. Margaret Thatcher, Press Conference for Washington Press Club, 26 Feb. 1981, in Margaret Thatcher, Complete Public Statements, 1945–1990.

11. Margaret Thatcher, TV Interview for ABC News 'Issues and Answers', 28 Feb. 1981, in Margaret Thatcher, Complete Public Statements, 1945–1990.

12. Statement in Knesset by Foreign Minister Shamir, 19 June 1980, *Israel Documents*, Vol. 6, p. 283.

13. On the Israeli response to the Community abstention on UNGA resolution ES-7/2, 29 July 1980, see statement in Knesset by Foreign Minister Shamir, 30 July 1980, *Israel Documents*, Vol. 6, p. 318.

14. Seiler, '"King of the Armed Ghetto"', p. 284.

15. Mark Stuart, *Douglas Hurd: Public Servant*, Edinburgh and London: Mainstream Publishing, 1998, p. 119.

16. Robert Swann, 'Hague Meeting Underlines Shift in Dutch Opinion on Palestine', *MEI*, 135, 10 Oct. 1980, p. 4.

17. Foreign Ministry reaction to the transfer of the Dutch embassy from Jerusalem to Tel Aviv, 26 Aug. 1980, *Israel Documents*, Vol. 6, p. 339.

18. E.E. Wynne, 'Uninhibited: Greece and the PLO', *MEI*, 166, 15 Jan. 1982.

19. *Kathimerini*, 9 Jan. 1985.

20. Greilsammer and Weiler, *Europe's Middle East Dilemma*, pp. 35–45. Also see *Athens News Agency Bulletin*, 3 Nov. 1981.

21. *Athens News Agency Bulletin*, 10 Dec. 1981.

22. See Said K. Aburish, *Arafat, from Defender to Dictator*, London: Bloomsbury, 1998. Also see *New York Times*, 15 Nov. 1981.

23. Sir Anthony Parsons, 'The Middle East', in Peter Byrd (ed.), *British Foreign Policy Under Thatcher*, New York and London: St Martin's Press, 1989, pp. 76–95, p. 88.

24. Cabinet Statement on Sinai Multinational Force, 8 Nov. 1981, *Israel Documents*, Vol. 7, p. 183; Interview with Foreign Minister Shamir, *Ma'ariv*, 4 Dec. 1981.

25. Statement by the four European countries on their decision to join the multinational force in Sinai, 23 Nov. 1981 and statement by the Ten member governments of the European Economic Community, 23 Nov.1981, reprinted in *MEI*, 163, 27 Nov. 1981, p. 15.

26. *New York Times*, 7 Nov. 1981.

27. See J.W. Friend, *The Long Presidency: France in the Mitterrand Years, 1981–1995*, Boulder, CO: Westview Press, 1998.

28. Interview with Jean Lacouture, *Al-Nahar*, 26 Oct. 1974.

29. Yves Azeroul and Yves Derai, *Mitterrand, Israël et les juifs*, Paris: Éditions Robert Laffont, 1990, p. 86.

30. *New York Times*, 1 July 1981.

31. Statement by Prime Minister Begin to Herut Convention, 3 June 1979, *Israel Documents*, Vol. 6, p. 45.

32. *Yedioth Achronot*, 28 Sept.1981.

33. Interview with Prime Minister Begin on French Television, 25 Nov. 1981, *Israel Documents*, Vol. 7, p. 195; Interview with Prime Minister Begin on Israel Radio, 7 May 1981, *Israel Documents*, Vol. 7, p. 28.

34. Dominique Moisi, 'La France de Mitterrand et le conflit du Proche-Orient: comment concilier emotion et politique', *Politique Etrangère*, 47, 2, 1982, pp. 395–402, p. 395.

35. Interview with Yasser Arafat, *MEI*, 167, 29 Jan. 1982, p. 14.

36. *Athens News Agency Bulletin*, 15 Jan. 1982.

37. *New York Times*, 17 Aug. 1981. See also Raymond Barre, *Au Tournant du siècle*, p. 56.

38. See, for example, Ben Soetendorp, *Foreign Policy in the European Union, Theory History and Practice*, London: Addison Wesley Longman, 1999, p. 108; Pia Christina Wood, 'France and the Israeli-Palestinian Conflict: the Mitterrand Policies, 1981–1992', *Middle East Journal*, 47, 1, Winter 1993, pp. 21–40, p. 22 and Philippe Rondot, 'France and Palestine', p. 96.

39. Fritz Stern, 'Germany in a Semi-Gaullist Europe', *Foreign Affairs*, 58, 4, Spring 1980, pp. 867–86, p. 878.

40. A.W. DePorte, 'France's New Realism', *Foreign Affairs*, 63,1, Fall 1984, pp. 144–65.

41. *Le Monde*, 19 July 1981.

42. *The Times*, 31 Aug. and 8 Nov. 1981.

43. Robert Swann, 'France and Israel: The Balance is Negative', *MEI*, 170, 12 March 12, 1982, p. 3.

44. E.A. Kolodziej, 'France and the Arms Trade', *International Affairs*, 56, 1, 1980, pp. 58–9; *New York Times*, 28 Sept. 1981.

45. Quoted in Ronald Tiersky, *François Mitterrand*, New York: St Martin's Press, 2000, p. 366.

46. *New York Times*, 4 March 1982.

47. *New York Times*, 10 June 1981.

48. LaPorte, 'France's New Realism', p. 159.

49. Azeroul and Derai, *Mitterrand, Israël et les juifs*, p. 216.

50. Andrew Gowers and Tony Walker, *Arafat: The Biography*, London: Virgin Books, 1990, pp. 237–8.

51. *Athens News Agency Bulletin*, 20 Sept. 1982.

52. Adopted as resolution 508 (1982) at UN Security Council meeting 2374, 5 June 1982, *UN Security Council Official Records*, 37th Year, p. 3.

53. Address by Prime Minster Begin in the Knesset, 12 Aug. 1982, *Israel Documents*, Vol. 8, p. 137.

54. Statement by Ambassador Dorr, meeting 2375 of the UN Security Council, 6 June 1982, *UN Security Council Official Records*, 37th Year, p. 2.

55. See UN Security Council Resolution 509 (1982), 6 June 1982, *UN Security Council Official Records*, 37th Year, Supplement for April, May and June 1982, p. 148.

56. See meeting 2381 of the UN Security Council, 26 June 1982, *UN Security Council Official Records*, 37th Year, p. 2

57. See Israeli cabinet communiqué, 27 June 1982, *Israel Documents*, Vol. 8, p. 87.

58. See draft resolution submitted by Egypt and France, 28 July 1982, document S/15317, *UN Security Council Official Records*, 37th Year, Supplement for July, August and September 1982, p. 25.

59. See resolution 518 (1982) adopted at UN Security Council meeting 2392, 12 August 1982, *UN Security Council Official Records*, 37th Year, p. 9.

60. Alain Dieckhoff, 'Europe and the Arab World: The Difficult Dialogue', p. 278.

61. Pamela Ann Smith, 'The European Reaction to Israel's Invasion', *Journal of Palestine Studies*, XI-XII, 4–5, Summer-Fall, 1982, pp. 38–47, pp. 44–5.

62. *Le Monde*, 22 and 23 June 1982.

63. *New York Times*, 21 Dec. 1983.

64. Statement on the Situation in the Middle East issued by the Ministers for Foreign Affairs of the EEC member states, 20 Sept. 1982, reprinted in *UN*

Security Council Official Records, 37th Year, Supplement for July, August and September 1982, p. 91.

65. Address to the 37th General Assembly of the UN by the Minister for Foreign Affairs Collins, 30 Sept. 1982, *Statements and Speeches*, No. 4, Dublin: Department of Foreign Affairs, 1982.

66. Wayne Northcutt, *Mitterrand: A Political Biography*, New York and London: Holmes & Meier, 1992, p. 123

67. P. Rondot, 'France and Palestine', p. 97.

68. *New York Times*, 14. Aug 1982.

69. See *Report on the Danish EC-Presidency in the Second Half of 1982*, Copenhagen: Ministry of Foreign Affairs, 1983, pp. 33–4.

70. Sir Anthony Parsons, 'The Middle East', p. 89.

71. European Council, Conclusions of meeting, Brussels, 21–22 March 1983, http://aei.pitt.edu/1432/01/Brussels_march_1983.pdf

72. R.B. Soetendorp, 'The Netherlands', in *European Foreign Policy Making and the Arab Israeli Conflict*, p. 44; *The Times*, 7 Feb. 1983; *New York Times*, 23 March 1983.

73. See *Athens News Agency Bulletin*, 23 June 1983 and Elie A. Salem, *Violence and Diplomacy in Lebanon, The Troubled Years, 1982–1988*, London: I.B. Tauris, 1995, pp. 62, 89.

74. *Athens Information Office Newsletter*, 10 Nov. 1983.

75. Shada Islam, 'Greece and Middle East: Silencing Papandreou', *MEI*, 215, 23 Dec. 1982, p. 3.

76. Ibid.

77. Jawad, *Euro-Arab Relations*, p. 237.

78. *Le Monde*, 15 May 1986.

79. See Press Conference after London European Council, 6 Dec. 1986, Margaret Thatcher, Complete Public Statements, 1945–1990, p. 24.

80. Beate Lindermann, 'Votes of EU United Nations on Questions Related to Israel, in Europe and Israel', in Greilsammer and Weiler (eds), *Israel and Europe*, pp. 303–12, pp. 310, 311.

81. Margaret Thatcher, *The Downing Street Years*, London: HarperCollins, 1993, p. 511.

82. Statement in the Knesset by Prime Minister Peres, 28 October 1985, *Israel Documents*, Vol. 9, p. 295.

83. Interview with Defence Minister Rabin on Israel Television, 30 Dec. 1985, *Israel Documents*, Vol. 9, p. 374.

84. Sir Anthony Parsons, 'The Middle East', p. 90.

85. Interview with Prime Minister Peres on Israel Television, 27 Oct. 1985, *Israel Documents*, Vol. 9, p. 291.

86. *New York Times*, 23 Aug. 1986.

87. Comments by Shamir on talks with Prime Minister Thatcher, 4 June 1985, *Israel Documents*, Vol. 9, p. 198. See also Address by Prime Minister Thatcher at State Dinner held in her Honour, Jerusalem, 25 May 1986, *Israel Documents*, Vol. 9, p. 457.

88. *New York Times*, 21 Feb. 1983. Also see Interview with Vice Premier and Foreign Minister Shamir on Israel Radio, 23 Oct. 1985, *Israel Documents*, Vol. 9, p. 285.

89. Address by President Herzog to the European Parliament, 12 Feb. 1985, *Israel Documents*, Vol. 9, p. 135.

90. Gideon Rafael, *Destination Peace*, p. 359.

91. Miguel Angel Moratinos, 'A shared past: Spain and Israel', *Ha'aretz*, 12 April 2004.

92. *New York Times*, 26 Sept. 1979.

93. Text of Early Day Motion, House of Commons, 5 June 1980, reprinted in *MEI*, 127, 20 June 1980, p. 2.

94. Address by Vice Premier and Foreign Minister Shamir to World Jewish Conference, 28 Jan. 1986, *Israel Documents*, Vol. 9, p. 397.

95. Prime Minister's bureau statement on ties with Spain, 17 Jan. 1986, *Israel Documents*, Vol. 9, p. 394. See also N. Lorch, 'Israel and Spain: Diplomatic Relations', in Yegar, Govrin, and Oded (eds), *Israel's Foreign Policy*, Jerusalem: Ministry for Foreign Affairs, pp. 398–403.

96. Esther Barbe, 'Spain and CSFP: The Emergence of a Major Player?', *Mediterranean Politics*, 5, 2, Summer 2000, pp. 44–63, p. 48.

97. Patrick Keatinge, *A Place Among the Nations*, Dublin: Institute of Public Administration, 1978, p. 274.

98. *Kathimerini*, 20 May 1983.

99. E.E. Wynne, 'Unimpressed: Greece and Israel', *MEI*, 202, 10 June 1983, p. 8.

100. See Richard Clogg, A *Concise History of Greece*, Cambridge: Cambridge University Press, 1992.

101. *Athens News Agency Daily Bulletin*, 23 June 1983.

102. *MEI*, 280, 25 July 1986, p. 9.

103. Aaron S. Klieman, *Israel and the World After 40 Years*, New York and London: Pergamon-Brassey's, 1990, pp. 95–6.

104. Statement in Knesset by Prime Minister Shamir, 12 March 1984, *Israel Documents*, Vol. 9, p. 538; Statement to the Press by Foreign Minister Peres, 28 January 1987, *Israel Documents*, Vol. 9, p. 585.

105. Michel Rocard, *A l'épreuve des faits: Textes politiques, 1979–1985*, Paris: Éditions du Seuil, 1986, p. 83.

106. Prime Minister Margaret Thatcher, Interview with *Al-Ahram*, 12 Sept. 1985.

107. Majjed al-Sheik, 'Europe and the Zionists', *Al-Watan*, 27 May 1986.

108. Mattityahu Peled, 'Why Europe must Act', *MEI*, 284, 26 Sept. 1986, p. 15.

109. See foreword by Mahmoud S. Rabbani, to Lakhdar Brahimi, 'Who is Speaking to Whom in the Euro-Arab Dialogue', *Euro-Arab Dialogue Lectures II*, The Hague: The Luftia Rabbani Foundation, 1986, p. 9.

110. Shada Islam, 'The Honest Broker', *MEI*, 276, 30 May 1986, p. 13.

111. *New York Times*, 23 Aug. 1986.

112. Shada Islam, 'Conference Time', *MEI*, 295, 6 March 1987, p. 10.

113. See the Brussels European Declaration, 23 Feb. 1987, reprinted in Yeduda Lukacs (ed.), *The Israeli-Palestinian Conflict: a Documentary Record*, p. 27.

114. Shada Islam, 'Disappointed Tindemans', *MEI*, 303, 27 June 1987, p. 14.

115. *New York Times*, 12 Feb. 1987.

116. Statement by Israeli Prime Minister's spokesman, 13 May 1987, *Israel Documents*, Vol. 9, p. 650.

117. *The Times*, 24 Feb. 1987.

118. *New York Times*, 13 March 1988.

119. See Elfriede Regelsberger, 'The Dialogue of the EC/Twelve with Other Groups of States', *The International Spectator*, 23, 4, Oct. 1988, pp. 252–69.

120. Jean-Bernard Raimond, *Le Quai d'Orsay à l'épreuve de la cohabitation*, Paris: Flammarion, 1989, p. 191.

121. *MEI*, 334, 23 Sept. 1988, p. 5.

7. THE BOSNIA COMPLEX

1. See the Palestine National Council Political Communiqué, Algiers, 15 Nov. 1988, reprinted in Yeduda Lukacs (ed.), *The Israeli-Palestinian Conflict: a Documentary Record*, pp. 415–19.

2. Israel foreign ministry statement on the PNC Decision, 15 Nov.1988, *Israel Documents*, Vol. 10, p. 998; Statement by Prime Minister Shamir on PNC decisions, 15 Nov. 1988, *Israel Documents*, Vol. 10, p. 999.

3. See EEC statement on PNC's Algiers Declaration, 21 Nov. 1988, reprinted in *Athens News Agency Daily Bulletin*, 22 Nov. 1988.

4. *Athens News Agency Bulletin*, 15 Sept.1988, p. 4.

5. *Athens News Agency Bulletin*, p. 2.

6. Ibid.

7. EEC statement on PNC's Algiers Declaration, 21 Nov. 1988.

8. *MEI*, 339, 2 Dec. 1988, p. 7 and *New York Times*, 24 Dec. 1988.

9. *New York Times*, 18 Nov. 1988.

10. See Yasser Arafat's Geneva Press Statement, 15 Dec. 1988, reprinted in

Yeduda Lukacs (ed.), *The Israeli-Palestinian Conflict: a Documentary Record*, p. 434.

11. Shada Islam, 'European Community: Time for a Gesture', *MEI*, 340, 16 Dec. 1988, p. 5.

12. Ibid.

13. *New York Times*, 20 Dec. 1988.

14. *New York Times*, 28 Jan. 1989.

15. *New York Times*, 4 May 1989.

16. *New York Times*, 27 Jan. 1986.

17. *Le Monde Diplomatique*, 13 Dec. 1988.

18. Bassam Abu Sharif, *Arafat and the Dream of Palestine: An Insider's Account*, New York: Palgrave Macmillan, 2009, p. 189.

19. *New York Times*, 16 Dec. and 24 Dec. 1988.

20. *New York Times*, 6 Dec. 1988.

21. T.D. Allman, 'On the Road with Arafat', *Vanity Fair*, Feb. 1989, p. 180.

22. *New York Times*, 28 Jan. 1989.

23. See Elisha Efrat, 'Jewish Settlements in the West Bank: Past, Present and Future', *Israel Affairs*, 1, 1, Autumn 1994, pp. 135–48, p. 147.

24. See *Ireland 1990-Irish Presidency of the European Community January-June 1990*, Annex V, Dublin: Department of Foreign Affairs, p. 63.

25. Tonra, *The Europeanisation of National Foreign Policy*, p. 198.

26. For a breakdown of EEC nationals held hostage in Kuwait and Iraq during the crisis see Lawrence Freedman and Efraim Karsh, *The Gulf Conflict: 1990–1991*, London and Boston: Faber and Faber, 1993, p. 250.

27. Declaration on the Gulf Crisis, Annex II, Conclusions, European Council Summit, Rome, 27–28 October 1990, http://www.europarl.europa.eu/summits/rome1/default_en.htm

28. For a detailed examination of Saddam's motives for going to war see Efraim Karsh, 'Reflections on the Gulf Conflict', *Journal of Strategic Studies*, 19, 3, Sept. 1996, pp. 303–32. Also see editors of US News & World Report, *Triumph Without Victory: The Unreported History of the Persian Gulf War*, New York: New York Times Books, 1992, pp. 7–26.

29. *Economist*, 5 Jan. 1991, p. 51.

30. *Economist*, p. 13.

31. Michael Eppel, 'Syria: Iraq's Radical Nemesis' in Amatzia Baram and Barry Rubin (eds), *Iraq's Road to War*, London: Macmillan, 1993, pp. 177–98, p. 184.

32. Fouad Ajami, 'The Summer of Arab Discontent', *Foreign Affairs*, 69, 5, Winter 1990/1991, pp. 1–20, p. 6.

33. Stanley Reed, 'Jordan and the Gulf Crisis', *Foreign Affairs*, 69, 5, Winter 1990–1991, pp. 21–35.

34. *New York Times*, 7 Sept. 1990.

35. *New York Times*, 10 Aug. 1990. In a post-war interview Mitterrand called Saddam's refusal to find a diplomatic solution 'a kind of political and military suicide', *New York Times*, 25 Feb. 1991.

36. *New York Times*, 25 Sept. and 28 Sept. 1990.

37. Armand Clesse, 'Europe and the Gulf War as Seen by the Luxembourg Presidency of the EC', in Nicole Gnesotto and John Roper (eds), *Western Europe and the Gulf*, Paris: The Institute of Security Studies, Western European Union, 1992, pp. 89–96, p. 93.

38. *Economist*, 19 Jan. 1991, p. 60.

39. Bassam Abu Sharif, *Arafat and the Dream of Palestine*, p. 216.

40. *New York Times*, 10 Jan. 1991.

41. Freedman and Karsh, *The Gulf Conflict: 1990–1991*, p. 272.

42. *Economist*, 19 Jan. 1991, p. 60; *New York Times*, 24 Jan. 1991.

43. Gilles Kepel, 'Self and Other: The Heart of the Franco-Arab Paradox', p. 324.

44. *Libération*, 11 Feb. 1991.

45. *Le Monde*, 12 March 1991.

46. Charles Krauthammer, 'The Unipolar Moment', *Foreign Affairs*, 70, 1, 1991, pp. 23–33, p. 24.

47. Louise Fawcett and Robert O'Neill, 'Britain, the Gulf crisis and European Security', in Gnesotto and Roper (eds), *Western Europe and the Gulf*, pp, 141–58, p. 142.

48. Phebe Marr, 'The United States, Europe, and the Middle East: An Uneasy Triangle', *Middle East Journal*, 48, 2, Spring 1994, pp. 211–25. See also Michael Smith, '"The Devil you Know": the United States and a Changing European Community', *International Affairs*, 68, 1, 1992, pp. 103–20.

49. François D'Alançon, 'The EC Looks to a New Middle East', *Journal of Palestine Studies*, 23, 2, Winter 1994, p. 43.

50. *Economist*, 19 Jan 1991, p. 23.

51. See Freedman and Karsh, *The Gulf Conflict: 1990–1991*, chapter 30.

52. Martin Indyk, 'Watershed in the Middle East', *Foreign Affairs*, 71, 1, pp. 70–93, p. 83.

53. For an eye-witness account of Baker's efforts at this time see Aaron David Miller, *The Much Too Promised Land: America's Elusive Search for Arab-Israeli Peace*, New York: Bantam Books, 2008, pp. 200–03.

54. *International Herald Tribune*, 14 March 1991.

55. *Le Monde*, 5 Nov. 1991.

56. David Bar-Ilan, 'Israel's New Pollyannas', in Neal Kozodoy (ed.), *The Mideast Peace Process: An Autopsy*, New York: Encounter Books, 2001, pp. 1–12, p. 3.

57. Statement by Mr Hans van den Broek, Minister of Foreign Affairs of The Netherlands and Acting President of the Council of Ministers of the European Communities, 1 Nov. 1991, Madrid, http://www.mfa.gov.il/MFA/ Archive/Peace%20Process/1991/STATEMENT%20BY%20MR%20 HANS%20VAN%20DEN%20BROEK%20-%201-Nov-91

58. Tonra, *The Europeanisation of National Foreign Policy*, p. 189.

59. See Communication by Manuel Marin, Vice President of the European Commission, on the role of the EU in the Peace Process, 16 Jan. 1998, http:// www.congreso.es/estrella/documentos/marin98e.doc.

60. Indyk, 'Watershed in the Middle East', pp. 91–2.

61. Communication by Manuel Marin on the role of the EU in the Peace Process, 16 Jan. 1998, p. 2.

62. See the address to the Knesset by Prime Minister Rabin Presenting his Government, 13 July 1992, *Israel Documents*, Vol. 13, p. 2.

63. Bar-Ilan, 'Israel's New Pollyannas', p. 6.

64. Michel Rocard, *Un Pays comme le nôtre—textes politiques, 1986–1989*, Paris: Éditions du Seuil, 1989, p. 238

65. Pierre Lellouche, 'France in Search of Security', *Foreign Affairs*, 72, 2, Spring 1993, pp. 122–31, p. 123.

66. Ellen Laipson, 'Europe's Role in the Middle East: Enduring Ties, Emerging Opportunities', *Middle East Journal*, 44, 1, Winter 1990, pp. 7–17, p. 7.

67. Malcolm, 'The Case Against "Europe"', p. 68.

68. Interview with David Owen on the Balkans, *Foreign Affairs*, 72, 2, Spring 1993, pp. 1–9, p. 6.

69. Warren Zimmermann, 'The Last Ambassador', *Foreign Affairs*, 74, 2, March-April 1995, pp. 2–20, p. 16.

70. Marc Epstein and Alain Louyot, 'L'Europe engluée dans le cauchemar yougoslave', *Les Cahiers de l'Express*, 31, Feb. 1995, pp. 57–8.

71. Interview with David Owen, p. 2.

72. *Le Monde*, 8 April 1992.

73. Rt. Hon. Douglas Hurd, *Our Future in Europe*, London: Conservative Political Centre, 1993, p. 9.0

74. Josef Joffe, 'The New Europe: Yesterday's Ghosts', *Foreign Affairs*, 72, 1, 1992–93, pp. 29–43, p. 32.

75. Leon Brittan, *A Diet of Brussels: The Changing Face of Europe*, London: Little, Brown and Company, 2000, p. 156.

76. *Le Monde*, 23 Nov. 1995.

77. Lawrence F. Kaplan, 'Surrender', *The New Republic*, 20 Nov. 2000, p. 13.

78. Known as the Israel-PLO Declaration of Principles on Interim Self-Government Arrangements (also known as DOP or Oslo 1), reprinted in *Journal of Palestine Studies*, XXIII, 1, Autumn 1993, pp. 115–21.

79. King Hussein, 'Prospects for Peace in the Middle East', *Journal of Palestine Studies*, IXX, 3, Spring 1990, pp. 3–13, p. 6.

80. Robert Fisk, 'Breaking Ranks: the EU, the US and the Middle East', in Ben Tonra and Eilis Ward (eds), *Ireland in International Affairs: Interests, Institutions and Identity*, Dublin: Institute of Public Administration, 2002, pp. 176–92, p. 184.

81. Address by Foreign Minister Shamir in Honour of German Foreign Minister Genscher, 3 June 1982, *Israel Documents*, Vol. 7, pp. 356–7.

82. P. Kidron, 'Not a Resounding Success', *MEI*, 439, 4 Dec. 1992, pp. 9–10; *New York Times*, 27 Nov. 1992.

83. Statement in the Knesset by Prime Minister Peres, 28 Oct. 1985, *Israel Documents*, Vol. 9, p. 985.

84. Éric Aeschimann and Christophe Boltanski, *Chirac d'Arabie: les mirages d'une politique française*, Paris: Bernard Grasset, 2006, p. 209.

85. See address by PLO Chairman Yasser Arafat to a special meeting of the Oireachtas Joint Committee on Foreign Affairs, 16 Dec. 1993, quoted in Rory Miller, *Ireland and the Palestine Question, 1948–2004*, Dublin: Irish Academic Press, 2005, p. 35.

8. PAYER, NOT PLAYER

1. Communication by Manuel Marin on the role of the EU in the Peace Process, 16 Jan. 1998.

2. See Udo Diedrichs, 'National Views and European Cleavages: From Single European Act to the Treaty of European Union' in Franco Algieri and Elfriede Regelsberger (eds), *Synergy at Work: Spain and Portugal in European Foreign Policy*, Bonn: Europa Union Verlag, 1996, pp. 233–58.

3. Robins, 'Always the Bridesmaid', p. 78.

4. Communication by Manuel Marin on the role of the EU in the Peace Process, 16 Jan. 1998.

5. *Unfinished Peace: Report of the International Commission on the Balkans*, Washington, DC: Carnegie Endowment for International Peace, 1996.

6. D'Alançon, 'The EC Looks to a New Middle East', p. 46.

7. *The Sunday Business Post*, 21 April 1996.

8. Pia Christina Wood, 'Chirac's "New Arab Policy" and Middle East Challenges: The Arab-Israeli Conflict, Iraq and Iran', *Middle East Journal*, 52, 4, Autumn 1988, pp. 563–80, p. 567.

9. *Le Monde*, 19 April 1996.

10. *Irish Times*, 16 April 1996.

11. Dominique Moïsi, 'Chirac of France: A New Leader of the West?', *Foreign Affairs*, 74, 6, Nov.-Dec. 1995, pp. 8–13, p. 8.

12. *Economist*, 2 Nov. 1996, p. 51.

13. See Benjamin Netanyahu, *Fighting Terrorism: How Democracies can Defeat Terrorist Networks*, New York: Noonday Press, 1997, pp. 99–121. Also see Address by Prime Minister Netanyahu to Israeli Editors' Association, 27 Nov. 1997, *Israel Documents*, Vol. 16, p. 417.

14. Eric Rouleau, 'Reflections on the Peace Process and a Durable Settlement', *Journal of Palestine Studies*, XXVI, 1, Autumn 1996, pp. 5–26, p. 22.

15. See 'Tanaiste's Mission to the Middle East', *Ireland 1996: Presidency of the European Union Bulletin*, 6, Dublin: Department of Foreign Affairs, Nov. 1996, p. 1.

16. Raimond, *Le Quai d'Orsay*, p. 190.

17. Aeschimann and Boltanski, *Chirac d'Arabie*, p. 195.

18. *Le Monde*, 5 April 1996.

19. Avram Pazner, 'Choosing between Israel and the Arabs', in Manfred Gerstenfeld (ed.), *Israel and Europe: An Expanding Abyss?*, Jerusalem: Jerusalem Center for Public Affairs, 2005, pp. 159–68, p. 165.

20. *Irish Times*, 10 April 2002.

21. President Chirac's speech at Technion University, reprinted in *Jerusalem Post*, 22 Oct. 1996.

22. Freddy Eytan, 'French History and Current Attitudes to Israel' in Gerstenfeld (ed.), *Israel and Europe: An Expanding Abyss?*, p. 177. See also R. Tiersky, 'Mitterrand's Legacies', *Foreign Affairs*, 74, 1, 1995, pp. 112–21.

23. Paul-Marie de La Gorce, 'Europe and the Arab-Israeli Conflict: A Survey', *Journal of Palestine Studies*, XXVI, 3, Spring 1997, p. 6.

24. *New York Times*, 26 Oct. 1996.

25. Ibid.

26. *Economist*, 2 Nov. 1996, p. 51.

27. Address by M. Hervé de Charette, Minister of Foreign Affairs, Marseille, 26 November 1996, Embassy of France: Washington DC, March 1997.

28. An interview with Joschka Fischer, *Jerusalem Post*, 31 May 2002. See also Marc Otte, 'Europe has a central role to play in the Middle East', *Europe's World*, 13 April 2009, www.europesworld.org/NewEnglish/Home/Article/tabid/191/ArticleType/articleview/ArticleID/21436/Default.asp.

29. 'Peace Monitor: 16 November 1996–15 February 1997', *Journal of Palestine Studies*, XXVI, 3, Spring 1997, pp. 111–22, p. 115.

30. John Kampfner, *Robin Cook*, London: Victor Gollancz, 1998, p. 220.

31. *Le Monde*, 2 July 1997.

32. de La Gorce, 'Europe and the Arab-Israeli Conflict: A Survey', p. 6.

33. Miller, *Ireland and the Palestine Question*, p. 165.

34. Quoted in Kenneth W. Stein, 'Imperfect Alliances': Will Europe and America Ever Agree?', *Middle East Quarterly*, March 1997, pp. 39–45, p. 43.

35. Communication by Manuel Marin on the role of the EU in the Peace Process, 16 Jan. 1998, p. 3.

36. *Jerusalem Post*, 1 April 1997 and *Washington Post*, 1 April 1997. For a detailed examination of Oslo's multilateral track see Dalia Dassa Kaye, *Beyond the Handshake: Multilateral Cooperation in the Arab-Israeli Peace Process*, New York: Columbia University Press, 2001.

37. Communication by Manuel Marin on the Role of the EU in the Peace Process, 16 Jan. 1998, p. 3.

38. Ibid.

39. Address in the Knesset by Prime Minister-elect Netanyahu presenting his government to the Knesset, 18 June 1996, *Israel Documents*, Vol. 16, pp. 15–16.

40. Joseph Alpher, 'Israel's Security Concerns in the Peace Process', *International Affairs*, 70, 2, 1994, pp. 229–41, p. 235.

41. *Le Monde*, 13 Sept. 1997.

42. Remarks by Prime Minister Netanyahu to Conference of Mayors, 9 April 1997, *Israel Documents*, Vol. 16, p. 317.

43. European Union, Presidency Conclusion, part IV, Berlin, 25 March 1999, http://www.europarl.europa.eu/summits/ber2_en.htm#partIV

44. *Financial Times*, 26 March 1999.

45. *Le Monde*, 12 April 1997.

46. *Jerusalem Report*, 27 Nov. 1997, p. 8.

47. *The Europa World Year Book: 2004*, London: Europa Publications, 2005, p. 247.

48. *Ha'aretz*, 10 Oct. 1996.

49. See *Jerusalem Report*, 12 April 1996, p. 6.

50. Ibid., 4 Jan. 1999, p. 18.

51. See conversation between Prime Minister Netanyahu and President Mubarak of Egypt, 26 Feb. 1997, *Israel Documents*, Vol. 16, p. 250.

52. Aaron David Miller, 'The False Religion of Middle East Peace', *Foreign Policy Magazine*, May-June 2010, p. 3.

53. *Jerusalem Report*, 4 Jan. 1999, p. 18.

54. Robert Satloff, 'Undone Deal', *The New Republic*, 2 Nov. 1998, p. 12.

55. *New York Times*, 30 Nov. 1998.

56. *Jerusalem Report*, 4 Jan. 1999, pp. 14–6.

57. Communication by Manuel Marin on the Role of the EU in the Peace Process, 16 Jan. 1998.

58. Stein, 'Imperfect Alliances', p. 39.

59. Robert K. Olson, 'Partners in the Peace Process: The United States and Europe', *Journal of Palestine Studies*, XXVI, 4, Summer 1997, pp. 78–89, p. 78.

60. See Joint interview with President Sadat and Prime Minister Begin on French Television, 7 Sept. 1979, *Israel Documents*, Vol. 6, pp. 116–23.

61. 'An Interview with William Waldegrave', *Journal of Palestine Studies*, XX, 1, Autumn 1990, p. 86.

62. Bassam Abu Sharif, *Arafat and the Dream of Palestine*, p. 228.

63. *Jerusalem Report*, 4 Jan.1999, pp. 14–16.

64. *Irish Times*, 18 May 1999.

65. European Union, Presidency Conclusion, part IV, Berlin, 25 March 1999.

66. ArabicNews.Com, 2 June 1999, http://www.arabicnews.com/ansub/Daily/Day/990602/FP.html.

67. European Council, Presidency Conclusions, Cologne, 3–4 June 1999, http://www.consilium.europa.eu/ueDocs/cms_Data/docs/pressData/en/ec/kolnen.htm

68. European Council, Presidency Conclusions, Helsinki, 10–11 Dec. 1999, http://www.consilium.europa.eu/uedocs/cms_data/docs/pressdata/en/ec/ACFA4C.htm

69. See Geoffrey R. Watson, *The Oslo Accords: International Law and the Israeli-Palestinian Peace Agreements*, Oxford: Oxford University Press, 2000, pp. 385–9.

70. Eytan, 'French History and Current Attitudes to Israel', p. 181.

71. Quoted in Robert Fisk, 'Breaking Ranks', p. 190.

72. See, for example, the widely reported article defending the Palestinian position at Camp David by Hussein Agha and Robert Malley, 'Camp David: the Tragedy of Errors', *New York Review of Books*, 9 Aug. 2001, and Robert Fisk's scathing attack on Israel and the United States at Camp David in 'War Without End', *Irish Times Magazine*, 11 Aug. 2001. See also Akram Hanieh, 'The Camp David Papers', *Journal of Palestine Studies*, XXX, 2, Winter 2001, pp. 75–97.

73. See, for example, transcript of Ross' televised interview with Brit Hume on Fox News Special Report, 11 April 2002, and his article 'Making Reform A Reality', *Washington Post*, 23 May 2002. See also Nabil Amer's 'Open Letter to Yasser Arafat', *Al-Hayat*, 2 Sept. 2002 and *Ha'aretz*, 9 Sept. 2002.

74. Communication by Manuel Marin on the role of the EU in the Peace Process, 16 Jan. 1998.

9. THE CHORUS OF REFORM

1. Declaration by Heads of State and Government of the European Union on the Situation in the Middle East, Biarritz, France, 13 Oct. 2000, http://www.consilium.europa.eu/uedocs/cms_data/docs/pressdata/en/ec/04686-r3.en0.htm.

2. The EU's relations with West Bank and Gaza Strip: Overview, European Commission External Relations Department, Brussels, July 2000.

3. European Council Presidency Conclusions, Part II, The Middle East, Barcelona, 15–16 March 2002, http://www.consilium.europa.eu/uedocs/cms_data/docs/pressdata/en/ec/71025.pdf

4. *Irish Times*, 10 Oct. 2000.

5. *Economist*, 17 Oct. 1998, p. 60.

6. European Council, Presidency Conclusions Annex III, Laeken, 14 & 15 Dec. 2001, http://ec.europa.eu/governance/impact/background/docs/laeken_concl_en.pdf

7. Chris Patten, Situation in the Middle East, Speech to European Parliament, 12 Dec. 2001, http://europa.eu/external relations/news/patten/sp01627.htm

8. General Affairs and External Relations, Middle East Statement, 2397st Council meeting, Brussels, 10 Dec. 2001 http://europa.eu/rapid/pressReleasesAction.do?reference=PRES/01/460&format=HTML&aged=0&lg=bg&guiLanguage=en

9. See Thomas L. Friedman, 'An Intriguing Signal from the Saudi Crown Prince', *New York Times*, 17 Feb. 2002

10. *Irish Times*, 6 Feb. 2002.

11. *Guardian*, 28 Feb. 2002.

12. *Ha'aretz*, 27 Feb. 2002.

13. Javier Solana, 'The EU's role in the Middle East', *Politiken*, 23 May 2002.

14. *Washington Post*, 25 Feb. 2002.

15. *Financial Times*, 10 Feb. 2002.

16. *Independent*, 10 April 2002.

17. Nicholas Lemann, 'The Iraq Factor', *New Yorker*, 22 Jan. 2002, p. 37.

18. Lawrence F. Kaplan, 'State Unfair', *The New Republic*, 14 May 2001, p. 23.

19. *Le Monde*, 14 Sept. 2001.

20. *Independent*, 7 Nov. 2001.

21. White House, Office of the Press Secretary, 'President speaks on war effort to Citadal cadets', 11 Dec. 2001, available at http://www.whitehouse.gov/news/releases/2001/12/20011211–6.html.

22. White House, Office of the Press Secretary, 'President Bush delivers graduation speech at West Point', 1 June 2002, available at http://www.whitehouse.gov/news/releases/2002/06/20020601–3.html.

23. See *The National Security Strategy of the United States of America*, Washington DC, 2002, available at http://www.whitehouse.gov/nsc/nss.pdf (20 January 2004) and *The National Strategy for Combating Terrorism*, Washington DC, 2003, available at http://www.whitehouse.gov/news/releases/2003/02/counter_terrorism/intent.pdf (20 January 2004).

24. *Le Monde*, 10 Sept. 2002.

25. *Guardian*, 9 Feb. 2002.

26. *Guardian*, 6 Aug. 2002.
27. *Guardian*, 9 Feb. 2002.
28. Anne Applebaum, 'Farewell, New Europe', *Slate*, 5 June 2007, http://politics.slate.msn.com
29. *International Herald Tribune*, 31 Jan. 2003; *Time International*, 3 March 2003.
30. Bret Stephens, 'Why is Europe anti-Israel?', *Wall Street Journal*, 26 April 2002.
31. Geoffrey Kemp, 'Europe's Middle East Challenges', *The Washington Quarterly*, 27, 1, Winter 2003, pp. 163–77, p. 163.
32. *Ha'aretz*, 27 Feb. 2002.
33. *Ha'aretz*, 4 Feb. 2002.
34. *Irish Times*, 13 April 2002.
35. *Irish Times*, 7 Feb. 2002.
36. Jim Hoagland, 'Europe's Mideast Mellowing', *Washington Post*, 14 July 2002
37. *Guardian*, 9 Feb. 2002.
38. Interview with Joschka Fischer, *Jerusalem Post*, 31 May 2002.
39. *Ha'aretz*, 16 Dec. 2002.
40. President's Address to the Public Affairs Council of the European Union, 24 January 2000, PLO Negotiations Affairs dept, speeches & statements.
41. CNN.com, 21 Aug. 2001, http://edition.cnn.com/2001/WORLD/asiapcf/east/08/23/arafat.asia/
42. *Irish Times*, 7 Feb. 2002.
43. *Guardian*, 21 May 2002.
44. *Irish Times*, 7 Feb. 2002.
45. *Irish Times*, 5 Dec. 2001.
46. Ivo H. Daalder and James M. Lindsay, *America Unbound: the Bush Revolution in Foreign Policy*, Washington, DC: Brookings Institution Press, 2003, p. 15.
47. Lawrence F. Kaplan, 'Surrender', *The New Republic*, 20 Nov. 2000.
48. *New York Times*, 7 Feb. 2002.
49. *Guardian*, 26 Feb. 2002.
50. BBCNews.com, 4 April 2002.
51. *Washington Post*, 25 Feb. 2002.
52. *Financial Times*, 23 April 2002.
53. *Financial Times*, 21 Jan. 2002.
54. Interview with Joschka Fischer, *Jerusalem Post*, 31 May 2002.
55. *Ha'aretz*, 4 July 2002.
56. *Ha'aretz*, 18 July 2003.
57. Chris Patten, 'A Road Map paid for in euros', *Financial Times*, 17 July 2003.

58. *Jerusalem Post*, 2 July 2002.
59. Denis Bauchard, 'Europe's Role in Averting a Middle East Tragedy', *Europe's World*, Autumn 2009, p. 134.
60. *Jerusalem Post*, 29 Aug. 2002.
61. *New York Times*, 15 July 2003.
62. P. David Hornik, 'Alistair Crooke's Meeting with Sheik Yassin', FrontPageMagazine.com, 15 April 2005.
63. *Financial Times*, 15 Dec. 2001.
64. *Le Monde*, 29 Jan. 2002.
65. Solana, 'The EU's role in the Middle East'.
66. *The Times*, 9 May 2002.
67. *Irish Examiner*, 5 April 2002
68. *Financial Times*, 18 Nov. 2003.
69. *Jerusalem Post*, 25 June 2003.
70. *Los Angeles Times*, 26 Jan. 2002.
71. *Ha'aretz*, 4 July 2002
72. *Economist*, 27 June 2002, p. 42.
73. *Economist*, 13 July 2002, p. 52.
74. *Irish Times*, 28 June 2002.
75. *Financial Times*, 17 March 2003.
76. Philip H. Gordon, 'Bush's Middle East Vision', *Survival*, 45, 1, Spring 2003, pp. 155–65, p. 159.
77. Dennis Ross, 'Taking Stock: The Bush Administration and the Roadmap to Peace', *The National Interest*, Fall 2003, pp. 11–21, 15.
78. Hoagland, 'Europe's Mideast Mellowing'.
79. Solana, 'The EU's role in the Middle East'.
80. Middle East Debate: Should Washington Actively Promote an Israeli-Palestinian Peace Settlement, Council on Foreign Relations, 2 May 2003, http://www.cfr.org/publication/5906/middle_east_debate.html?breadcrumb=%2Fpublication%2Fpublication_list%3Ftype%3Dvideo%26page%3D26
81. *Daily Telegraph*, 19 Sept. 2003.
82. *Guardian*, 9 Feb. 2004.
83. *Ma'ariv International*, 3 June 2004.
84. Khalil Shikaki, 'Let us vote', *Wall Street Journal*, 30 July 2004.
85. *Ha'aretz*, 10 Aug. 2004.
86. Reuters News Agency Report, 11 Aug. 2004.
87. Colin Shindler, *A History of Modern Israel*, Cambridge: Cambridge University Press, 2008, p. 300.
88. Eytan, 'French History and Current Attitudes to Israel', in Manfred Gerstenfeld (ed.), *Israel and Europe: An Expanding Abyss?*, p. 176.
89. Interview with Harry Kney-Tal, *Ha'aretz*, 21 Aug. 2002.

90. *Ha'aretz*, 4 Feb. 2002.
91. *Ha'aretz*, 14 Feb. 2002.
92. *Jerusalem Post*, 14 Feb. 2002.
93. *Jerusalem Post*, 14 May 2002.
94. *Guardian*, 19 Jan. 2003.
95. Reuters News Agency, 22 July 2004.
96. See, for example, Rachel Ehrenfeld, 'Where Does the Money GO? A Study of the Palestinian Authority' on behalf of the New York-based American Centre for Democracy and commissioned by B'nai Brith Europe, Oct. 2002.
97. OLAF investigation into EU assistance to the Palestinian Authority budget, summary of conclusions, 17 March 2005, http://www.europa-eu-un.org/articles/es/article_4486_es.htm
98. *Spectator*, 2 Nov. 2002.
99. *Independent*, 3 June 2003.
100. *Ha'aretz*, 13 Oct. 2003.
101. *Ha'aretz*, 14 Oct. 2003.
102. *Financial Times*, 15 Oct. 2004.
103. 'Flash Eurobarometer 151', European Commission, Nov. 2003, p. 81.
104. Zvi Shtauber, 'British Attitudes Towards Israel and the Jews', in Manfred Gerstenfeld (ed.), *Israel and Europe: An Expanding Abyss?*, pp. 169–92, p. 191.
105. *Jerusalem Post*, 13 July 2003.
106. *Washington Post*, 25 Feb. 2005.
107. Interview with Jimmy Carter, *Irish Times*, 19 June 2007.
108. Anthony Seldon, *Blair Unbound*, London, New York: Simon & Schuster, 2007, p. 65.
109. *Guardian*, 5 Oct. 2002.
110. 'President welcomes Palestinian President Abbas to the White House' White House Press Statement, 26 May 2005, http://www.whitehouse.gov/news/releases/2005/05/20050526.html.
111. See Trevor Asserson and Cassie Williams, 'The BBC and the Middle East: The Documentary Campaign, 2000–2004', July 2004, bbcwatch.com
112. *Guardian*, 24 April 2002.
113. *Daily Telegraph*, 3 Jan. 2005.
114. *Jerusalem Post*, 7 March 2007.
115. Interview with Prime Minister Tony Blair, *The Times*, 21 May 2002.
116. *Irish Times*, 8 Feb. 2004.
117. *The Times*, 21 May 2002.
118. *New York Times*, 30 March 2002.
119. *The Times*, 3 July 2003.

120. *Jerusalem Post*, 16 July 2003.
121. *Ha'aretz*, 27 March 2003.
122. Efraim Karsh, 'Arafat Lives', *Commentary Magazine*, Jan. 2005, p. 33.
123. *Washington Post*, 10 Aug. 2005.
124. Miller, *Ireland and the Palestine Question*, p. 249, note 134.
125. See 'PM Sharon Meets with French President Chirac', Israeli Foreign Ministry Press Statement, 27 July 2005, http://www.mfa.gov.il/MFA/Government/Communiques/2005/PM+Sharon+meets+with+French+President+Chirac+27-Jul-2005.htm.
126. *Libération*, 31 March 2006.
127. *Jerusalem Post*, 17 Aug. 2005.
128. *Jerusalem Post*, 30 Aug. 2005.
129. *Ha'aretz*, 18 Aug. 2005.
130. Jewish Telegraphic Agency (JTA), 20 Sept. 2005, http://www.jta.org.
131. Jewish Telegraphic Agency (JTA), 6 Oct. 2005, www.jta.org.
132. General Affairs and External Relations, 'Conclusions on the Middle East Peace Process, 2691 Council meeting, Brussels, 21–22 Nov. 2005'. http://www.consilium.europa.eu/uedocs/cms_Data/docs/pressdata/en/gena/87093.pdf
133. *Jerusalem Post*, 6 Nov. 2005.
134. *Ha'aretz*, 18 Aug. 2005.
135. Javier Solana, 'Europe is ready to commit more after disengagement', *Daily Star* (Beirut), 10 Sept. 2005.
136. Jewish Telegraphic Agency (JTA), 22 Sept. 2005, http://www.jta.org.

10. THE BEST LAID PLANS

1. Jewish Telegraphic Agency (JTA), 20 Sept. 2005, www.jta.org.
2. *New York Times*, 28 Jan. 2006.
3. Jonathan Schanzer, 'The Challenge of Hamas to Fatah', *Middle East Quarterly*, Spring 2003, pp. 29–38, p. 30.
4. Khaled Abu Toameh, 'From Cradle to Grave', *The Jerusalem Report*, 4 Sept. 1997, p. 4.
5. *US News & World Report*, 20 Sept. 1993.
6. *Ha'aretz*, 9 Nov. 1994.
7. Amos Perlmutter, 'Arafat's Police State', *Foreign Affairs*, 73, 4, July-Aug. 1994, pp. 8–11, p. 11.
8. Wendy Kristianasen, 'Challenge and Counterchallenge: Hamas' Response to Oslo', *Journal of Palestine Studies*, XXVIII, 3, Spring 1999, pp. 19–36, p. 24.
9. Jeroen Gunning, *Hamas in Politics: Democracy, Religion, Violence*, London: Hurst & Company, 2007, p. 48.

10. Schanzer, 'The Challenge of Hamas to Fatah', p. 32.

11. Dan Ephron, 'Power Play', *The New Republic*, 17 Jan. 2005; *Daily Star* (Beirut), 6 May 2005.

12. Jamil Hilal, 'Hamas's Rise as charted in the Polls, 1994–2005', *Journal of Palestine Studies*, XXXV, 3, Spring 2006, pp. 6–19, p. 7.

13. *New York Times*, 17 Dec. 2005.

14. Jewish Telegraphic Agency (JTA), 22 Sept. 2005, http://www.jta.org.

15. *Al-Jazeera*, 21 Sept. 2005, http://english.aljazeera.net/NR/exeres/49507A87-B6ED-40A9-BB71–9DAA6053D155.htm.

16. *Washington Post*, 8 May 2003.

17. *Daily Telegraph*, 16 Dec. 2002.

18. *Jerusalem Post*, 26 Aug. 2003.

19. *Independent*, 27 Aug. 2003.

20. *The Times*, 26 June 2003.

21. *Financial Times*, 25 Aug. 2003.

22. *New York Times*, 7 Sept. 2003.

23. *EU Observer*, 25 Nov. 2004.

24. *Independent*, 26 Nov. 2004.

25. See Efraim Karsh and Rory Miller, 'Group Dynamics', *The New Republic*, 12 May 2005, http://tnr.com/doc.mhtml?i=w050509&s=karshmiller051205.

26. *Arutz 7*, 21 Aug. 2005, http://www.arutzsheva.org/news.php3?id=88053.

27. *Sunday Times*, 27 March 2005.

28. On Crooke's high-profile promotion of this argument see *Daily Telegraph*, 2 Feb. 2004; *Sunday Times*, 12 Dec. 2004. See also Alastair Crooke and Mark Perry, 'How to lose the War on Terror', *Asia Times*, parts I & II, 31 March and 1 April 2006 and Crooke and Beverley Milton-Edwards, 'Hamas and the Peace Process', *Journal of Palestine Studies*, XXXIII, 4 Summer 2004, pp. 39–52.

29. *The Times*, 10 May 2005.

30. *Guardian*, 20 May 2005.

31. *Ha'aretz*, 16 June 2005.

32. *USA Today*, 16 June 2005.

33. Chris Patten, 'West's boycott of Hamas a recipe for disaster', *Irish Times*, 15 March 2007.

34. Quoted in Seldon, *Blair Unbound*, p. 467.

35. *EurActiv*, 27 Jan. 2006, http://www.euractiv.com/en/security/eu-hamas-renounce-violence-recognise-israel/article-151982

36. Aaron D. Pina, 'Fatah and Hamas: the New Palestinian Factional Reality', Washington DC: Congressional Research Service, 3 March 2006, http://www.fas.org/sgp/crs/mideast/RS22395.pdf.

37. See Israeli Foreign Ministry Press Release on EU Contacts with Hamas, 19 June 2005, http://www.mfa.gov.il/mfa/mfaarchive/2000_2009/2005/

38. *European Jewish News*, 15 Feb. 2006.

39. *Turkish Weekly News*, 6 April 2006.

40. *European Jewish News*, 15 Feb. 2006.

41. Ibid.

42. Pina, 'Fatah and Hamas: the New Palestinian Factional Reality'.

43. *Tripoli Post*, 13 Aug. 2007.

44. *European Jewish News*, 1 Sept. 2006, http://www.ejpress.org/

45. Patten, 'West's boycott of Hamas a recipe for disaster'.

46. *Jerusalem Post*, 26 Oct. 2006 47Ynetnews, 15 Dec. 2006 http://www.ynet-news.com/home/0,7340,L-3083,00.html

48. *Jerusalem Post*, 30 Jan. 2006.

49. *Ha'aretz*, 19 April 2005.

50. Interview with Mahmoud Zahar, *The Times*, 6 April 2006.

51. Agence France-Presse (AFP), 17 May 2006.

52. *WorldNetDaily*, 6 Dec. 2009, http://www.wnd.com.

53. BBCNews.com 14 July 2007, http://news.bbc.co.uk/1/hi/6754499.stm.

54. *Guardian*, 15 June 2007.

55. *BBCNews.Com*, 18 June 2007, http://news.bbc.co.uk/1/hi/world/middle_east/6762777.stm

56. *Euractiv*, 27 Jan. 2006.

57. Ibid.

58. Pina, 'Fatah and Hamas: the New Palestinian Factional Reality'

59. House of Lords European Union Committee, 'The EU and the Middle East Peace Process, 26th Report of Session 2006–07', http://www.publications.parliament.uk/pa/ld200607/ldselect/ldeucom/132/132i.pdf

60. Clara Marina O'Donnell, *The EU, Israel, and Hamas*, London: Centre for European Reform Working Paper, 2008, http://www.cer.org.uk/pdf/wp_820.pdf.

61. Chris Patten, 'West's boycott of Hamas a recipe for disaster'.

62. *Ynetnews*, 15 Dec. 2006, http://www.ynetnews.com/home/0,7340,L-3083,00.html

63. *Irish Times*, 15 May 2007

64. *2009 Report of the United Nations Fact Finding Mission on the Gaza Conflict* (hereinafter, the Goldstone Commission report), http://www2.ohchr.org/english/bodies/hrcouncil/docs/12session/A-HRC-12–48.pdf, p. 381.

65. *The Times*, 15 Sept. 2007.

66. 'Breaching the Peace—Will the Hamas-Israel Ceasefire Hold?', *Jane's Intelligence Review*, 18 July 2008

67. PEGASE: Helping to build a Palestinian State, Jerusalem: European Commission Technical Assistance Office, 2009, http://ec.europa.eu/delegations/westbank/documents/eu_westbank/governance_en.pdf

68. Gunning, *Hamas in Politics*, p. 193.
69. *Ha'aretz*, 20 Sept. 2008.
70. Augustus Richard Norton, 'The Gaza War: Antecedents and Consequences' Elcano Royal Institute Feb. 2009 http://www.realinstitutoelcano.org/wps/portal/rielcano_eng/Content?WCM_GLOBAL_CONTEXT=/elcano/elcano_in/zonas_in/mediterranean+arab+world/ari21–2009#sdfootnote18anc
71. Hillel Frisch, 'The Need for a Decisive Victory over Hamas', *BESA Perspectives on Current Affairs*, 57, 12 January 2009, http://www.biu.ac.il/Besa/perspectives57.html
72. Herb Keinon, 'The Gaza operation's unstated goal: Anarchy', *Jerusalem Post*, 1 Jan. 2009.
73. Almut Moller, 'After Gaza: A New Approach to Hamas', Maria Enzersdorf: Austrian Institute for European Security Policy, Feb. 2009, p. 2.
74. *BBCNews.Com*, 26 Jan. 2006, http://news.bbc.co.uk/1/hi/world/middle_east/7851545.stm
75. *The Times*, 20 Jan. 2009.
76. Moller, 'After Gaza: A New Approach to Hamas', p. 3.
77. *Jerusalem Post*, 28 Dec. 2008.
78. *Jerusalem Post.*, 9 Jan. 2008.
79. See European Parliament press release on Mahmoud Abbas at the European Parliament', 4 Feb. 2009.
80. *New York Times*, 25 March 2009.
81. *Guardian*, 26 May 2008.
82. *Jerusalem Post*, 25 June 2005.
83. EU/Palestinian Authority Action Plan, 2004 http://trade.ec.europa.eu/doclib/docs/2010/june/tradoc_146237.pdf
84. See Raffaella A. Del Sarto, 'Wording and Meaning(s): EU-Israeli Political Cooperation according to the ENP Action Plan', *Mediterranean Politics*, 11, 1, 2007, pp. 59–74.
85. 'European Neighbourhood Policy', European Commission statement, http://europa.eu.int/comm/world/enp/faq_en.htm#1.5.
86. *Jerusalem Post*, 26 Aug. 2004.
87. Press Conference to launch the first seven action plans under the European Neighbourhood Policy, 9 Dec. 2004, http://www.europa.eu.int/comm/external_relations/news/ferrero/2004/sp04_529.htm; Benita Ferrero-Waldner, 'Ce que les Européens ont à dire aux Israéliens et aux Palestiniens', *Le Monde*, 9 Feb. 2005.
88. See Dan Senor and Saul Singer, *Start-up Nation: The Story of Israel's Economic Miracle*, New York: Twelve Books, 2009. See also, Dan Breznitz, *Innovation and the State: Political Choice and Strategies for Growth in Israel, Taiwan and Ireland*, New Haven and London: Yale University Press, 2007.

89. 'EU Bilateral Trade Relations-Israel', http://europa.eu.int/comm/trade/issues/bilateral/countries/israel/index_en.htm.

90. *Newsweek*, 8 April 1996, p. 36.

91. 'EU Bilateral Trade Relations-Israel'.

92. 'The Relationship between France and Israel', Press release, Embassy of France in the United States, 30 September 2004, http://www.ambafrance-us.org/news/statmnts/2004/france_israel073004.asp.

93. Aeschimann and Boltanski, *Chirac d'Arabie*, pp. 315–16.

94. Laurent Fabius, *Le Coeur du Futur*, Paris: Calmann-Lévy, 1985, p. 250.

95. 'France and Israel: Economic Relations', French Foreign Ministry, http://www.diplomatie.gouv.fr/en/country-files_156/israel-palestinian-territories_290/israel_2157/france-and-israel_4067/economic-relations_6303/index.html

96. *New York Times*, 5 June 2008.

97. *Jerusalem Post*, 17 June 2008.

98. *Ha'aretz*, 9 Dec. 2008.

99. 'The European Union Upgrades its relations with Israel', Israeli Ministry of Foreign Affairs Press Release, 16 June 2008, http://www.mfa.gov.il/MFA/About+the+Ministry/MFA+Spokesman/2008/The+EU+and+Israel+upgrade+relations++16-June-2008.htm

100. Sharon Pardo, 'Narrowing gaps', *Jerusalem Post*, 2 Jan. 2004, p. 9.

101. Michael Brecher, *The Foreign Policy System of Israel: Settings, Images, Process*, London: Oxford University Press, 1972, p. 348.

102. Statement by Foreign Minister Allon to Knesset on EEC-Israel Trade Agreement, 26 May 1975, *Israel Documents*, 2, pp. 218–21.

103. Howard M. Sachar, *Israel and Europe: An Appraisal in History*, New York: Alfred A. Knopf, 1999, p. 212.

104. *Ha'aretz*, 30 April 2009.

105. *EUobserver.com*, http://euobserver.com/9/28310

106. See for example, Marc Otte, 'Europe has a central role to play in the Middle East', Europe's World, 13 April 2009, http://www.europesworld.org/NewEnglish/Home/Article/tabid/191/ArticleType/articleview/ArticleID/21436/Default.aspx. At the time of writing Otte was the EU's Special Representative for the Middle East peace process.

107. *Al-Jazeera*, 6 Nov. 2008, http://english.aljazeera.net/news/americas/2008/11/20081155293464248.html

108. Miller, 'The False Religion of Peace', p. 3.

109. See President Obama's interview with *Al-Arabiya*, 26 Jan. 2009, http://www.alarabiya.net/articles/2009/01/27/65087.html

110. 'Remarks by the President on a New Beginning', Cairo University, Cairo, Egypt, 4 June 2009, The White House, Office of the Press Secretary, http://

www.whitehouse.gov/the_press_office/Remarks-by-the-President-at-Cairo-University-6–04–09/

111. Oded Eran, 'Why Europe and Israel Need to Bury the Hatchet', *Europe's World*, 13, Autumn 2009, p. 140.

BIBLIOGRAPHY

Primary sources

Archives
British National Archives
National Archives of Ireland

Official Publications

Foreign Relations of the United States, 1964–1968, XVIII, Arab-Israeli Dispute 1964–1967, Washington, DC: US Government Printing Office.
Israel's Foreign Relations: Selected Documents, Vol. 1–17, 1947–1999, Jerusalem: Ministry of Foreign Affairs.
United Nations General Assembly Official Records, New York: United Nations.
United Nations Security Council Official Records, New York: United Nations.

Internet sources

European Commission Statements, Declarations, Press Releases, http://ec.europa. eu/index_en.htm
European Council Presidency Conclusions, http://ec.europa.eu/archives/european-council/index_en.htm
French Ministry of Foreign Affairs, http://www.diplomatie.gouv.fr/en/
Hansard: House of Commons Debates, http://www.publications.parliament.uk/ pa/cm/cmhansrd.htm
Hansard: House of Lords Debates http://www.parliament.uk/business/publications/hansard/lords/ Israeli Foreign Ministry Press Office http://www.mfa. gov.il/MFA Palestinian Authority Negotiations Affairs Department, http:// www.nad-plo.org/ US State Department, http://www.state.gov/ White House Press Office http://www.whitehouse.gov/briefing-room/statements-and-

Newspapers, Magazines and News Services

Agence France-Presse (AFP)
Al-Ahram Weekly

Al-Arabiya
Al-Jazeera
ArabicNews.Com
Athens News Agency Bulletin
BBCNews.com
Bulletin of the European Communities
Commentary
Corriere della Sera
Daily Star (Beirut)
Daily Telegraph
Der Spiegel
Die Welt
Economist
Encounter
Euobserver.com
European Jewish News
European News Agency
Financial Times
France-Pays Arabes
Frankfurter Allgemeine Zeitung
Foreign Policy
Guardian
Ha'aretz
Independent (London)
International Herald Tribune
Irish Independent
Jerusalem Post
Jerusalem Report
Jewish Telegraphic Agency (JTA)
Le Figaro
Le Monde
Le Monde Diplomatique
Los Angeles Times
Ma'ariv International
Middle East International
National (Abu Dhabi)
National Interest
New Republic
New York Times
New Yorker
Reuters News Agency
Spectator
Sunday Business Post

The Times
Wall Street Journal
Washington Post
Yediot Aharonot
Ynetnews

Memoirs

Abu Sharif, Bassam *Arafat and the Dream of Palestine: An Insider's Account*, New York: Palgrave Macmillan, 2009.

Barre, Raymond, *Au tournant du siècle*, Paris: Plon, 1988.

Barzani, Luigi, *The Impossible Europeans*, London: Weidenfeld & Nicolson, 1983.

Callaghan, James, *Time and Chance*, London: Collins, 1987.

Carrington, Peter, *Reflect on Things Past: The Memoirs of Lord Carrington*, London: Collins, 1988.

Chaban-Delmas, Jacques, *Mémoires pour demain*, Paris: Flammarion, 1997.

Clinton, Bill, *My Life*, New York: Knopf, 2004.

Debré, Michel, *Gouverner autrement: Mémoires, Vol. IV, 1962–1970*, Paris: Albin Michel, 1993.

Fawaz, Turki, *Exile's Return: The Making of a Palestinian-American*, New York: The Free Press, 1994.

Fitzgerald, Garret, *All in a Life: An Autobiography*, London: Macmillan, 1991

Giscard d'Estaing, Valéry (with Agathe Fourgnaud), *Mémoire vivante*, Paris: Flammarion, 2001

———, *Le Pouvoir et la vie, Vol. 1, La Rencontre*, Paris: Cie 12, 1988.

———, *Le Pouvoir et la vie, Vol. II, L'Affrontement*, Paris:Cie, 1991.

Haig Jr., Alexander M., *Caveat: Realism, Reagan, and Foreign Policy*, New York: Macmillan, 1984.

Heath, Edward, *The Course of My Life: My Autobiography*, London: Hodder & Stoughton, 1998.

Jobert, Michel, *Mémoires d'avenir*, Paris: Grasset, 1974.

Kissinger, Henry, *Years of Renewal*, New York: Simon & Schuster, 1999.

Lord Home, *The Way the Wind Blows: An Autobiography*, London: Collins, 1976.

Pompidou, Georges, *Entretiens et discours, 1968–1974, Vol. II*, Paris: Flammarion, 1984.

Rafael, Gideon, *Destination Peace: Three Decades of Israeli Foreign Policy, A Personal Memoir*, New York: Stein and Day, 1981.

Raimond, Jean-Bernard, *Le Quai d'Orsay à l'épreuve de la cohabitation*, Paris: Flammarion, 1989.

Salem, Elie A., *Violence and Diplomacy in Lebanon, The Troubled Years, 1982–1988*, London: I.B. Tauris, 1995.

Stewart, Michael, *Life and Labour: An Autobiography*, London: Sidgwick & Jackson, 1980.

Thatcher, Margaret, *The Downing Street Years*, London: HarperCollins, 1993.

Lectures, Speeches, and Published Interviews

Arafat, Yasser, Interview in *Middle East International*, 167, 29 Jan. 1982.

Blair, Tony, Interview in *The Times*, 21 May 2002.

———, Interview in *The National* (Abu Dhabi), 4 April 2009.

Carter, Jimmy, Interview in *The Irish Times*, 19 June 2007.

Couve de Murville, Maurice, Interview in *Revue d'Etudes Palestiniennes*, 39, Spring 1991.

Fischer, Joschka, Interview in *Jerusalem Post*, 31 May 2002.

Kney-Tal, Harry, Interview in *Ha'aretz*, 21 Aug. 2002.

Lacouture, Jean, Interview in *Al-Nahar*, 26 Oct. 1974.

Major Addresses, Statements and Press Conferences of General Charles de Gaulle, May 19, 1958-January 31, 1964, New York, Paris: French Foreign Ministry, Press & Information Division, 1964.

Obama, Barack, Interview with *Al-Arabiya*, 26 January 2009, http://www.alarabiya.net/articles/2009/01/27/65087.html

Owen, David, Interview in *Foreign Affairs*, 72, 2, Spring 1993.

Rocard, Michel, *A l'épreuve des faits: textes politiques, 1979–1985*, Paris: Éditions du Seuil, 1986.

———, *Un Pays comme le nôtre: textes politiques, 1986–1989*, Paris: Éditions du Seuil, 1989.

Thatcher, Margaret, Complete Public Statements, 1945–1990. Database and Compilation (CD-Rom) (cited in text as Thatcher, Complete Public Statements, 1945–1990), Oxford University Press, 1999

Tueni, Ghassan, in *Middle East International*, 9, December 1971.

Waldegrave, William, Interview in *Journal of Palestine Studies*, 20, 1, Autumn 1990.

Books (other than memoirs)

Aburish, Said K., *Arafat, from Defender to Dictator*, London: Bloomsbury, 1998.

Aeschimann, Éric and Christophe Boltanski, *Chirac d'Arabie: les mirages d'une politique française*, Paris: Bernard Grasset, 2006.

Ahiram, Ephraim and Alfred Tovias (eds), *Whither EU-Israeli Relations? Common and Divergent Interests*, Frankfurt: Peter Lang, 1995.

Al-Mani, Saleh A., *The Euro-Arab Dialogue: A Study in Associative Diplomacy*, London: Palgrave Macmillan, 1983.

Algieri, Franco and Elfriede Regelsberger (eds), *Synergy at Work: Spain and Portugal in European Foreign Policy*, Bonn: Europa Union Verlag, 1996.

BIBLIOGRAPHY

Allen, David Allen and Alfred Pijpers (eds), *European Foreign Policy Making and the Arab Israeli Conflict*, The Hague, Boston, Lancaster: Martinus Nijhoff Publishers, 1984.

Aron, Raymond, *De Gaulle, Israel and the Jews*, trans. from French by John Sturrock, London: Andre Deutsch, 1969.

Asuri, Naseer (ed.), *Palestinian Refugees, The Right of Return*, London: Pluto Press, 2001.

Azeroul, Yves and Yves Derai, *Mitterrand, Israël et les juifs*, Paris: Éditions Robert Laffont, 1990.

Balta, Paul and Claudine Rulleau, *La Politique arabe de la France: de Gaulle à Pompidou*, Paris: Sindbad, 1974.

Bar-Joseph, Uri, *The Watchman Fell Asleep: the Surprise of Yom Kippur and Its Sources*, Albany, NY: State University Press of New York, 2005.

Baram, Amatzia and Barry Rubin (eds), *Iraq's Road to War*, London: Macmillan, 1993.

Beker, Avi, *The United Nations and Israel: From Recognition to Reprehension*, Lexington, Mass., Toronto: Lexington Books, 1988.

Benchenane, Mustapha, *Pour un dialogue euro-arabe*, Paris: Berger-Levrault, 1983.

Bibes, Geneviève, *L'Italie a-t-elle une politique étrangère*, Paris: Centre d'Etudes des Relations Internationales, 1974.

Bossuat, Gerard and Andreas Wilkens (eds), *Jean Monnet, l'Europe et les chemins de la paix*, Paris: Sorbonne, 1999.

Brecher, Michael, *The Foreign Policy System of Israel: Setting, Images, Process*, London, Toronto: Oxford University Press, 1972.

Brittan, Leon, *A Diet of Brussels: The Changing Face of Europe*, London: Little, Brown and Company, 2000.

Brookings Institute, *Toward Peace in the Middle East*, Report of a Study Group, Los Angeles: Brookings Institute, 1975.

Brown, L. Carl and Mathew S. Gordon (eds), *Franco-Arab Encounters: Studies in Memory of David C. Gordon*, Syracuse, NY: Syracuse University Press, 1997.

Bunker, Robert J., (ed.), *Networks, Terrorism and Global Insurgency*, London, New York: Routledge, 2005.

Callaghan, James, *Challenges and Opportunities for British Foreign Policy*, London: Fabian Bureau, 1975.

Cobban, Helena, *The Palestinian Liberation Organization—People, Power and Politics*, Cambridge: Cambridge University Press, 1984.

Coll, Steve, *The Bin Ladens: The Story of a Family and its Fortune*, New York, London: Allen Lane, 2008.

Crosbie, Sylvia K., *A Tacit Alliance: France and Israel from Suez to the Six Day War*, Princeton University Press, 1974.

Daalder, Ivo H. and James M. Lindsay, *America Unbound: the Bush Revolution in Foreign Policy*, Washington, DC: Brookings Institution Press, 2003.

De Schoutheete, Phillippe, *La Coopération politique européenne*, Paris and Brussels: Fernand Nathan, 1980.

Eytan, Walter, *The First Ten Years: A Diplomatic History of Israel*, New York: Simon & Schuster, 1958.

Falkender, Marcia, *Downing Street in Perspective*, London: Weidenfeld & Nicolson, 1983.

Freedman, Lawrence, *A Choice of Enemies: America Confronts the Middle East*, London: Orion Books, 2008.

Freedman, Lawrence and Efraim Karsh, *The Gulf Conflict: 1990–1991*, London and Boston: Faber and Faber, 1993.

Freedman, Robert O. (ed.), *The Middle East Since Camp David*, Boulder, CO and London: Westview Press, 1984.

Friend, J.W., *The Long Presidency: France in the Mitterrand Years, 1981–1995*, Boulder, CO: Westview Press, 1998.

Gardner-Feldman, Lily, *The Special Relationship between West Germany and Israel*, Boston: Allen & Unwin, 1984.

Gerstenfeld, Manfred (ed.), *Israel and Europe: An Expanding Abyss?*, Jerusalem: Jerusalem Center for Public Affairs, 2005.

Gnesotto, Nicole and John Roper (eds), *Western Europe and the Gulf*, Paris: The Institute of Security Studies, Western European Union, 1992.

Greilsammer, Ilan and Joseph H.H. Weiler (eds), *Europe and Israel, Troubled Neighbours*, Berlin and New York: Walter De Gruyter, 1988.

———, *Europe's Middle East Dilemma: The Quest for a Unified Stance*, Boulder, CO and London: Westview Press, 1987.

Haines, Joe, *The Politics of Power*, London: Jonathan Cape, 1977.

Hatem, Abdel-Kader, *Information and the Arab Cause*, London: Longmans, 1974,

Hirst, David and Irene Beeson, *Sadat*, New York and London: Faber and Faber, 1981.

Hoffman, Bruce, *Inside Terrorism*, New York: Columbia University Press, 2006.

Hurd, Douglas, *Our Future in Europe*, London: Conservative Political Centre, 1993.

Israeli, Rafael, *The Public Diary of President Sadat. Vol. 3, The Road of Pragmatism: June 1975-October 1976*, Leiden: E.J. Brill, 1979.

Jansen, G.H., *Zionism, Israel and Asian Nationalism*, Beirut: The Institute for Palestine Studies, 1971.

Jawad, Haifaa A., *Euro-Arab Relations: A Study in Collective Diplomacy*, Reading: Ithaca Press, 1992.

Jobert, Michel, *Les Américains*, Paris: Albin Michel, 1987.

Kampfner, John, *Robin Cook*, London: Victor Gollancz, 1998.

Kaye, Dalia Dassa, *Beyond the Handshake: Multilateral Cooperation in the Arab-Israeli Peace Process*, New York: Columbia University Press, 2001.

Khouri, Fred, *The Arab-Israeli Dilemma*, Syracuse University Press, 1985.

Kissinger, Henry A., *The Troubled Partnership: A Re-Appraisal of the Atlantic Alliance*, New York: McGraw-Hill, 1965.

Klieman, Aaron S., *Israel and the World After 40 Years*, New York, London: Pergamon-Brassey's, 1990.

Korany, Bahgat and Ali E. Hillal Dessouki (eds), *The Foreign Policies of Arab States*, Boulder, CO and London: Westview Press, 1984.

Kozodoy, Neal (ed.), *The Mideast Peace Process: An Autopsy*, New York: Encounter Books, 2001.

Lacouture, Jean, *De Gaulle: The Ruler, 1945–1970*, trans. by Alan Sheridan, London: Harvill, 1992.

Lall, Arthur, *The UN and the Middle East Crisis, 1967*, New York: Columbia University Press, 1968.

Laqueur, Walter, *Confrontation: The Middle East War and World Politics*, London: Abacus, 1974.

Lavy, George, *Germany and Israel: Moral Debt and National Interest*, London: Frank Cass, 1996.

Levey, Zach, *Israel and the Western Powers, 1952–1960*, Chapel Hill and London: University of North Carolina Press, 1997.

Lukacs, Yeduda (ed.), *The Israeli-Palestinian Conflict: a Documentary Record, 1967–1990*, Cambridge and New York: Cambridge University Press, 1992.

Miller, Aaron David, *The Much Too Promised Land: America's Elusive Search for Arab-Israeli Peace*, New York: Bantam Books, 2008.

Miller, Rory, *Ireland and the Palestine Question, 1948–2004*, Dublin: Irish Academic Press, 2005.

Morgan, Kenneth O., *Callaghan: A Life*, Oxford University Press, 1997.

Northcutt, Wayne, *Mitterrand: A Political Biography*, New York and London: Holmes & Meier, 1992.

Noushci, André, *La France et le monde arabe depuis 1962*, Paris: Librairie Vuibert, 1994.

Péan, Pierre, *Les Deux bombes*, Paris: Fayard, 1981.

Quandt, William B., *Peace Process: American Diplomacy and the Arab-Israeli Conflict Since 1967*, Los Angeles: Brookings Institute Press and University of California Press, 3rd edition, 2005.

Roussel, Eric, *Jean Monnet, 1888–1979*, Paris: Fayard, 1996.

Said, Edward, *The End of the Peace Process*, 2nd edition, London: Granta, 2002.

Sayigh, Yezid, *Armed Struggle and the Search for State: The Palestinian National Movement, 1949–1993*, Washington, DC and Oxford: Oxford University Press, 1997.

Sayigh, Yusif A., *Arab Oil Policies in the 1970s: Opportunity and Responsibility*, London and Canberra: Croom Helm, 1983.

Segev, Tom, *1967: Israel, the War and the Year That Transformed the Middle East*, New York: Little, Brown, 2007.

Seguev, Samuel, *Israël, les arabes et les grandes puissances, 1963–1968*, Paris: Calmann-Lévy, 1968.

Seldon, Anthony, *Blair Unbound*, London and New York: Simon & Schuster, 2007.

Shindler, Colin, *A History of Modern Israel*, Cambridge: Cambridge University Press, 2008.

Shirabi, Hisham, *Palestine Guerrillas: Their Credibility and Effectiveness*, Beirut: Institute for Palestine Studies, 1970.

Soames, Christopher, *Three Views of Europe*, London: Conservative Political Centre, 1973.

Soetendorp, Ben, *Foreign Policy in the European Union, Theory History and Practice*, London: Addison Wesley Longman, 1999.

Stephens, Elizabeth, *US Policy towards Israel: The Role of Political Culture in Defining the "Special Relationship*, Brighton, Portland: Sussex University Press, 2006.

Stuart, Mark, *Douglas Hurd: Public Servant*, Edinburgh and London: Mainstream Publishing, 1998.

Tierksy, Ronald, *François Mitterrand: The Last French President*, New York: St Martin's Press, 2000.

US News & World Report, *Triumph Without Victory: The Unreported History of the Persian Gulf War*, New York: New York Times Books, 1992.

Wallace, William and W.E. Patterson (eds), *Foreign Policy Making in Western Europe: A Comparative Approach*, Farnborough: Saxon House, 1978.

Watson, Geoffrey R., *The Oslo Accords: International Law and the Israeli-Palestinian Peace Agreements*, Oxford: Oxford University Press, 2000.

Wilson, Harold, *The Chariot of Israel: Britain, America and the State of Israel*, London: Weidenfeld & Nicolson and Michael Joseph, 1981.

Wistrich, Robert S. (ed.), *Anti-Zionism and Antisemitism in the Contemporary World*, New York: New York University Press, 1990.

Yergin, Daniel, *The Prize: The Epic Quest for Oil, Money and Power*, London and New York: Simon & Schuster, 1991.

Yodfat, Aryeh Y. and Yval Arnon-Ohanna (eds), *PLO Strategy and Tactics*, New York: St. Martins Press, 1981.

Ziegler, Philip, *Wilson, The Authorised Life of Lord Wilson of Rievaulx*, London: Weidfenfeld and Nicolson, 1993.

Articles

Abadi, Jacob, 'Constraints and Adjustments in Italy's Policy toward Israel', *Middle Eastern Studies*, 38, 4, Oct. 2002, pp. 63–94.

Ajami, Fouad, 'The Summer of Arab Discontent', *Foreign Affairs*, 69, 5, Winter, 1990–1991, pp. 1–20.

Al-Dajani, Ahmad Sidqi, 'The PLO and the Euro-Arab Dialogue', *Journal of Palestine Studies*, IX, 3, Spring 1980, pp. 81–98.

Allman, T.D., 'On the Road with Arafat', *Vanity Fair*, Feb. 1989.

Alpher, Joseph, 'Israel's Security Concerns in the Peace Process', *International Affairs*, 70, 2, 1994, pp. 229–41.

Atkins, James E., 'The Oil Crisis: This Time the Wolf is Here', *Foreign Affairs*, 51, 3, April 1973, pp. 462–90.

Artner, Stephen J., 'The Middle East: A Chance for Europe?', *International Affairs*, 56, 3, Summer 1980, pp. 420–42.

Barbe, Esther, 'Spain and CSFP: The Emergence of a Major Player?', *Mediterranean Politics*, 5, 2, Summer 2000, pp. 44–63.

Bauchard, Denis, 'Europe's Role in Averting a Middle East Tragedy', *Europe's World*, Autumn 2009, pp. 134–9.

Brahimi, Lakhdar, 'Who is Speaking to whom in the Euro-Arab Dialogue', *Euro-Arab Dialogue Lectures II*, The Hague: The Luftia Rabbani Foundation, 1986, pp. 1–15.

Colord, Daniel, 'La Politique méditerranéene et proche-oreintale de G. Pompidou', *Politique Etrangère*, 43, 3, 1978, pp. 283–96.

D'Alançon, François, 'The EC Looks to a New Middle East', *Journal of Palestine Studies*, XXIII, 2, Winter, 1994, pp. 41–50.

De La Gorce, Paul-Marie, 'Europe and the Arab-Israeli Conflict: A Survey', *Journal of Palestine Studies*, XXVI, 3, Spring 1997, pp. 5–16.

Del Sarto, Raffaella A., 'Wording and Meaning(s): EU-Israeli Political Cooperation according to the ENP Action Plan', *Mediterranean Politics*, 11, 1, 2007, pp. 59–74.

Eban, Abba, 'Camp David-The Unfinished Business', *Foreign Affairs*, 57, 2, Winter, 1978–1979, pp. 343–54.

Efrat, Elisha, 'Jewish Settlements in the West Bank: Past, Present and Future', *Israel Affairs*, 1, 1, Autumn 1994, pp. 135–48.

Epstein, Marc and Alain Louyot, 'L'Europe engluée dans le cauchemar yougoslave', *Les Cahiers de l'Express*, 31, Feb. 1995, pp. 57–8.

Fisk, Robert, 'Breaking Ranks: the EU, the US and the Middle East', in Ben Tonra and Eilis Ward (eds), *Ireland in International Affairs: Interests, Institutions and Identity*, Dublin: Institute of Public Administration, 2002, pp. 176–92.

Fontaine, André, 'Transatlantic Doubts and Dreams', *Foreign Affairs*, 59, 3, 1980, pp. 578–93.

Goldsborough, James O., 'France, the European Crisis and the Alliance', *Foreign Affairs*, 52, 3, April 1974, pp. 538–56.

Gordon, Philip H., 'Bush's Middle East Vision', *Survival*, 45, 1, Spring 2003, pp. 155–65.

Hartley, Anthony, 'Europe Between the Superpowers', *Foreign Affairs*, 49, 2, Jan. 1971, pp. 271–82.

Heikal, Mohamed Hassanein, 'Egyptian Foreign Policy', *Foreign Affairs*, 56, 4, July 1978, pp. 714–27.

Hilal, Jamil, 'Hamas's Rise as Charted in the Polls, 1994–2005', *Journal of Palestine Studies*, XXXV, 3, Spring 2006, pp. 6–19.

Hourani, Cecil, 'The Moment of Truth: Towards a Middle East Dialogue', *Encounter*, XXIX, 5, Nov. 1967, pp. 3–14.

Howard, Michael, 'The World of Henry Kissinger', *Encounter*, LIX, 5, Nov. 1982, pp. 52–5.

Hussein, King, 'Prospects for Peace in the Middle East', *Journal of Palestine Studies*, IXX, 3, Spring 1990, pp. 3–13.

Indyk, Martin, 'Watershed in the Middle East', *Foreign Affairs*, 71, 1, 1991–92, pp. 70–93, p. 83.

Joffe, Josef, 'The New Europe: Yesterday's Ghosts', *Foreign Affairs*, 72, 1, 1992–93, pp. 29–43.

Kaiser, Karl, 'Europe and America: A Critical Phase', *Foreign Affairs*, 52, 4, July 1974, pp. 725–841.

Karsh, Efraim, 'Reflections on the Gulf Conflict', *Journal of Strategic Studies*, 19, 3, Sept. 1996, pp. 303–32.

Kemp, Geoffrey, 'Europe's Middle East Challenges', *The Washington Quarterly*, 27, 1, Winter 2003, pp. 163–77.

Kepel, Gilles, 'Self and Other: The heart of the Franco-Arab Paradox', in L. Carl Brown and Mathew S. Gordon (eds), *Franco-Arab Encounters: Studies in Memory of David C. Gordon*, Syracuse, NY: Syracuse University Press, 1997, pp. 306–26.

Kolodziej, E.A., 'France and the Arms Trade', *International Affairs*, 56, 1, 1980, pp. 58–9.

Krauthammer, Charles, 'The Unipolar Moment', *Foreign Affairs*, 70, 1, 1991, pp. 23–33.

Kristianasen, Wendy, 'Challenge and Counterchallenge: Hamas' Response to Oslo', *Journal of Palestine Studies*, XXVIII, 3, Spring 1999, pp. 19–36.

Laipson, Ellen, 'Europe's Role in the Middle East: Enduring Ties, Emerging Opportunities', *Middle East Journal*, 44, 1, Winter 1990, pp. 7–17.

Laqueur, Walter, 'Israel, the Arabs, and World Opinion', *Commentary Magazine*, Aug. 1967, pp. 49–59.

Lellouche, Pierre, 'France in Search of Security', *Foreign Affairs*, 72, 2, Spring 1993, pp. 122–31, p. 123.

Levy, Walter J., 'Oil Power', *Foreign Affairs*, 49, 4, July 1971, pp. 652–68.

———, 'Oil and the Decline of the West', *Foreign Affairs*, 58, 5, Summer 1980, pp. 999–1015.

Lewis, Bernard, 'The Anti-Zionist Resolution', *Foreign Affairs*, 55, 1, Oct. 1976, pp. 54–64.

Lord Carrington, 'European Political Co-Operation: American Should Welcome it', *International Affairs*, 58, 1, Winter 1981–82, pp. 1–6.

Lord Gladwyn, 'Atlantic Dreams and Realities, *Encounter*, XXI, 6, Dec. 1963, pp. 57–63.

Lowenthal, Richard, 'A World Adrift', *Encounter*, XXXVIII, 2, Feb. 1972, pp. 22–9.

Marr, Phebe, 'The United States, Europe, and the Middle East: An Uneasy Triangle', *Middle East Journal*, 48, 2, Spring 1994, pp. 211–25.

Miller, Rory and Ashraf Mishrif, 'The Barcelona Process and Euro-Arab Economic Relations: 1995–2005', *Middle East Review of International Affairs*, 9, 2, June 2005.

Minerbi, Sergio, 'Israel et l'Europe', *Politique Etrangère*, 46, 2, 1981, pp. 429–40.

Moïsi, Dominique, 'La France de Mitterrand et le conflit du Proche-Orient: comment concilier émotion et politique', *Politique Etrangère*, 47, 2, 1982, pp. 395–402.

———, 'Chirac of France: A New Leader of the West?', *Foreign Affairs*, 74, 6, Nov.-Dec. 1995, pp. 8–13.

Otte, Marc, 'Europe has a Central Role to Play in the Middle East', *Europe's World*, 13 April 2009.

Parsons, Sir Anthony, 'The Middle East', in Peter Byrd (ed.), *British Foreign Policy Under Thatcher*, New York and London: St Martin's Press, 1989, pp. 76–95.

Peretz, Don, 'Arab Palestine: Phoenix or Phantom?', *Foreign Affairs*, 48, 2 Jan. 1970, pp. 322–33.

Pinkus, Binyamin, 'Atomic Power to Israel's Rescue: French-Israeli Nuclear Cooperation, 1949–1957', *Israel Studies*, 7, 1, 2002, pp. 104–38.

Prodi, Romano and Alberto Clo, 'Europe', in *The Oil Crisis in Perspective*, DAEDALUS, 14, 4, Fall 1975, pp. 91–112.

Quandt, William B., 'The Middle East Crises', *Foreign Affairs*, 58, 3, 1979, pp. 540–62.

Reed, Stanley, 'Jordan and the Gulf Crisis', *Foreign Affairs*, 69, 5, Winter 1990–1991, pp. 21–35.

Robins, Philip, 'Always the Bridesmaid: Europe and the Middle East Peace Process', *Cambridge Review of International Affairs*, 10, 2, Winter-Spring, 1997, pp. 69–83.

Rondot, Philippe, 'France and Palestine: From Charles de Gaulle to François Mitterrand', *Journal of Palestine Studies*, XVI, 3, Spring 1987, pp. 87–100.

Ross, Dennis, 'Taking Stock: The Bush Administration and the Roadmap to Peace', *The National Interest*, Fall 2003, pp. 11–21.

Rouleau, Eric, 'The Palestinian Quest', *Foreign Affairs*, 53, 2, Jan. 1975, pp. 264–83.

———, 'Reflections on the Peace Process and a Durable Settlement', *Journal of Palestine Studies*, XXVI, 1, Autumn 1996, pp. 5–26.

Safran, Nadav, 'The War and the Future of the Arab-Israeli Conflict', *Foreign Affairs*, 52, 2, Jan. 1974, pp. 215–36.

———, 'Engagement in the Middle East', *Foreign Affairs*, 53, 1, Oct. 1974, pp. 45–63.

Serpell, Christopher, 'Europe and the Middle East: A Time for Re-appraisal', *MEI*, 31, Jan. 1974, pp. 6–7.

Sicherman, Harvey, 'Politics of Dependence: Western Europe and the Arab-Israeli Conflict', *Orbis*, 23, 4, Winter 1980, pp. 845–57.

Simonet, Henri, 'Energy and the Future of Europe', *Foreign Affairs*, 53, 3, April 1975, pp. 450–63.

Smith, Michael, '"The Devil you Know": the United States and a Changing European Community', *International Affairs*, 68, 1, 1992, pp. 103–20.

Smith, Pamela Ann, 'The European Reaction to Israel's Invasion', *Journal of Palestine Studies*, XI-XII, 4–5, Summer-Fall, 1982, pp. 38–47.

Sommer, Theo, 'The Community is Working', *Foreign Affairs*, 51, 4, July 1973, pp. 747–60.

———, 'Europe and the American Connection', *Foreign Affairs*, 58, 3, 1979, pp. 622–36.

Stein, Kenneth W., 'Imperfect Alliances: Will Europe and America Ever Agree?', *Middle East Quarterly*, March 1997, pp. 39–45.

Stern, Fritz, 'Germany in a Semi-Gaullist Europe', *Foreign Affairs*, 58, 4, Spring 1980, pp. 867–86.

Stewart, Michael, 'Britain, Europe and the Alliance', *Foreign Affairs*, 48, 4, July 1970, pp. 648–59.

Tiersky, Ronald, 'Mitterrand's Legacies', *Foreign Affairs*, 74, 1, 1995, pp. 112–21.

Turner, Louis, 'The Politics of the Energy Crisis', *International Affairs*, 50, 3, July 1974, pp. 404–15.

Ullman, Richard H., 'After Rabat: Middle East Risks and America Roles', *Foreign Affairs*, 53, 2, Jan. 1975, pp. 284–96.

Wood, Pia Christina, 'Chirac's "New Arab Policy" and Middle East Challenges: The Arab-Israeli Conflict, Iraq and Iran', *Middle East Journal*, 52, 4, Autumn 1998, pp. 563–80.

———, 'France and the Israeli-Palestinian Conflict: the Mitterrand Policies, 1981–1992', *Middle East Journal*, 47, 1, Winter 1993, pp. 21–40.

"Z", 'The Year of Europe?' *Foreign Affairs*, 52, 1, Jan. 1974, pp. 237–48.

Zimmermann, Warren, 'The Last Ambassador', *Foreign Affairs*, 74, 2, March-April 1995, pp. 2–20.

PhD Thesis

Seiler, Fiorella, '"King of the Armed Ghetto": Israel in the West German National Press during Menachem Begin's First Government (1977–1981)', Unpublished PhD thesis, University of London, 2001.

INDEX

121, 175, 182; accepted by Israel as legitimate Palestinian representatives (1993), 134; and EAD, 67; and Fatah, 17, 92; call for increased role in negotiations, 90–1; Central Committee, 80; expansion of (1971–2), 52; expelled from Kingdom of Jordan (1970), 17; *Filastin al-Thawra*, 85; founded (1964), 16; Hebron Agreement (1997), 144, 154; information offices of, 36, 99, 107; Israel-PLO Cairo Agreement (1994), 138; leaders of, 103, 114; operation in Tunis, 130; Palestine National Fund, 60; participation in UN, 54; personnel of, 52, 69, 72, 79, 99; political department, 60, 79; recognised by Italy (1979), 82; representations of, 5; Research Centres, 64; retaliation attacks on Galilee (1982)view of Camp David peace discussions (1978), 72; view of US-Israeli special relationship, 4

Palestine National Council (PNC): 117–18, 177; controlled by Fatah, 17; personnel of, 67

Papandreou, Andreas: 107; administration of, 108; and Yasser Arafat, 99–100, 102; criticisms of, 100; electoral success of (1981), 99; foreign policy of, 100; Greek Prime Minister, 117; invitation to Yasser Arafat (1981), 99–100; leader of PASOK party, 99

Papoulias, Carolos: Greek Foreign Minister, 114

Parliamentary Association for Euro-Arab Co-operation: established (1974), 45; ideology of, 47; open letter to Jimmy Carter (1980), 88; organisation of Damascus meeting (1974), 46–7; personnel of, 45

Patten, Chris: 166, 180; and Tony Blair, 169; EU Commissioner for External Relations, 155, 182; member of House of Lords, 182; speech to European Parliament (2001), 155

Pazner, Avi: Israeli Ambassador to France, 142

Peled, Mattityahu: criticism of EEC, 112

Pelletreau, Robert H.: US Ambassador to Tunisia, 120

Peres, Shimon: 110–12, 120; foreign policy of, 134; Israeli Foreign Minister, 92, 133; Israeli Prime Minister, 139; leader of Labour party, 80, 92, 109, 121, 139; supporters of, 147

Persian Gulf War (1990–1): 139; diplomatic attempts to end, 123; effects of, 124; outbreak of, 121

Pique, Josep: Spanish Foreign Minister, 160, 162

Plumb, Lord Charles Henry: President of European Parliament, 114

Pompidou, Georges: 144; criticisms of, 23; death of (1974), 53; foreign policy of, 22–3, 41, 53, 101–2; President of France, 22, 43, 50, 101

Poos, Jacques: Luxembourgian Foreign Minister, 123, 131

Popular Front for the Liberation of Palestine (PFLP): criticisms of Valéry Giscard D'Estaing, 85; hijacking of El Al aircraft (1968), 17; led by George Habash, 64, 91